HOSTELS
AUSTRIA &
SWITZERLAND

SECOND EDITION

"Put this book in your pack before your trip to Europe—you'll return with more money and better memories than those who didn't."

—*Big World* magazine

HELP US KEEP THIS GUIDE UP TO DATE

Every effort has been made by the authors and editors to make this guide as accurate and useful as possible. However, many things can change after a guide is published—establishments close, phone numbers change, facilities come under new management, etc.

We would love to hear from you concerning your experiences with this guide and how you feel it could be improved and kept up to date. While we may not be able to respond to all comments and suggestions, we'll take them to heart and we'll also make certain to share them with the authors. Please send your comments and suggestions to the following address:

The Globe Pequot Press
Reader Response/Editorial Department
P.O. Box 480
Guilford, CT 06437

Or you may e-mail us at:

editorial@globe-pequot.com

Thanks for your input, and happy travels!

HOSTELS
AUSTRIA &
SWITZERLAND

SECOND EDITION

The Only Comprehensive,

Unofficial,

Opinionated

Guide

Paul Karr

and Martha Coombs

The Globe Pequot Press

Guilford, Connecticut

Cover design, text design, and maps by M. A. Dubé
Contributing freelancer: Hiro Nakajima
Other assistance: Evan Halper

ISBN 0-7627-2183-9

Printed in Canada
Second Edition/First Printing

CONTENTS

ACKNOWLEDGMENTS

Paul Karr thanks Martha once again for companionship and editorial assistance. She is simply stunning. Martha thanks Senja St. John and Richard Coombs for guidance and support.

From both of us, thanks to the following, who went far beyond the call of duty: Klaus Heindl in Vienna, Stephan Frölich in Bregenz, Lottie in Lugano, Evelyne Mock of Switzerland Tourism, and Gabriele Wolf of the Austrian National Tourist Office gave patient answers to our frequent questions. Special thanks to our European friends: Clive, Mandy, and Jonathan Pease; Stephan, Maud, Mikael, and Oskar Mangold; the extended Leichel family; and Helen Tharsgaard.

We both again thank the Karr, Coombs, Couture, and Bottinger families; our long-standing and new friends in New England, Georgia, Canada, and Japan and their various children. Thank you all for bringing light and joy to our travels, for being our homes away from home.

Thanks to the good folks at Magellan's for kindly helping sponsor the work with incredibly useful travel supplies; to TravelSmith for supplying travel products; to TravelGuard for attending to our travel insurance needs; to the Parker Company for smoothly handling all our communication needs during the trip; to Econophone and PrestoCard for providing us with long-distance service; and to Toby Pyle of American Youth Hostels for a world of help, as well as continuous encouragement and assistance.

DER Travel of Chicago, a topflight tour company, gets our hearty thanks for lots of information and assistance and for making rail travel throughout Austria and Europe a real pleasure.

And thanks, finally, to a world (literally) of new friends met or made on the road. So many of you have taught us about your corner of the world or otherwise made this work enjoyable and useful.

Thank you all.

HOW TO USE THIS BOOK

What you're holding in your hands is the first-ever attempt of its kind: a fairly complete listing and rating of all the hostels we could find in Austria and Switzerland. Dozens of hostellers from all over the globe were interviewed in the course of putting this guide together, and their comments and thoughts run throughout its pages. Who knows? *You* might be quoted somewhere inside.

We wrote this guide for two pretty simple reasons:

First, we wanted to bring hostelling to a wider audience. Hostels continue to grow in popularity, but many North American travelers still don't think of them as options when planning a trip. We wanted to encourage that because—at its best—the hostelling experience brings people of greatly differing origins, faiths, and points of view together in a convivial setting. You learn about these people, and also about the place in which the hostel is situated, in a very personal way that no textbook could ever provide.

Second, we wanted very much to give people our honest opinions of the hostels. You wouldn't send your best friend to a fleabag, and we don't want readers traveling great distances only to be confronted with filthy kitchens, nasty managers, or dangerous neighborhoods. At least, we thought, we could warn them about unsafe or unpleasant situations ahead of time.

On the other hand, of course, we would also tip our friends off to the truly wonderful hostels—the ones with treehouses, cafes, free breakfasts; the ones with real family spirit. So that's what we've done. Time after time on the road, we have heard fellow travelers complaining that the guidebooks they bought simply listed places to stay but didn't rate them. Well, now we've done it—and we haven't pulled a single punch or held back a bit of praise.

HOW WE WROTE THIS BOOK

The authors, along with a cadre of assistants, fanned out across Austria and Switzerland with notebooks and laptops in hand during 2001. Sometimes we identified ourselves in advance as authors; sometimes we just popped in for surprise visits. We counted rooms, turned taps, tested beds. And then we talked with managers and staff.

Before we left, we also took the time to interview plenty of hostellers in private and get their honest opinions about the places they were staying or had already stayed.

The results are contained within this book: actual hosteller quotes, opinions, ratings—and more.

WHAT IS A HOSTEL?

If you've picked up this book, you probably know what a hostel is. On the other hand, a surprising number of people interviewed for this book weren't sure at all what it means.

So let's check your knowledge with a little pop quiz. Sharpen up your pencils, put on your thinking caps, and dive in.

1. A hostel is:

    A. a hospital.

    B. a hospice.

    C. a hotel.

    D. a drunk tank.

    E. none of the above.

        (correct answer worth 20 points)

2. A hostel is:

    A. a place where international travelers bunk up.

    B. a cheap sleep.

    C. a place primarily dedicated to bunks.

    D. all of the above.

        (correct answer worth 20 points)

3. You just turned 30. Word on the street has it that you'll get turned away for being that age. Do you tell the person at the hostel desk the grim news?

    A. No, because a hostel is restricted to students under 30.

    B. No, because a hostel is restricted to elderly folks over 65.

    C. No, because they don't care about your midlife crisis.

        (correct answer worth 10 points)

4. You spy a shelf labeled FREE FOOD! in the hostel kitchen. What do you do?

    A. Begin stuffing pomegranates in your pockets.

    B. Ask the manager how food ended up in jail.

    C. Run for your life.

        (correct answer worth 5 points)

5. Essay question. Why do you want to stay in a hostel?

        (extra credit; worth up to 45 points)

Done? Great! And the envelope, please . . .

1. **None of the above.** The word *hostel* is originally German, and it means "country inn for youngsters" or something like that.

2. **All of the above.** You got that one, right?

3. **C.** No age limits or restrictions here! (Only in Bavaria—the south of Germany—is there an age limit.)

4. **A.** Free means free.

5. Give yourself 15 points for every use of the word "friends," "international," or "cool," okay? But don't give yourself more than 45. Yes, we mean it. Don't make us turn this car around right now. We will. We mean it.

What? All you wrote was "It's cheap"? Okay, okay, give yourself 20 points.

So how did you do?

100 points:	Born to be wild
80–100:	Get your motor runnin'
40–80:	Head out on the highway
20–40:	Lookin' for adventure
0–20:	Hope you don't come my way

Don't be embarrassed if you flunked this little quiz, though. Hostel operators get confused and blur the lines, too. You'll sometimes find a campground, retreat center, or college setting aside a couple bunks—and calling itself a hostel anyway. In those cases we've used our best judgment about whether a place is or isn't a hostel.

Also, we excluded some joints—no matter how well-meaning—if they (a) exclude men or women, (b) serve primarily as a university residence hall (with a very few special exceptions), or (c) serve you a heavy side of religious doctrine with the eggs in the morning.

In a few cases our visits didn't satisfy us either way; those places were either left out, set aside for a future edition, or briefly described here but not rated.

The bottom line? If it's in this book, it probably is a hostel. If it isn't, it's not, and don't let anyone tell you otherwise. There. 'Nuff said.

UNDERSTANDING THE RATINGS

All the listings information in this book was current at press time. Here's the beginning of a sample in the book, from a hostel in Bregenz, Austria, near the Swiss border:

JUGENDGÄSTEHAUS BREGENZ

(Bregenz Guest House Hostel)

Mehrerauerstrasse 3–5; A–6900 Bregenz

Telephone Number: 05–574–42867

Fax Number: 05–574–428–674
E-mail: jgh.bregenz@jgh.at
Rates: €17–26 (about $17–$26 US) per HI member;
doubles €44 (about $44 US)
Credit cards: Yes
Beds: 142
Season: May 1–December 31
Office hours: 7:00 A.M. to midnight
Lockout: None
Curfew: None
Affiliation: Hostelling International-ÖJHV
Extras: Meals ($), breakfast, bar, snacks, Internet access, play
area, volleyball, currency exchange, TV

See those little pictures at the bottom? Those are icons, and they signify something important we wanted you to know about the hostel. We've printed a key to these icons on the facing page.

The overall hostel rating consists of those hip-looking thumbs sitting atop each entry. It's pretty simple: Thumbs up means good. Thumbs down means bad.

We've used these thumbs to compare the hostels to one another. Only a select number of hostels earned the top rating of two thumbs up, and a few were considered unpleasant enough to merit a thumb down. You can use this rating as a general assessment of a hostel.

Sometimes we didn't rate a hostel that was a mixed-bag experience. Or maybe, for one reason or another—bad weather, bad luck, bad timing, remoteness, an inability to get ahold of the staff, or our own confusion about the place—we just didn't feel we collected enough information to properly rate that hostel for you. These hostels are designated by [NR].

That said, here's a key to what these ratings mean:

 Cream of the crop, recommended

 Pretty good

 So-so

 Only if you're desperate

 Bad news; don't even *think* of staying here

 Not rated

KEY TO ICONS

 Attractive natural setting

 Ecologically aware hostel

 Superior kitchen facilities or great cafe/restaurant

 Offbeat or eccentric place

 Superior bathroom facilities

 Romantic private rooms

 Comfortable beds

 A particularly good value

 Handicapped-accessible

 Good for business travelers

 Especially well suited for families

 Good for active travelers

 Visual arts at hostel or nearby

 Music at hostel or nearby

 Great hostel for skiers

 Bar or pub at hostel or nearby

 Among our very favorite hostels

The rest of the information is pretty much self-explanatory:

Address is usually the hostel's street address; occasionally we add the mailing address if that's different from the physical address.

Telephone Number is the primary phone number as dialed within the country.

Fax Number is the primary fax number as dialed within the country.

E-mail is the staff's e-mail address, for those who want to get free information or (sometimes) book a room by computer.

Web site (this hostel didn't have one) indicates a hostel's World Wide Web address.

Rates are the cost per person to stay at the hostel—when all the currency converting's said and done, expect to pay somewhere around $15 per person, more in cities or popular tourist areas. For private or family rooms, we've listed the total price for two people to stay in the room; usually it's higher than the cost of two singles, sometimes considerably so. Single or triple room rates will vary; ask ahead if you're unsure what you'll pay.

Note that these rates sometimes vary by season or by membership in a hostelling group such as Hostelling International (HI); we have tried to include a range of prices where applicable. Most HI-member hostels, for instance, charge $2.00 to $4.00 extra per day if you don't belong to one of Hostelling International's worldwide affiliates.

Also, a few hostels might charge you about $1.00 to supply sheets or towels if you haven't brought your own. (Sleeping bags, no matter how clean you think they are, are often frowned upon.) Finally, various local, municipal, or other taxes might also add slightly to the rates quoted here.

Credit cards can be a good way to pay for a bed in a foreign country (you get the fairest exchange rates on your home currency). We have noted whether cards are accepted by the hostels. That usually means Visa, Mastercard, or American Express. More and more hostels are taking them, and even if we haven't listed a hostel as accepting credit cards, things may have changed. When in doubt, call ahead and ask.

Beds indicates the number of beds available to hostellers.

Season indicates what part of the year a hostel is open—if it's closed part of the year. We've made our best effort at listing the seasons of each hostel, but schedules sometimes change according to weather or a manager's vacation plans. Call if you're unsure whether a hostel will be open when you want to stay there.

Office hours indicate the hours when staff are at the front desk and answering the phones—or at least would consider answering the phones. Keep in mind that nothing is fixed in stone, however; some hostel staffs will happily field calls in the middle of the night if you're reasonable, while others can't stand it. Try to call within the listed hours if possible.

A good rule of thumb to follow: The smaller a place, the harder it is for the owner/manager to drag him/herself out of bed at four in the morning just because you lost your way. Big-city hostels, however, frequently operate just like hotels—somebody's always on duty, or at least on call.

Austria and Switzerland are notorious for their strict attitudes toward time and punctuality; don't expect the front desk to stay open a few minutes late and end the lockout ten minutes early. Don't knock it; adapt and deal. It's just their way.

Private rooms or **family rooms** are rooms for a couple, a family with children, or (sometimes) a single traveler. Sometimes it's nice to have your own room on the road: It's more private, more secure, and your snoring won't bother anyone. They're becoming more common in Europe but are still hard to snag during the busy season. Book months ahead for one if you're going to a popular place like Interlaken, Geneva, Vienna, or Salzburg. Really.

Kitchen available simply indicates whether the hostel allows hostellers to cook in a kitchen or not. In North America and the U.K., almost every hostel has a kitchen—but the situation changes in Austria and Switzerland. Probably half of all these hostels have some sort of kitchen setup; just as many serve a delicious meal instead, so take advantage and fill 'er up.

Lockout or **curfew:** Many hostels have hours during which you are locked out of the place; in other words, you're not permitted on the premises. Many also have a curfew; be back inside before this time, or you'll be locked out for the night.

Affiliation indicates whether a hostel is affiliated with Hostelling International or not. For more information about what these organizations do, see "A Word about Affiliation" in "A Short History of Hostelling."

Extras list some of the other amenities that come with a stay at the hostel. A dollar sign in parentheses after an item indicates that you must pay for it. However, some—but not all—will be free; there's an amazing variety of services, and almost as big a variety in managers' willingness to do nice things for free. Laundries, on the other hand, are never free, and there's almost aways a charge for meals, lockers, bicycle or other equipment rentals, and other odds and ends. Some hostels maintain free information desks, and a few will pick you up at rail stations and the like.

With each entry we've also given you a little more information about the hostel to make your stay a little more informed—and fun. The sidebar (see right) contains more of the hostel entry that began above: What does all that stuff mean?

Best bet for a bite tells you where to find food in the area. Usually, we'll direct you to the cheapest and closest supermarket. But sometimes, in the interest of variety—and good eatin'—we'll point you toward a surprising health food store, a farmers' market rich with local color, or even a fancy place well worth the splurge.

Insiders' tip is a juicy secret about the area, something we didn't know until we got to the hostel ourselves.

Best bet for a bite:
Bella Napoli, downtown

Insiders' tip:
Underwear outlet store next door

What hostellers say:
"More of everything!"

Gestalt:
Bregenz Sie Deutsch?

Hospitality: 👍

Cleanliness: 👍

Party index:

What hostellers say relates what hostellers told us about a hostel—or what we imagine they would say.

Gestalt is the general feeling of a place—our (sometimes humorous) way of describing what it's about.

Safety describes urban hostels only; the example hostel is not in a big city, so there's no safety rating. If it had been, we would have graded it based on both the quality of the neighborhood and the security precautions taken by the hostel staff, using this scale:

No worries

Keep an eye out

Dial 911

Hospitality rates the hostel staff's friendliness toward hostellers (and travel writers):

Smile city

Grins & growls

Very hostile hostel

Cleanliness rates, what else, the general cleanliness of a place. Bear in mind that this can change—rapidly—depending on the time of year, turnover in staff, and so forth. Use it only as a general guide.

Spic-and-span

Could be cleaner . . .

Don't let the bedbugs bite

The **party index** is our way of tipping you off about the general scene at the hostel:

Rage all night

Party hearty

Lively

Mellow

Downright quiet

How to get there includes directions to many hostels—by car, bus, train, plane, or even ferry. Subway directions are given in big cities if applicable. Often these directions are complicated, however. In those cases managers have asked (or we recommend) that you call the hostel itself for more precise directions.

How to get there:

By car: Call hostel for directions.

By train: From Bregenz Station, walk up to long corridor in station crossing tracks. Follow signs toward AM SEE (away from CITY); walk to end of corridor, down stairs, and turn left. Walk past casino and through casino parking lot to main road (Meeraurergasse); cross street. Hostel entrance is just across road.

By bus: Call hostel for transit route.

A SHORT HISTORY OF HOSTELLING

Hostelling as we know it started around 1907, when Richard Schirmann, an assistant schoolteacher in Altena, Germany, decided to make one of the empty classrooms a space for visiting students to sleep. That was not a completely unique idea; Austrian inns and taverns had been offering reduced rates and bunk space to students since 1885. But Schirmann would develop much grander plans. He was about to start a movement.

His idea was to get students out of the industrial cities and into the countryside. Schirmann was a strong believer that walking and bicycling tours in the fresh air were essential to adolescent development and learning. But such excursions were impossible without a place to spend the night. His logic was simple: Since rural schoolhouses were deserted during weekends and holidays, why not make use of those spaces?

The caretakers of the school he chose agreed to serve as houseparents, and some fast ground rules were established. Students were responsible for piling up the tables and benches in the classroom and laying out thin straw sacks on the floor. At some ungodly early-morning hour, the students were to restack the straw mats and reorganize the classroom as they found it. Boys and girls slept in separate rooms but were treated as equals. Detractors cried scandal, wondering aloud what was going on in these schoolrooms after dark.

The experiment worked, sort of. Altena became a haven for student excursions into the countryside, but finding shelter in other communities proved to be difficult. Sometimes the situation would become dire. Late one night in the summer of 1909, Schirmann decided it was time to expand his movement beyond Altena. His goal was to establish a network of hostels within walking distance of one another. Beginning in a schoolhouse with straw mats, Schirmann eventually acquired the use of a castle. It still stands—the Ur-hostel, if you will—in Altena, and it's still used as a hostel, believe it or not.

After World War I the movement really began to spread. By 1928 there were more than 2,000 hostels worldwide. Today tens of thousands of hostellers stay at HI-affiliated hostels each year, hailing from everywhere from Alaska to Zaire. Thousands more stay at independent hostels.

The goal of a single association of hostels located within a day's walk of one another will probably never be realized. Still, you're likely to find a promising brew of cultural exchange and friendship over pots of ramen noodles and instant coffee almost anywhere you go.

In that sense, perhaps, Richard Schirmann's dream has been realized after all.

A WORD ABOUT AFFILIATIONS

A majority of hostels in this book are affiliated with Hostelling International (HI); the rest, we've labeled independent hostels.

SCHWEIZER JUGENDHERBERGEN (HI–SJ) is Switzerland's Hostelling International affiliate. The organization is part of the International Youth Hostel Federation, which has 5,000 member hostels in seventy countries. Member hostels are held to a number of regulations, such as maximum number of beds per shower, even a minimum amount of space that must exist between top bunks and the ceiling. To get into an HI hostel you must sometimes have an HI membership card (see below).

These hostels are incredibly strict with rules, and we found staff at the official hostels to be some of the least friendly hostel people in the world. Maybe "hostile" applies instead. The home office in Zürich isn't much help, either. We got the distinct feeling that all they care about is making money by packing in busloads of schoolkids or tourists; they don't seem to care much for the individual backpacker.

That said, the hostels are uniformly clean, safe, and absolutely blah. There are a few exceptions—member hostels that are still basically independently run, as in Lugano and Geneva—and these places are terrific. We'd avoid big-city HI-Swiss hostels otherwise, though.

Austria has two separate branches of Hostelling International, closely related but located in two different offices—they split along political lines long ago, one of them right-wing and the other basically Communist. They get along just fine now, but the result is sometimes chaos. To make matters worse (or better), a chain of Hostelling International–affiliated joints in the province of Styria (known here as Steiermark) has created its own distinct miniorganization. Confusing indeed.

To contact either of the official Austrian organizations, abbreviated as **HI-OEHJV** and **HI-OEJHW** (we won't even try spelling the real names), see below. There aren't any independent hostel groups in Austria—yet.

Drawbacks to the HI hostels include the nonproximity of these villas to the cities and towns (count on half an hour by public transport for many). Also, virtually every one of these hostels kicks you out very early for the entire day. And they're strict about it. However, a breakfast is often included for free, and the dinner (which you pay for) is almost always good and filling.

Many of the giant HI urban hostels in Austria and Switzerland are purpose-built facilities owned by the associations themselves and often resemble well-equipped college dormitories. Some of these HI-owned hostels have developed impressive educational programs that incorporate volunteers from the local community and so forth.

The bulk of the HI hostels, however, are still independently owned. These joints are as varied in personality as their owners are. A common thread that runs through them is a respect for the educational dimension of hostelling. Owners reiterate that hostels offer more than just a cheap sleep; they often join HI out of respect for the organization and its goals.

But sometimes you want a break from all that. Thank goodness, then, for **Swiss Backpackers,** a terrific fledgling organization headquartered in Zürich that administers a growing list of really fine and interesting places. They also publish a helpful, free newspaper you can find here and there. See below for contact information.

Independents are what we call the others. Some owners opt not to join Hostelling International. Membership costs are high, and they feel the return on such an investment isn't enough. Such a decision—in and of itself—does not reflect on the quality of the hostel. It would be foolish to write a hostel off simply because it is not affiliated.

Things in an independent hostel are usually more laid-back—and that's not always a good thing. Some of them are just Party Central, twenty-four hours a day and night.

Liquor isn't always officially off-limits at these places. (In HI joints you must often buy alcohol at the hostel bar or restaurant or forget about it.) Some independent hostels do the lockout thing, but it's not as common or as long-lasting as the one at HI hostels. Rooms are probably homier but also more crowded and smoky. There's no guarantee of quality, and the standards, upkeep, noise level, and beer flow tend to vary wildly from place to place. Some are outstandingly fun; some are grungy beyond belief.

A few independent hostels in Austria and Switzerland are run by church organizations such as convents. These places obviously have stricter lockouts, curfews, and alcohol rules than anyone else in this book. Most also ban unmarried couples from sharing a bed. If they do, we have banned *them* from this book.

HOSTEL MEMBERSHIPS
AND INTERNATIONAL BOOKING

First things first. We advise you to get a Hostelling International membership *before* you set out on your trip.

How do you do that? Easy. Contact the home office of your country's Hostelling International chapter (we've listed a few below) and get a membership card plus other goodies like individual country hostelling guides. Individual memberships cost about $18 US, about $25 for a family (it varies according to country), and are good for one year. If there's a Hostelling International hostel in your neck of the woods, ask about buying the card there instead.

If you want to try some hostels before committing to the responsibility of owning a card, you can also obtain a guest membership. You pay a small supplement of about $3.00 US at an "official" hostel, which stamps your "guest card" each night you pay it. After six stamps, presto! You're a member. As a bonus, many hostels have established discounts for hostellers at businesses in the towns where hostels are located. You might get 10 percent off a meal at a restaurant, discounted train tickets or museum entrance fees, or other perks.

Hostelling International–American Youth Hostels
733 Fifteenth Street NW #840
Washington, DC 20005
Phone: (202) 783–6161, ext. 136
Fax: (202) 783–6171
E-mail: hiayhserv@hiayh.org
Web site: www.hiayh.org

Hostelling International–Canada
400–205 Catherine Street
Ottawa, ON K2P 1C3
Phone: (613) 237–7884
Fax: (613) 237–7868
E-mail: info@hostellingintl.ca
Web site: www.hostellingintl.ca

Youth Hostels Association of England and Wales
8 St. Stephen's Hill
St. Albans, Hertfordshire A11 2DY
Phone: +44 (0) 870 870 8808
Web site: www.yha.org.uk

Scottish Youth Hostels Association
7 Glebe Crescent
Stirling FK8 2JA Scotland
Phone: +44 (0)1786 891400
Fax: +44 (0)1786 891333
E-mail: info@syha.org.uk
Web site: www.syha.org.uk

An Óige (Irish Youth Hostel Association)
61 Mountjoy Street
Dublin 7, Republic of Ireland
Phone: +353 (0) 1 8304555
Fax: +353 (0) 1 8305808
E-mail: mailbox@anoige.ie
Web site: www.irelandyha.org

Hostelling International–Northern Ireland
22 Donegall Road
Belfast BT12 5JN, Northern Ireland
Phone: +44 (0) 28 90324733
Fax: +44 (0) 28 90439699
E-mail: info@hini.org.uk
Web site: www.hini.org.uk

If you're the type who needs the security of knowing where you're staying each night of your trip, you might also want to participate in the International Booking Network (IBN), whereby certain participating hostels—usually located in big cities or major tourist areas—call ahead to another IBN hostel (located in the same sorts of areas) and secure your bunk, even in high season if it's humanly possible. Most ask for an advance notice of three to seven days; if there's any room, you'll get priority. You need only to pre-pay for your bed with a VISA, MasterCard, or Discover (plus a $5.00 US booking fee) and you're in. The system is fairly straightforward. However, *be prepared to eat the cost of the whole bed if you need to cancel on short notice.*

HOW TO HOSTEL

Hostelling is, generally speaking, easy as pie. Plan ahead a bit and use a little common sense, and you'll find check-in goes pretty smoothly.

RESERVING A BED

Getting a good bunk will often be your first and biggest challenge, especially if it's high season. Summer is usually high season, but in some areas—the Alps, Tyrol, and the Bernese Oberland, for instance—winter is the toughest time to get a bed. And popular cities like Vienna or Salzburg seem to be busy almost year-round. Hostellers often have an amazingly laissez-faire attitude about reservations; many simply waltz in at midnight expecting that a bed will work out.

Sometimes it does. Sometimes it doesn't.

Almost every Hostelling International abode takes reservations of some form or another, so if you know where you're going to be, use this service. Be aware that you might need a credit card number to hold a bed, and other hostels require you to mail them a deposit check. You might also need to show up by a certain hour like 6:00 P.M. to get in. Some HI hostels are also affiliated with the worldwide International Booking Network.

Independent hostels can be more strict or more lax about taking solid reservations. Note that they're often much faster to fill up than HI joints because of the wild popularity of no-rules places.

If you can't or won't reserve, the best thing to do is get there superearly. Office opens at 8:00 A.M.? Get there at 7:00. No room, but checkout ends at 11:00? Be back at 11:05 in case of cancellations or unexpected checkouts. The doors are closed again till 4:30 in the afternoon? No problem. Come back around 4:00 with a paperback and camp out on the doorstep. That's your only shot if you couldn't or wouldn't reserve ahead, and hostellers are somewhat respectful of the pecking order: It really is first come, first served. So come first.

PAYING THE PIPER

Once you're in, be prepared to pay for your night's stay immediately—before you're even assigned a bunk. Take note ahead of time which hostels take credit cards, checks, and so forth. And don't expect every little hostel to change your 100-euro note for a couple bucks' worth of laundry.

You will almost always be required to give up your passport and (if you have one) Hostelling International card for the night. Don't sweat it; it's just the way it's done over there, and in fact they have good reasons. For example, if an emergency happens (nah, no chance), the passport might help hostel staff locate your significant others.

Remember to pay ahead if you want a weekly stay, too. Often you can get deep discounts, though the downside is that you'll almost never get even a partial refund if you decide you can't stand the place and leave before the week is up.

If you're paying by the day, rebook promptly each morning; hostel managers are very busy during the morning hours, keeping track of check-ins, checkouts, cleaning duties, and cash. You'll make a friend if you're early about notifying them of your plans for the next day. Managers hate bugging guests all morning or all day about whether they'll be staying on. Don't put the staff through this.

All right, so you've secured a bed and paid up. Now you have to get to it. This may be no easy task at some hostels, where staff and customers look and act like one and the same. A kindly manager will probably notice you bumbling around and take pity. As you're being shown to your room, you're also likely to get a short tour of the facilities and a briefing on the ground rules.

On checkout, you'll get your card and passport back. You might need to pay a small amount if you lose your room key—usually about $5.00 US, but sometimes as much as $25.00 US.

KNOWING THE GROUND RULES

There's one universal ground rule at every hostel: You are responsible for serving and cleaning up after yourself. And there's a corollary rule: Be courteous. So, while you're welcome to use the kitchen facilities, share the space with your fellow guests—don't spread your five-course meal out over all the counter space and rangetop burners if other hungry folks are hanging around waiting. And never ever leave a sinkful of dirty pots and pans behind. That's bad form.

Hostel guests are almost always asked to mark their name and check-in date on all the food they put in the refrigerator. Only a shelf marked FREE FOOD is up for grabs; everything else belongs to other hostellers, so don't touch it. Hostellers might get very touchy about people stealing their grub. Some of the better-run hostels have a spice rack and other kitchen essentials on hand. If you're not sure whether something is communal, ask. Don't assume anything is up-for-grabs unless it is clearly marked as such.

Then there's the lockout, a source of bitter frustration among non-European hostellers. Many hostels in Austria and Switzerland kick everybody out in the morning and don't let them back in until the afternoon or early evening; big-city joints are sometimes but not always immune to this rule. Lockouts tend to run from around 9:30 A.M. (which is ungodly, we say, but pretty typical) to 5:00 or 6:00 P.M., during which time your bags might be inside your room—but *you* won't be. A few places let you back in around 2:00 or 3:00 P.M. Oooooooh, the generosity.

The practice has its pros and cons. Managers usually justify a lockout by noting that it forces travelers to interact with the locals and also allows their staff to "meticulously clean" the rooms. The real reason is usually that the hostel can't or won't pay staff to hang around and baby-sit you all day. On the upside, these hostels never become semiresidential situations stuffed with couch potatoes like many U.S. hostels, so maybe the lockouts solve that problem.

Curfews are also very common; usually the front doors lock between 11:00 P.M. and midnight, and they won't give you a key. Big-city joints generally have some system in place to let you get in twenty-four hours: a guard, a numbered keypad, a room key that also opens the main door. But check first.

In the reviews we've tried to identify those hostels that enforce lockouts. Usually you wouldn't want to be hanging out in the hostel in the middle of the day anyway, but after several sleepless nights of travel—or when you're under the weather—daytime downtime sure is appreciated. So beware. Note that even if we haven't listed a lockout or a curfew, it might exist. These things change. Assume that you *will* get kicked out at 9:00 A.M. for the day, and—except in big cities—will need to be back by midnight.

Finally, some hostels also enforce a maximum limit on your stay— anywhere from three days, if the hostel is really popular, to about two weeks. Savvy budget travelers have learned how to get around this unfortunate situation, of course: They simply suck it up and spend a night at the "Y" or a convenient motel—then check back into the cheaper hostel first thing in the morning. But we didn't tell you to do that. Uh-uh.

ETIQUETTE AND SMARTS

Again, to put it simply, use common sense. Hostellers are a refreshingly flexible bunch. All these people are able to make this system work by looking after one another; remember, in a hostel you're a community member first and a consumer second. With that in mind, here are some guidelines for how to act:

- The first thing you should do after check-in is get your bed made. When you're assigned a bed, stick to it. Don't spread your stuff out on nearby bunks, even if they are empty. Someone's going to be coming in late-night for one of 'em, you can bet the backpack on it.

- Be sure to lock your valuables in a locker—or in a safe if they've got one. Good hostels offer lockers as a service; it might cost a little, but it's worth it. Bring a padlock in case the hostel has run out or charges an arm and a leg.

- Set toiletries and anything else you need in a place where they are easily accessible. This avoids your having to paw through your bag late at night, potentially disturbing other guests from their slumber. The same goes for early-morning departures: If you're taking off at the crack of dawn, take precautions not to wake the whole place.

- If you're leaving early in the morning, try to make all arrangements with the manager before going to bed the night before. Managers are usually accommodating and pleasant folks, but guests are expected to respect their privacy and peace of mind by not pushing things too far. Dragging a manager out of bed at four in the morning to check out—or for some other trivial matter—is really pushing it.

- Be sure to mind the bathroom. A quick wiping of the shower floor with a towel after you use it is common courtesy.

- Finally, be sure to mind the quiet hours. Some hostels have curfews, but very few force lights-out. If you are up after-hours, be respectful. Don't crank the television or radio too loud; don't scream in the hallways late at night. (Save that for the beach, and annoy people staying in much nicer digs.)

PACKING

Those dainty hand towels and dapper shaving kits and free soaps you get at a hotel won't be anywhere in sight at the hostel. In fact, even some of the basic essentials may not be available—kitchens are *not* a given in Austria or Switzerland, for instance. Bring everything you need to be comfortable.

There are only a few things you can expect the hostel to supply:

- A bed frame with a mattress and pillow

- Shower and toilet facilities

- A common room with some spartan furniture

- Maybe a few heavy blankets

Some of the more chic hostels we've identified in this guide may be full-service. But they are the exceptions to the rule.

Bring stuff like this to keep your journey through hostel territory comfortable:

- If you're traveling abroad from the United States, you obviously need a passport. Unlike U.S. hostels, a Euro-hostel will often take your passport as collateral when you check in. Don't get nervous; this is extremely common. It's the European equivalent of taking down your driver's license number when you write a check. However, in the unlikely event that someone loses your passport, make sure you've got backup copies of the issuing office, date, and passport number—both in your luggage and back home.

- Hostelling International membership cards are a good thing to have on hand. They can be purchased at many foreign HI hostels for about $25 annually per person, or $35 for a family membership. You can also buy them at U.S. hostels ahead of time or from American Youth Hostels in Washington, D.C. This card identifies you as a certified superhosteller and gets you the very cheapest rate for your bed in all HI (and also some unaffiliated) hostels. With discounts of $2.00 to $4.00 per night, the savings can add up fast. Sometimes that membership card also gets you deals at local restaurants, bike shops, and tours. Again, it will be easier to deal with the front desk at some of the more cautious hostels (even nonmember ones) if you can flash one of these cards.

- Red Alert! Do not plan on using a sleeping bag in most hostels. A good number of places simply won't allow it—problems with ticks and other creatures dragged in from the great outdoors have propelled this prohibition into place. The alternative is a sleepsack, which is basically two sheets sewn together with a makeshift pillowcase. You can find them at most budget travel stores, or you can make your own. Personally, we hate these confining wraps and rarely get through the night in one without having it twist around our bodies so tight that we wake up wanting to charge it with attempted manslaughter. Our preferred method is to bring our own set of sheets, though that might be too much extra stuff to pack if you're backpacking. Some hostels give you free linen; most that don't will rent sheets for about $1.00 to $3.00 US per night. You don't get charged for use of the standard army surplus blankets or the musty charm that comes with them.

- Some people bring their own pillows, as those supplied tend to be on the frumpy side. Small pillows are also useful for sleeping on trains and buses.

- We definitely suggest earplugs for light sleepers, especially for urban hostels—but also in case you get caught in a room with a heavy snorer.

- A small flashlight is a must, not only for late-night reading but also to find your bed without waking the entire dorm.

- A little bit of spice is always nice, especially when you have had one too many plates of pasta. You'll find the cost of basil, oregano, and the like way too high to stomach once you're on the road. Buy it cheap before you leave and bag it in jars or small Ziploc® bags.

- Check to see which hostels have laundry facilities. Most won't, and then you'll need to schlep your stuff to the local laundromat. It'll be expensive, so bring lotsa money.

- Wearing flip-flops in the shower might help you avoid a case of athlete's foot.

- Be sure your towel is a quick-drying type. Otherwise you'll wind up with mildew in your pack—and in your food.

TRAVEL INSURANCE

Travel insurance might seem like a useless expenditure, but it might come in handy. This insurance typically covers everything from baggage loss and injuries in an air travel accident (nah, that won't happen, don't even think about it) to medical expenses incurred while you're traveling. It's also helpful if someone puts a dent in that rental car and you waived the damage coverage to save bucks.

We'd recommend buying some sort of travel insurance. The best we've found so far for European traveling is from a company in Wisconsin called Travel Guard (800–826–1300).

TRANSPORTATION

Take a careful look at your transportation options when planning a hostel journey. You should be able to hop from city to city by bus or train without a problem, but you could have trouble getting to rural hostels without a car.

GETTING TO AUSTRIA AND SWITZERLAND BY PLANE

The airline business is volatile. Airlines are in business one day and in bankruptcy the next. Great deals and rip-off fares come and go with a regularity that is frightening to behold. Supply, demand, season, the stock market, and random acts of cruelty or kindness all appear to contribute to the quixotic nature of fares.

As a result there is no one piece of simple advice we can give you, other than this one: Find a darned good travel agent who cares about budget travelers, and trust your agent with all the planning. You can cruise the Internet if you like, and you might find an occasional great deal your agent doesn't know about. Just make sure that the sellers are reputable before giving out your credit-card number.

FROM NORTH AMERICA

A couple tips:

- **Charters** are the cheapest way to go, though it's no-frills all the way.

- From the United States, most direct routes are run by the **national airlines** of the two countries. Austrian Airlines (800–843–0002) flies to Vienna; Swissair (800–221–4750 in the United States; 800–267–9477 in Canada) flies to Geneva and Zürich, though at press time the airline was in deep financial trouble. Both are more expensive than average European flight tickets, so consider flying into Paris, Nice, Munich, or Milan and then taking a train if that's cheaper. You might also be able to get a good deal connecting through Germany on Lufthansa (800–645–3880) or LTU (800–888–0200), which flies to Düsseldorf, Frankfurt, and Munich from New York, Orlando, and Miami.

- From eastern Canada, you can sometimes get very cheap flights on Air Canada (800–776–3000) from Montréal, Toronto, or Halifax. Or try connecting out of eastern Canada through a European hub—use KLM, for instance, to get from Canada to Amsterdam to wherever. In summer there are more flights, but they're superpopular, so book early.

- **Cheap-ticket brokers** (also called consolidators or bucket shops) are a great bet for saving money, but you have to be fast on your feet to keep up, as the deals appear and disappear literally daily.

London and New York are major centers for bucket shops. The introduction to *Europe: The Rough Guide* is the best source of material we've found on hubs, connections, and consolidators to Europe from just about anywhere in the world. Hit the library and make some notes. (It's mighty thick to be carrying around.)

- **Flying as a courier** comes highly recommended by some folks who've tried it. Others are nervous about it. It works this way: You agree to carry luggage for a company in exchange for a very cheap round-trip ticket abroad. You must be flexible about your departure and return dates, and you can't change those dates once assigned to you—and you usually can bring only carry-on luggage.

There isn't nearly as much demand for couriers from smaller destinations to Europe as there is from places like New York or Los Angeles; but it's still worth a shot. Check out guidebooks and Web sites on the subject.

Here's one more tip: If you're flying into Switzerland and don't want to schlep stuff around to your first hotel, there are airport services that will **check it through** and ensure that it will arrive at your bunk (probably ahead of you). It costs a bit but might be worth checking out.

FROM EUROPE

Planes within Europe used to be fantastically expensive. However, times are changing: A raft of cut-rate short-hop airlines have sprung up—like Go!, Easyjet, British Midland, and Virgin Express. Check out the papers and travel agents for the latest-breaking deals, and be prepared to sometimes fly into or out of a weird airport to save the dough.

Austria and Switzerland have not yet been much served by these new Euro-cheapies, so you might end up flying into Munich or Milano, for example, and then taking a short flight or train ride from there.

BY TRAIN

Most folks go by train around Europe, and it's a sensible choice. Services and connections are generally good, so getting to Austria and/or Switzerland by rail is normally a straightforward matter of booking and then taking a long-distance journey, possibly with a change or two en route. You've got two choices: (1) Buy point-to-point tickets for every leg of the journey, or (2) buy a Europe-wide pass.

If you're math-and-map friendly, definitely buy a copy of the *Thomas Cook European Rail Timetable* before you go—or in an English-language bookstore in London, Paris, or elsewhere in Europe after you arrive. It's an invaluable reference to the train schedules of Great Britain and Eastern and Western Europe.

FROM ENGLAND

There's only one way to get to Switzerland from England by train: **Eurostar** (102–104 Victoria Street, London SW1 5J1; phone: +44–0990–1861 86 or +44–1233–6175 75; 800–387–6782 in the United States; Web site: www.eurostar.com). They've got a monopoly on the sub-Chunnel service that takes you from England to Brussels in under three hours, but they run it well: You'll never get onto a faster or more efficiently run train. You can have breakfast in SoHo and lunch in Paris—without the delays of airport check-in and checkout and with pretty minimal customs and immigration formalities. From there you could take a daytime or overnight train to Switzerland.

Of course you pay extra for the privilege. Tickets tend to run from as little as £99 (about $175 US) off-season, booking in advance, to much more if you book on short notice or travel during a summer weekend. And—bummer—buying a single one-way ticket isn't much cheaper than purchasing a round-tripper. So you might as well go whole hog.

At least there are discounts for Eurail and BritRail pass holders and for young travelers.

Always check ahead for price information. Book ahead by fifteen days and you might save as much as 50 percent! It's easiest to book ahead through your travel agent at home, but Eurostar also has offices in London's Waterloo Station, Paris's Gare du Nord, and Brussels' Gare du Midi.

The Eurostar runs from London to Paris about twenty times a day, and to Brussels about ten times a day—both less frequently on weekends—and you've gotta have a reservation. One additional plus with Eurostar: If you somehow manage to miss your train (you oaf), they will let you reschedule your ride for another convenient and available time—within certain limits—at no penalty if you bought a full-fare ticket. Wouldn't it be nice if the airlines worked that way? Yep. It sure would.

FROM CONTINENTAL EUROPE

From elsewhere in Europe, getting to Austria or Switzerland by rail is a straightforward matter of booking and then taking a long-distance journey, possibly with a change or two en route. You've got three choices: (1) Buy point-to-point tickets for every leg of the journey, (2) get a regional pass, or (3) buy a Europe-wide pass.

Eurail passes can be key if you're touring Austria and Switzerland en route to someplace else in Europe. Here's the rule: If you're seeing them as part of a long trip, get the Eurail. In our experience these passes are a great deal for covering big distances. DER Travel (888–337–7350; www.dertravel.com), a German company with offices in Chicago, sells Eurail passes and really impressed us as experts on travel in this area, especially Austria. You can also get a Eurail pass from Rail Europe (888–382–7245 in the United States; 800–361–7245 in Canada; www.raileurope.com).

Sure, they're not cheap, but they're superconvenient and cover almost everything. If you do get the Eurail pass, you've gotta play by the rules: Wait until the first day you're gonna use it, then go to the station early and have it validated (stamped) by a ticket agent. Write the current date into the first square (it should have a "1" beneath it), and remember to put the day first (on top), European-style.

Now it gets easier. Just show it to ticket agents when you want to reserve a seat on a train (which is crucial in summer season, on weekends, and during rush hours). That smiling person will print you out a seat reservation, which you show to the conductor. You must reserve seats before the train arrives, and since you'll have no idea where or when that is, it's best to reserve a day or two ahead as you're getting off the train.

If you can't or won't get a reservation, just show your pass to the conductor. Sometimes he'll let you get on anyway.

Finally, don't fold, bend, or otherwise mangle the long cardboard pass (and that can be difficult to achieve while fumbling for your money belt at the station as the train whips in). That might invalidate the whole thing.

The cost of these passes depends on a few things: (1) how long you're traveling and (2) how much comfort you want. First-class passes, which few hostellers buy, cost 50 percent more and give you a little more legroom. Call one of the railpass vendors listed above for the very latest pricing information.

Point-to-Point Tickets might be the best route to go if you're just blowing through these countries in a hurry. Get them at stations, either at ticket windows or—if you have cash, coins, or credit cards—automatic machines.

A few more tips on cross-European train travel:

- If you're buying just point-to-point tickets, go for second-class. Why pay 50 percent more for a little extra legroom?

- From distant countries, like Denmark or Spain, you can sometimes take a sleeper car (also known as a couchette); at less than $20 per person (quite a bit more for a double), it saves you a night in a hotel or hostel and gets you closer to where you want to go. The drawback is that you sleep four or, more likely, six to a car.

- From Paris the high-speed TGV lines make a great way to connect quickly through Europe. France's train system is one of the world's best, with superfast bullet trains blasting you from Paris out into the countryside at upwards of 100 miles an hour. TGV trains always cost extra, but they're covered by the Eurail pass. It's important to remember that you must reserve a ticket at least ten minutes before departure. That will cost a pittance, usually about €4.00 or (about $4.00 US) per ticket, for the reservation—well worth it.

- TGV trains run from Paris to Geneva (four per day, three and one-half hours), Lausanne (five per day, four hours), and Zürich (one per day, six hours).

- Remember that trains don't run as frequently on weekends; Saturday is usually the worst day to travel. International trains and sleeper cars usually run seven days a week, and Friday and Sunday are feast or famine; check schedules and think like a local.

BY BUS

Eurolines is a Europe-wide company running comfortable long-distance buses around Europe for very competitive rates, certainly cheaper than trains and planes if you're booking on short notice. They serve quite a network of cities.

GETTING AROUND AUSTRIA AND SWITZERLAND

BY TRAIN

Trains are still king in Europe. Sure, the car dominates everyday life for locals, but when you're a tourist you just can't beat the iron horse.

Swiss and Austrian train lines aren't always fast, but, boy, are they scenic. And they always run on time. SNTO, Switzerland's rail company, is as efficient as a Swiss watch; its trains and tracks are world renowned for their comfort and scenery. Austrian trains are only good quality, not great—too many cars have six-seated compartments, where you're staring down five people you don't know for the next six hours or so.

While these rail systems cross an incredible variety of landscape, even the iron horse can't get everywhere. It's likely that at some point you will need to supplement your train travel with some form of gondola, lift, bus, cog railway, steam train . . . something. All part of the fun.

TICKETS AND PASSES

What to buy? If you're going to be doing lots of short city-to-city hops, just buy tickets each day; it's cheaper. But chances are you'll be in the area for a week or two; in that case get a pass.

Swiss Railpasses are one of the best deals in the world. They come in bunches of four, eight, fifteen, and thirty days; like other country railpasses, they confer free passage on all state railroads and most private ones, too. They get you free passage on terrifically scenic rides like the Glacier Express, Bernina Express, Panorama Express, and more; you pay only for a seat reservation.

Get this: As a great bonus, they're also good on the postbus system (see bus section below) and ferryboats that ply Swiss lakes. As if that weren't enough, many mountain railways and gondolas—which are *not* covered by this otherwise amazing pass—will *still* give you a 25 percent discount for holding one.

Other options include a Half-Fare Travel Card (for 90 SF/about $63 US, you get half off all train tickets for a month), a Swiss

Flexipass, a Swiss Card, a Rail 'n' Drive Pass, and a Family Card. Contact the tourism offices or travel offices listed in this book for the latest pricing info, or just stand in line at any Swiss train station ticket office; the staff are exceptionally knowledgeable about this stuff.

Austrian railpasses are also available in various changing packages, which a travel agent can better fill you in on.

Always remember to punch your train ticket before you get on the train; there will be a machine in every station that stamps the current date and time on the ticket, showing the conductor that it has been "used up."

Oh, and let's not forget this important side note: Train station toilets—marked with a wc—almost always require you to cough up something like 1.50 SF (that's about $1.00 US!). As a bonus (we guess), these same joints sell shampoo, shaving kits, and what have you; use one of the nice sinks and you could even spruce up before a big meeting or date in one of these places. Suddenly that buck isn't hurting quite so much.

The Bern, Switzerland, train station even has pay showers, though we haven't noticed them anywhere else in the country.

BY BUS

Buses can be a cheaper ride than the train or more expensive, depending on local whims. They're extremely useful in places where trains simply don't go—reasonably on time, scenic, and with lots of locals riding alongside you happy to give advice or opinions or soccer scores.

It might take you all day to make connections, but most bus drivers are helpful and knowledgeable. They'll sometimes let you off where you want to go even if there isn't an actual scheduled bus stop there. They are also quite accustomed to hostellers asking, "Where's my stop??" and handle the situation calmly and professionally. Usually. (In small towns, though, anything goes.)

Both the Swiss and the Austrians have an interesting system of getting you to the sticks while delivering mail at the same time. It's called a postbus, and the only other place we've seen it is in Scotland, where it's supplemental to bigger bus companies. In Switzerland and Austria the post office–owned buses ARE the bus. Long, sleek, and comfortable, they'll take you up mountain passes and into tiny hamlets where no train would dare venture. They're cheap, too.

In Austrian cities you often buy tickets from the bus or streetcar conductor or from the local ticket office. In small-town Switzerland it's the same, but in cities you might be able to buy one from a streetside automatic ticket machine right at the stop.

Always remember to punch your ticket, for local bus rides; there will be a machine either at the bus stop or on the bus. Most are good for one hour. Longer-distance tickets don't need to be punched, just shown to the driver when you get on.

BY BOAT

There are a few occasions when you might be cruising lakes or rivers, and your Eurail pass covers some (though not all) of these journeys.

Donaudamfschiffarhtsgesellschaft (DDSG), the tongue-twisting transport organization, for instance, runs one ferry a day on summer weekends from Vienna up the Danube to Krems and Dürnstein and then back. It leaves Vienna (on the river, obviously, just on the bridge next to the U-Bahn stop) at 9:00 in the morning, starts back in midafternoon, and finally arrives at around 8:30 P.M. Other ferry companies run boats along the more pastoral stretch of the river between Krems and Melk.

Other ferries run around Lake Konstanz (Constance, Bodensee) between Switzerland, Austria, and Germany; there's a popular steamer service on Lake Luzern, too.

BY CAR

Renting a car is definitely the most expensive way to see Europe, and yet it has advantages: You can cover the hamlets a whole lot quicker, you have complete freedom of movement, and you get that cool feeling of the wind and rain rushing past your ears.

Just bring your wallet: Car rentals are incredibly expensive in Switzerland, less so in Austria but still certainly not inexpensive. And the gas isn't cheap, either. At least their small autos get great gas mileage. By all means—we can't stress this enough—book your rental *ahead* from your home country. It's so much cheaper. Rentals will set you back a stiff $60 to $100 US a day for a small car, and that price might or might not include heavy taxes and insurance.

If you can, rent or lease long-term through a company such as Kemwel (800–678–0678; www.kemwel.com), which books long-term rentals for a fraction of the daily rate if you book ahead from your home country. You may have to pick the car up in Germany, but who cares? The other usual American companies also rent in Austria and Switzerland.

Speeds and distance in continental Europe are measured in kilometers. Just to remind you, 1 kilometer is a little less than ⅔ mile; 100 miles equal roughly 160 kilometers. Here are some common speed limits you might see on road signs, with their U.S. equivalents:

40 kph = 25 miles per hour
100 kph = 62 miles per hour
50 kilometers away = 31 miles away

Stop signs are round and red and, surprisingly, they say STOP in English. Can't get much clearer than that. Streetlights are also simple: Red means stop, yellow means slow down, green means go. A green or blinking green arrow means go ahead and turn left; a yellow arrow means slow down.

Gas is measured in liters, and there are roughly four liters to the U.S. gallon. Gas prices are listed per liter, so multiply by four and then convert into home currency to estimate the price per gallon you'd pay back home—you'll be shocked at how much it is. Want a bike yet?

What else? Well, as elsewhere in Europe, drivers tend to be rather aggressive—even in hairpin mountain situations, even in civilized countries like these two. So be careful. Also note that in all of Switzerland and some of Austria, you *must stop at crosswalks* even if someone has put just a big toe on the walk. (Kids don't even need to be in the crossing yet.) Take crosswalks very seriously, or you'll get busted big-time.

PHONES

Two words: *phone card.* Dealing with three different kinds of pay phones can be frustrating, so don't bother pumping change unless you're truly desperate. Instead buy phone cards at tobacco shops, train station windows, or small markets, and stick 'em into the slots in the phones.

Don't bother trying to call Mom and Dad back home with these cards, however. Get a phone card from the United States (or other home country) before you arrive. It'll be cheaper and easier, though a few phones might block your phone card.

When calling the hostels to book a bunk, you dial differently depending on whether you are in the country or not. Inside the countries, dial the numbers exactly as shown in this book. To call from outside the country, you'll need to add a few prefixes.

To call Switzerland from North America, dial 011 (the international long-distance code when calling from the United States or Canada), then dial 41 (the country code), and DROP THE FIRST ZERO from the numbers printed in this book.

To call Austria from North America, dial 011, then 43 (the country code for Austria), and DROP THE FIRST ZERO from the numbers printed in this book.

To call Austria or Switzerland from any other European country, substitute 00 as the international long-distance code. To call back home to the United States, Canada, or wherever else you might hail from, dial 001 and then the number you are calling.

Special note: You cannot make toll-free calls from public pay phones in Austria. Instead you have to go to the post office, where there are phone booths designed to make international or long-distance calls, and must use AT&T, MCI, or Sprint.

Remember that it's cheaper to make coin calls at night and that directory assistance is invariably expensive (dial 111 in Switzerland).

Currently the three giant communications corporations appear to have monopolized the way you call home; many of the larger hostels in Europe have special phones that have been installed by companies like AT&T, MCI, and Sprint. The calls come with a weighty per-call charge, which can add up real fast, in addition to the exhorbitant rates they already charge per minute. What's more, you can use these phones only if you have an existing account with the specific phone company. The situation is made more frustrating because these phones sometimes won't accept a credit card.

Your best bet is to purchase a prepaid calling card at any Austrian post office—or newsstand or tobacco shop, if a post office isn't handy—then stick it into the slot in a pay phone. What could be easier?

Even cooler, on many phones there's a visual graph displaying your call time as a line that shrinks as you talk. The only drawback: You can't recharge these cards mid-call, so if that line disappears—let's say you're on hold with Mom, waiting for her to find a pen and get you're Western Union details—you're toast.

MONEY

You'll need it, that's for sure, especially in Switzerland—one of the most expensive countries in Europe, and that means everything from your hostel bed to your train ticket to your groceries. Don't even *think* about eating out on the cheap. Austria is a much better value—bigger portions, lower prices.

Always get money from an ATM if possible rather than changing money. If you must change, use a big bank instead of a tourist office, train station, bureau de change, or small bank; their rates are all terrible, and they figure you won't know the difference. Try to spend all your change before you leave one country for another unless you're coming back, or unless you've got euros, since you can't exchange coins—only bills.

The euro will be the only currency used in participating countries, including Austria, after February 2002. Credit card charges might appear in euros before then—although the final result will still be converted back to dollars on your monthly statement.

One euro is roughly equal to one U.S. dollar. At press time, it wasn't known precisely what all the new euro denominations would be—but it was known that each country would get to design one face of their local coins and bills.

Swiss money consists of solid, heavy change—just as you'd expect from such a prosperous and efficient land—plus a selection of paper bills. The change weighs a ton when you're traveling, so get in the habit of paying for purchases with the coins whenever possible; save a few for lockers at train stations, too, which take only coins. At press time there were about 1.4 Swiss francs (SF) to the U.S. dollar (the rate fluctuates, of course). Here's a quick primer:

- Five-franc coins are enormous barbells; they're worth about $3.50 US at this writing.

- Two-franc coins are smaller but also weighty and are worth something like $1.40 US.

- One-franc coins are thinner than the twos and are worth perhaps 70 cents US.

- The half-franc is an oddball, tiny and thin, yet worth about 35 cents US.

Swiss francs get split up into 100 centimes (or rappen, in German) for the purposes of making change. The twenty-centime pieces are solid but not worth much, just 14 cents each or so. And the skinny five- and ten-centime coins aren't worth your time of day; though they're light, give 'em to street musicians—or else be stuck with an ever-growing pocket of souvenirs.

The paper is easier to carry, obviously, and to keep straight in your head. That's because you'll normally be dealing only with the four kinds of bills noted below; ATMs give only the first two. That long blue 100-franc note is worth about $70.00 US—enough for a hostel night and a dinner, about what you'd probably spend in a typical day on the road. The slightly shorter 50-franc note is worth half as much, about $35.00 US. Twenty-franc notes—shorter again, and pinkish—are worth about $14.00 US, and the yellowish-orange ten-franc notes, really short, are worth about $7.00 US.

No sweat, right? The real challenge, as we've said, is to keep your balance with all that really heavy change weighing down your pockets.

SPEAKING FRENCH, GERMAN, AND ITALIAN

English will get you by in touristed areas of Austria and Switzerland, which probably covers most of the places you're going. However, occasionally you'll want to get way off the beaten track, where you might have a little more trouble. Just think: This might be your only chance to forge a meaningful bond while getting the right bus tickets, too.

Austria pretty much speaks one language: German. English is well understood by some, *poorly understood* by others, and not understood at all by still others. Don't assume that just because someone happens to work in, say, a train ticket office he or she will know your language. We've found many a hostel manager in rural Austria who couldn't speak a word of English, so learn a little German before you go.

The Swiss are the polyglots of Europe—they speak *four* languages without any seeming effort at all: German in the north and east (the biggest part, including Zürich, Interlaken, Tyrol, Bern, and Basel); French in the west (Geneva, Lausanne, Montreux); Italian in the far south (Lugano, Locarno); plus a fourth tongue called Romansch in the far southeastern corner that looks and sounds like a blend of all three, though you'll rarely encounter this language.

Don't despair. You'll be OK with a bit of brushing up on your language skills and a little sign or body language where necessary. Hereforth, a short primer.

Bon courage! E buona fortuna! Viel Glüeck!

FRANCAIS (FRENCH)
WESTERN SWITZERLAND

WHAT THEY SAY	HOW THEY SAY IT (approximately)	WHAT THEY MEAN
oui	we	yep
non	no!	nope
peut-être	put ed	maybe
un	uh	one
deux	do	two
trois	twa	three
quatre	cat	four
billet/billets	B.A.	ticket/tickets
première classe	premier class	first class
deuxième classe	do-zyem class	second class
autobus	aw toe booze	bus
non fumer	naw foo may	non-smoking
passe d'Eurail	pass door rail	Eurail pass
train	tren	train
quai/voie	kay/vwa	platform
voiture	vwa-choor	car number of a train
voiture-lit	vwa-choor leet	sleeping car of a train
place	plass	seat
pardon	par don	excuse me/I'm sorry
de Nice	de niece	from Nice
à Paris	ah, pear "E"	to Paris
je voudrais	zhuh food ray	I'd like...
j'ai besoin de	J.B. swan, duh	I need...
merci	mare "C"	thank you
merci bien	mare CBN	thanks a lot!
bonjour	bon shoo	good morning, good afternoon
bon soir	bon swar	good evening, good nigh
au revoir	oh, vwar	goodbye
à bientôt	ah, be in toe	see ya soon
de rien	darien	you're welcome
monsieur	miss yew	sir
madame	ma damn	m'am
mademoiselle	madam was hell	miss
mesdames	may damn	ladies
messieurs	may sure	sirs
ceci	sir see	this one
cela	sir la	that one

ITALIANO (ITALIAN)
SOUTHERN SWITZERLAND

WHAT THEY SAY	HOW THEY SAY IT (approximately)	WHAT THEY MEAN
si	see/she	yes
no	no	no means no
una/uno	ooh nah/ooh no	one
due	do "A"?	two
tre	tray	three
quattro	kwa-tro	four
biglietta/biglietti	Billy eta/Billy A.T.	ticket/tickets
prima classe	preema class "A"	first class
seconda classe	sick on da class "A"	second class
non fumatori	naw foo ma tory	nonsmoking
passa di treno	passa the traino!	train pass
treno	traino	train
binario	beanario	platform/track number
scusami	skooza me	excuse me
mi dispiace	me "D" spee-ah-chee	I'm sorry
grazie	gratsy	thank you
grazie mille	gratsy mealy	thanks a lot!
bongiorno	bon journo	good morning
buona sera	wanna Sara	good afternoon, good evening
ciao	chow	hi;bye
ciao-ciao	chow-chow	bye-bye
arrivaderci	a-riva-dare-chay	goodbye
prego	prego	you're welcome
pronto	pronto!	yes?
da	"D"	Rome
per	pear	to
Vorrei	Vhooray	I'd like . . .
Ho bisogno di	obi sanyo "D"	I need . . .
Questa	kwest-ah	this one
Quella	kwell-ah	that one

DEUTSCH (GERMAN)
AUSTRIA and EASTERN SWITZERLAND

WHAT THEY SAY	HOW THEY SAY IT (approximately)	WHAT THEY MEAN
grussgött	groose got	hello (Austria)
gutten tag	goo ten tag	hello, good day (Switzerland)
bitte	beetah	please; excuse me; may I help you?
danke	Don "K"	thanks
danke schöne	Don KeShane	thank you very much
ein	ine	one
zwei	dzvye	two
drei	dry	three
zug	zoog	train
U-Bahn	oo baan	subway
S-Bahn	S baan	commuter/suburban tra
bahnof	baa-noff	train station
hauptbahnof	how baa-noff	main train station
bus	boose	bus
ich möchte . . .	eek mookta	I'd like . . .
ein fahrkarte	ine far carta	a ticket
jugendherberge	you get her burger	hostel
doppelzimmer	dopple zimmer	double room
platz	plats	square
sprechen	spricken	speak
sie Englisch	zee English	English

OTHER RESOURCES

There's surprisingly little out there about hostelling and hostels—that's why you're reading this, right?—but we did find a few sources. Most simply list phone numbers and addresses.
Remember that hostels are constantly opening, closing, renovating, being sold, and changing their policies. So not everything written in a guidebook will always still be true by the time you read it. Be smart and call ahead to confirm prices, availability, and directions, rather than rolling into town depending on a bed—and getting a nasty surprise like a vacant lot instead. We know; it has happened to us.

HOSTEL ASSOCIATION HEADQUARTERS

AUSTRIA

Both of the following groups are affiliates of Hostelling International; they are not competitors, and some hostels belong to both associations. You can get information for all Hostelling International Austrian hostels from either office.

Österreichischer Jugendherbergsverband (OEJHV)
Hauptverband
Schottenring 28, A–1010 Vienna
Phone: (43) (0)1–533–5353 or (43) (0)1–533–5354
Fax: (43) (0)1–535–0861
E-mail: oejhv-zentrale@oejhv.or.at
Web site: www.oejhv.or.at

Österreichische Jugendherbergswerk
Helferstorferstrasse 4, A–1010 Vienna
Phone: (43) (0)1–533–1833
Fax: (43) (0)1–533–1833–81
E-mail: oejhw@oejhw.or.at
Web site: www.oejhw.or.at

SWITZERLAND

SCHWEIZER JUGENDHERBERGEN
Schaffhauserstrasse 14, Postfach 161
CH–8042 Zürich
Phone: (41) (0)1–360–1414
Fax: (41) (0)1–360–1460
E-mail: bookingoffice@youthhostel.ch
Web site: www.youthhostel.ch
Home office of Hostelling International offices in Switzerland.

SWISS BACKPACKERS
P.O. Box 530
CH–8027 Zürich
Home office of the independent Swiss Backpackers chain.

TOURISM OFFICES

AUSTRIA

IN THE UNITED STATES:

Austrian National Tourist Office
500 Fifth Avenue, #800
New York, NY 10110
Phone: (212) 575–7723
Fax: (212) 730–4568
Web site: www.anto.com

IN ENGLAND:

Austrian National Tourist Office
14 Cork Street
London W1X 1PF
Phone: 0171–629–0461

SWITZERLAND

IN THE EASTERN UNITED STATES:

Switzerland Tourism
Phone: (212) 757–5944
Web site: www.switzerlandtourism.com

IN THE WESTERN UNITED STATES:

Switzerland Tourism
222 North Sepulveda Boulevard, Suite 1570
El Segundo, CA 90245–4300
Phone: (310) 640–8900
Web site: www.switzerlandtourism.com

WEB SITES

SWITZERLAND

There are also a few Web sites worth checking out. Twirl your browser to these coordinates:

> *www.youthhostel.ch*
> *www.jugitours.ch*

The well-designed home site of the otherwise extremely unhelpful "official" Switzerland hostel association. The design is humorous and interesting, you're always greeted with a quiz when you enter, and the hostel search engine actually works. *Some* of the pages are in English.

> *www.backpacker.ch*

Information about the good independent chain of Swiss Backpacker hostels, including member contact information, prices, bed counts, and such.

AUSTRIA

Mostly in German only, these are the Web pages of the two Austrian Hostelling International groups. They don't all overlap and aren't terribly helpful—or always translated. Oh, well.

> *www.jgh.at*
> *www.oejhv.or.at*
> *www.oejhw.or.at*

The prices and rates listed in this guidebook were confirmed at press time. We recommend, however, that you call establishments before traveling to obtain current information.

The Hostels

VIENNA (WIEN)

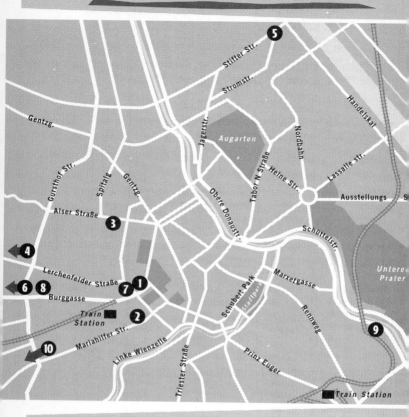

Page numbers follow hostel names.

VIENNA (WIEN)

Eastern Austria, for most travelers, can be defined in just one word.

Vienna.

Actually it's pronounced "Veen," or something like that, but no matter. This city is one of the world's distinctive places, as instantly recognizable as Venice and yet not a place stuck in the past: Thousands of locals live and breathe here, enjoying life with a fullness rarely seen elsewhere. Beer, wine, chocolate, lingerie, ice cream, clubs, discos, cafes . . . it goes on and on, in neighborhood after neighborhood of university students, well-heeled locals, and others.

The place has amazing history, too, of course—the Hapsburg emperors ruled this part of Europe with an iron hand for a time from the Hofburg Palace and assorted villas around town. For gosh sakes, there are even some Roman ruins here, in two places downtown. They're underneath the Hoher Markt at number 3 (very central, between Stephansplatz and Schwedenplatz), and then also at Am Hof 9 near Herrengasse Station on the U3 line of the U-Bahn.

Basically, independent travelers and backpackers flocking to Vienna can be divided into two camps: those seeking the old, historical city centered on palaces and cathedrals and those in the know who realize that this town is shaking off that dusty image with an explosion of trendy restaurants and cafes, clubs, and a local population who dress provocatively.

Those in the latter camp will be found snuffling through the district west of the city center, near the largest concentration of hostels. The area is dominated by Neubaugasse and Neustiftgasse Streets and is one of the most interesting and entertaining neighborhoods in Europe. You can do your grocery shopping, check out a cafe or bar, browse through a bookstore, or even convert to a different faith. Of course the hostels here are nearly always full at all times of the year, so it's best to *call well ahead* of your scheduled arrival—we would recommend at least six months to a year ahead if you're coming during the high season of June, July, and August.

The other camp comes to see what made Vienna a rival to Paris and London during the eighteenth and nineteenth centuries; that is, the stupendous architectural achievements brought to you by the Hapsburgs. Tourists can save themselves a lot of hassle by taking the #1 and #2 trams that circle Ringstrasse in opposite directions, giving a quick overview of the big sights. Or, if you take the U-Bahn to St. Stephan's Cathedral, just walk up the stairs to the exit and you will be within easy walking distance of the cathedral—which manifests itself immediately upon exit—as well as the pedestrian Kartnerstrasse, where you can watch humanity in all its glory or lameness.

Be prepared for milling crowds watching in awe as some guy manipulates a faux piano–playing puppet to the strains of Beethoven's *Fifth* or Kurdish political groups demonstrating against the capture of their leader. Either way, with milling crowds come the ubiquitous pickpockets, who are always on the lookout for clueless Americans stepping away from a handy ATM machine stuffing their wad of newly acquired bills into their already busting wallets.

Anyway, other places to hit in Vienna include the Prater amusement park and beaches on the Danube. Vienna gets way more sun than western Austria and is blessed with consistently good, warm weather, so sight-seeing isn't normally marred by rain.

Finally, if you've really got some serious problems, there's always the Sigmund Freud Museum in the ninth district at Berggasse 19. Check out the famous couch and reflect upon the meaning of cigars.

GETTING AROUND

Getting around Vienna is ridiculously easy. A comprehensive network of streetcar ("tram"), subway, electric railway, and bus lines crisscrosses the city, ensuring that you'll never have to walk too far for anything. At night, after the normal transit stops running, a series of "night buses" ferry partygoers from the action back out to their homes or hostels in the burbs. Good system. Cars are here, too, of course, but they aren't as thick on the ground as in some other cities.

To get the most out of the transit network, buy a twenty-four–hour ticket from a tobacco and cigarette shop ("Tabak"). It costs €4.00, about $5.00 US; you push it into an orange machine to stamp the time and date on it just before your first ride (not sooner), and then for the next twenty-four hours you can ride anywhere on the city transit system without a bother. Unlike in most other European cities, you don't have to keep buying tickets or even showing your ticket to the conductor—it works on the honor system. (If you get caught without a proper ticket by a surprise inspection, though, you could be fined up to $200 US. Ouch.)

Public transportation is very advanced in Vienna. Dig this, for instance: Cars have to stop for pedestrians in crosswalks (but if the walking signal's red, don't cross), and they have to stop for *any* child or elderly person crossing, even if it's not at a crosswalk. The city's network of trams, U-Bahns, and buses (bearing the Austrian flag) means that you'll never have to walk far.

Stephansplatz is the city's central node for subway lines going into and out of the historic center, and the Westbahnof train station is handy for many other destinations. All the instructions are usually in German, so make sure you get the correct information; try asking someone trustworthy to confirm train, track, or subway information.

VIENNA HOSTELS at a glance

	RATING	PRICE	IN A WORD	PAGE
HI-Wilhemininenberg Castle	👍👍	€17–26	beautiful	p.49
HI-Hutteldorf-Hacking	👍	€14–16	remote	p.51
HI-Myrthengasse	👍	€14–18	good	p.52
HI-Brigittenau	👍	€17–20	huge	p.50
HI-Ruthensteiner	👍	€11–18	central	p.46
Wombat's	👍	€14	crazy	p.56
Believe It or Not	👍👎	€8.00–12.00	tiny	p.45
Hostel Zöhrer	👍👎	€12–18	iffy	p.47
Panda Hostel	👍👎	€8.00–12.00	rubble	p.54
Don Bosco	👎	€7.00	horrible	p.55

BELIEVE IT OR NOT HOSTEL

7, Myrthengasse 10, Apartment #14, A-1070 Vienna

Telephone Number: 01–526–4658

Rates: €8.00–12.00 (about $9.00–$12.00 US) per person
Credit cards: No
Beds: 10
Private/family rooms: No
Kitchen available: Yes
Office hours: Vary, call ahead
Lockout: 10:30 A.M. to 12:30 P.M.
Affiliation: None

If you're into communal living situations, this would be an okay place to bunk down for the night in a neat area of Vienna. But it's so informal that you might have trouble reaching the staff.

This small place with the unusual name is located just across the street from two massive and group-filled "official" hostels. The crowd here, though, is vastly different—most guests are youthful adults traveling singly or in pairs; it's more like an apartment run by owner Gosha (a she), who won't answer the door or even the phone during the day. It's important that you call during the evening and ahead of arrival; a week before you plan to come to town isn't too early to secure a bed.

Best bet for a bite:
Naschmarkt

Insiders' tip:
Knock on the correct door

What hostellers say:
"Like sleeping with ten friends!"

Gestalt:
Believable

Safety:

Hospitality:

Cleanliness:

Party index:

It's basically a couple of apartments packed with laid-back hostellers. Most people love this place for such a cozy atmosphere (some say a little too cozy). There's a self-catering kitchen, with all you'll need for a spaghetti or ramen noodle feed. One word of warning, though, you may have to present proof of age since word on the street is that guests under age thirty sometimes aren't allowed.

How to get there:

By bus: Call hostel for transit route.
By car: Call hostel for directions.
By subway: Take U-Bahn U2 or U3 line to Volkstheater stop, or U6 line to Burggasse stop.
By train: From Westbahnof Station, take U-Bahn U6 line to Burggasse stop and change to 48A bus to Neubaugasse. From Sudbahnof Station, take 13A bus toward Haltestelle to Kellermanngasse stop.

HOSTEL RUTHENSTEINER

Robert Hamerlinggasse 24, A-1150 Vienna
Telephone Number: 01–893–4202 or 01–893–2796

Fax Number: 01–893–2796
E-mail: hostel.ruthensteiner@telecom.at
Rates: €11–18 (about $10–$19 US) per HI member; doubles €35 (about $34 US)
Credit cards: Yes (AMEX, MC, VISA)
Beds: 77
Private/family rooms: Yes
Kitchen available: Yes
Office hours: Twenty-four hours
Affiliation: Hostelling International-ÖJHV
Extras: Courtyard, Internet access, breakfast ($)

Best bet for a bite:
Nordsee (fish place)

Insiders' tip:
Zanoni & Zanoni ice cream

What hostellers say:
"Pretty groovy."

This hostel's odd. It's practically right next to Vienna's main train station and thus has decent location on a side street. The private rooms are nice, the attitude laid-back, and you hear lots of French from Canadian and French visitors—a bit of a surprise.

But there are problems with this indy-style backpacker joint, despite the efforts at making it a nice place. There's one enormous dorm room where hostellers are simply crammed in. We can tell that the very friendly staff cares, but things like cleaning just seem to have slid a bit. You have to pay extra for breakfast, too.

Gestalt:
Ruthless

Safety:

Hospitality:

Cleanliness:

Party index:

A kitchen, Internet terminal, and popular courtyard have to be counted as pluses, and this is certainly a very convenient place to sleep when you've gotten to town very late and the all-night reception is happy to let you in—it's just great to find the place open and convenient. There are no curfews, either.

Since it's so small, though, book well ahead of your arrival.

How to get there:

By bus: Call hostel for transit route.

By car: Call hostel for directions.

By train: From Westbahnof Station, walk out extreme right side, cross busy street, and continue to Robert Hamerlingasse on right. Turn right and walk down street to hostel on left.

HOSTEL ZÖHRER

Skodagasse 26

A-1080 Vienna

Telephone Number: (outside Austria) 1–406–0730;

(within Austria) 0222–406–0730

Fax Number: 01–222–408–0409

E-mail: info@zoehrer.com

Rates: €12–18 (about $12 US) per person, doubles €35 (about $34 US)

Credit cards: No

Beds: 45

Private/family rooms: Yes

Kitchen available: Yes

Office hours: 7:00 A.M. to 11:00 P.M.

Lockout: 11:00 A.M. to 2:00 P.M.

Affiliation: None

Extras: Breakfast, TV, lockers, laundry

S

Despite courteous management, the eleven-year-old Hostel Zöhrer could use a serious cleanup and facelift. Its location is pretty decent, though, with trams right down the street ready to whisk you to all the stuff you came to Vienna to see.

It's a small hostel with only forty-five beds, so it's often full. Please, we beg you, make reservations before you arrive in Vienna.

Two Canadian girls showed up with no clue about the tight hostel situation in summer and were disappointed to find the hostel was indeed full, although the clerk courteously phoned a few other hostels in town and landed them a bed.

Best bet for a bite:
EMMA grocery store

Insiders' tip:
Call wayyy ahead

What hostellers say:
"Um, like, do you have
any space?"

Gestalt:
Wiener dog

Safety:

Hospitality:

Cleanliness:

Party index:

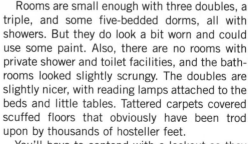

Rooms are small enough with three doubles, a triple, and some five-bedded dorms, all with showers. But they do look a bit worn and could use some paint. Also, there are no rooms with private shower and toilet facilities, and the bathrooms looked slightly scrungy. The doubles are slightly nicer, with reading lamps attached to the beds and little tables. Tattered carpets covered scuffed floors that obviously have been trod upon by thousands of hosteller feet.

You'll have to contend with a lockout so they can "clean," but it didn't appear from the looks of things that a very thorough job was carried out. Lockouts are usually unheard of in independent hostels, and people didn't like this.

We'd like to recommend this place for the location and the management, who does go above and beyond the call of duty—but we can't. Someone needs to renovate it before it can consider itself a big-league independent hostel.

How to get there:

By bus: From Wien-Mitte Station, take U-Bahn Landstrasse to get into town, then take either #5 or #33 tram.

By car: Call hostel for directions.

By plane: From airport, take S-Bahn line S7, which leaves every thirty minutes from 5:00 in the morning until 10:00 at night and arrives at Wien-Mitte train station. From Wien-Mitte Station take U-Bahn Landstrasse and then #5 or #33 tram.

By train: From Westbahnhof, Franz-Josefs-Bahnhor, or Nordbahnhof, take U-Bahn to Josephstadter Strasse or tram #5. From the Sudbahnhof, take bus #13A.

KEY TO ICONS

Attractive natural setting	Comfortable beds	Especially well suited for families
Ecologically aware hostel	Among our very favorite hostels	Good for active travelers
Superior kitchen facilities or cafe	A particularly good value	Visual arts at hostel or nearby
Offbeat or eccentric place	Handicapped-accessible	Music at hostel or nearby
Superior bathroom facilities	Good for business travelers	Great hostel for skiers
Romantic private rooms		Bar or pub at hostel or nearby

JUGENDGÄSTEHAUS SCHLÖSS— HERBERGE AM WILHEMININENBERG

(Wilhemininenberg Castle Guest House Hostel)

Savoyenstrasse 2, A-1160 Vienna

Telephone Number: 01–485–850–3700

Fax Number: 01–485–850–3702
E-mail: shb@wigast.com
Rates: €17–26 (about $16–$25 US) per HI member;
doubles €39–53 (about $42–$52 US)
Credit cards: Yes
Beds: 164
Private/family rooms: Yes
Kitchen available: Yes
Office hours: 7:00 A.M. to midnight
Lockout: 9:00 A.M. to 2:00 P.M.
Curfew: Midnight
Affiliation: Hostelling International-ÖJHV
Extras: Minigolf, table tennis, TV, laundry, breakfast, meals ($)

This nice way-out-of-the-way hostel gets big points for stunning surroundings and beautiful rooms. But being in the burbs, it sure does attract busloads of school groups. So consider yourself forewarned, and be aware that your journey will entail at least three changes of transportation and a long ride unless you've got a car. Also keep in mind that you'll turn into a pumpkin and be locked out if you stay out past 11:45 P.M., as that's the last bus out to this remote location.

Most rooms here are quads with their own bathrooms (yea!), and you can wash your duds in the hostel laundry. They've got a television lounge, meal service, free breakfast included with the expensive price, and even a minigolf course adjacent.

However, if you want to stay out past your bedtime or have an early train to catch, you may want to consider one of the more central Viennese hostels.

How to get there:

By bus: From Westbahnhof, take the U6 to Thaliastrasse, then tram #46 (Joachimsthalerplatz direction) to Ottakring. Then change to #46B or #146B bus to

Best bet for a bite:
Heurigen (wine cellars)

Insiders' tip:
24- or 72-hour
transportation pass

What hostellers say:
"Thought I'd never get here!"

Gestalt:
Savoy special

Safety:

Hospitality:

Cleanliness:

Party index:

Schloss Wilhelminenberg. Look for hostel on the left of big hotel.

From Sudbahnhof, take tram D to Dr.-Karl-Renner-Ring and follow bus directions as above.

By car: Call hostel for directions

By train: From Westbahnhof, take the U6 to Thaliastrasse, then tram #46 (Joachimsthalerplatz direction) to Ottakring. Then change to #46B or #146B bus to Schloss Wilhelminenberg. Look for hostel on the left of big hotel.

From Sudbahnhof, take tram D to Dr.-Karl-Renner-Ring and follow bus directions as above.

JUGENDGÄSTEHAUS WIEN-BRIGITTENAU

(Vienna Brigittenau Guest House Hostel)

Friedrich Engelsplatz 24, A-1200 Vienna

Telephone Number: 01–332–829–40 or 01–330–0598

Fax Number: 01–330–8379
E-mail: jgh.1200wien@chello.at
Rates: €17–20 (about $17–$19 US) per HI member; doubles €34–39 (about $33–$39 US)
Credit cards: Yes
Beds: 434
Private/family rooms: Yes
Kitchen available: No
Season: January 1–31; mid-February–December 31
Office hours: Twenty-four hours
Lockout: 9:00 A.M. to 1:00 P.M.
Curfew: 11:00 P.M.
Affiliation: Hostelling International-ÖJHV
Extras: TV, games, foosball, pool table, BBQ, vending machines, in-room lockers, Internet access

This hostel usually has tons of decent beds, a plus, but it's also overrun with school groups and is located in a really depressing and bland suburban neighborhood alongside a major traffic artery. It's a huge edifice with zero character but a lot of frills, including vegetarian meals, many rooms with private bathrooms and, for the most part, friendly and helpful staff—some of whom are native English speakers, which can be a relief for some. You make the call.

The hostel is actually two buildings, one of which is fairly new and is designated for families and couples. The main building is where the groups stay. Noise tends to travel through the walls here, and double rooms consist of a bunk bed instead of the two twins one would expect. At least some of the rooms are fairly spacious.

Given the out-of-the-way and bland location, you're not going to be hanging out in the neighborhood, so hop the U-Bahn or the S-Bahn (you get endless rides on both if you buy a twenty-four–hour pass) to other points. The Donauinsel riverside beach and park isn't far, for instance, nor is the Prater amusement park— fun for an afternoon—just a couple stops away by suburban train, which is covered by the city's twenty-four–hour tickets.

How to get there:

By bus: Take #11A or #5A bus to Friedrich Engels Platz and, following hostel logo sign, walk 50 yards to hostel.

By ferry: Take boat to Reichsbrucke dock, then walk 1½ miles to hostel.

By subway: Take U-Bahn subway U6 line to Handelskai stop and walk ⅓ mile to hostel, or take the #5a bus at the Handelskai stop for three stops, exit, and walk under overpass to hostel.

By tram: Take N, #31, or #32 streetcar to Friedrich Engels Platz and walk 50 yards to hostel.

Best bet for a bite:
Zielpunkt supermarket

Insiders' tip:
Buy that twenty-four–hour transport pass

What hostellers say:
"Too far from town."

Gestalt:
Outer space

Safety:

Hospitality:

Cleanliness:

Party index:

JUGENDGÄSTEHAUS WIEN HÜTTELDORF–HACKING

(Vienna/Hutteldorf-Hacking Guest House Hostel)

Schlossberggasse 8, A-1130 Vienna

Telephone Number: 01–877–1501

Fax Number: 01–877–02632
E-mail: jgh@wigast.com
Rates: €14–16 (about $13–$16 US) per HI member; doubles €37 (about $38 US)
Credit cards: Yes
Beds: 295
Private/family rooms: Yes
Kitchen available: No
Office hours: 7:00 A.M. to midnight
Lockout: 9:30 A.M. to 3:00 P.M.
Curfew: 11:45 P.M.
Affiliation: Hostelling International-ÖJHV
Extras: Laundry, TV, VCR, foosball, table tennis, meals ($), Internet access, lockers, information desk, garden, playground,

Best bet for a bite:
Duran sandwich joints
in town

Insiders' tip:
Satellite train station here

What hostellers say:
"Good place, so-so
location."

Gestalt:
Huttel house

Safety: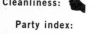

Hospitality:

Cleanliness:

Party index:

A huge six-story bunker on leafy grounds near Hütteldorf Station, this place is ruthlessly efficient and very well run, if distant.

A key-card system lets you in, where you'll find four singles, eleven doubles, three triples, eleven quads, twenty-four sixes, and six eight-bedded dorms—none with private bathrooms. They serve breakfast, maintain a television lounge, and really cater to families. Witness the playground area, game room, and meal service; kids will also love the new Internet access.

How to get there:

By bus: Take #53B bus and walk 20 yards to hostel.

By car: Call hostel for directions.

By subway: Take U-Bahn U4 line to Hütteldorf stop and walk ⅓ mile to hostel.

By train: Take U-Bahn U4 line to Hütteldorf stop and walk ⅓ mile to hostel.

JUGENDHERBERGE WIEN MYRTHENGASSE

(Vienna Myrthengasse Hostel)

Myrthengasse 7/Neustiftgasse 85, A-1070 Vienna

Telephone Number: 01–523–6329 or 01–523–6316–0

Fax Number: 01–523–5849
E-mail: hostel@chello.at
Rates: €14–18 (about $13–$17 US) per HI member; doubles €36 (about $36 US)
Credit cards: No
Beds: 260
Private/family rooms: Yes
Kitchen available: No
Office hours: Twenty-four hours
Lockout: 11:00 A.M. to 2:00 P.M.
Curfew: 1:00 A.M.
Affiliation: Hostelling International-ÖJHV
Extras: TV, lockers, store, information desk, meeting room, disco, patio, currency exchange, breakfast, meals ($), laundry, Internet access

If you're like most other hostellers, you'd probably think that a hostel with so many beds would be easy to waltz into and grab a bunk at the last minute.

Well, you couldn't be more wrong. You'll have to book it at least six months in advance if you have any hope of gracing its bunks during the summer. But it's not individual travelers who are booking the place out. It's school groups from all over Europe, sometimes in numbers totaling fifty or more. Multiply that by six, and there is no chance you'll get a bed. In fact management *prefers* groups because they bring in more money, what with the meals and all. So you'll just have to be really forward-thinking, because this is among the best-located hostels in town: It's right smack in the middle of the hippest district in Vienna, otherwise known as Neustiftgasse.

Best bet for a bite:
Amerling beer joint

Insiders' tip:
Book six months ahead

What hostellers say:
"No beds in July?
But it's February!"

Gestalt:
Group mentality

Safety: 👍

Hospitality: 👍

Cleanliness: 👍

Party index:

Staff are surprisingly laid-back and lack that authoritative look we've come to expect from a place dealing with gangly rugrats. Rooms are pretty accommodating, and there's even a single with its own shower. Of the sixteen doubles, twelve come with their own shower and toilet. The eight triples have a shower inside the room, and six of the thirty-two quads come with shower and toilet. There are also five- and six-bedded rooms with their own showers.

The hostel has organized a really useful information board, including many nearby cash machine locations and transportation information. They even recycle your used batteries. Common areas include a very tranquil patio with picnic tables, ivy-covered walls, and one of those antique-looking water fountains so common in Europe. There are several television lounges, each with cable TV. The meals are kept basic—stuff like spaghetti, soup, and local Viennese specialities.

KEY TO ICONS

Attractive natural setting

Ecologically aware hostel

Superior kitchen facilities or cafe

Offbeat or eccentric place

Superior bathroom facilities

Romantic private rooms

Comfortable beds

Among our very favorite hostels

A particularly good value

Handicapped-accessible

Good for business travelers

Especially well suited for families

Good for active travelers

Visual arts at hostel or nearby

Music at hostel or nearby

Great hostel for skiers

Bar or pub at hostel or nearby

Overall, management runs a good hostel despite the preference for groups. Maybe they can apply this efficiency and open a real hostel for travelers and backpackers that a great city like Vienna so richly deserves.

How to get there:

By car: Call hostel for directions.

By bus: Call hostel for transit route.

By subway: Take U-Bahn U2 or U3 line to Volkstheater stop, or take U6 line to Burggasse stop.

By train: From Westbahnof Station, take U-Bahn U6 line to Burggasse stop and change to #48A bus to Neubaugasse. From Sudbahnof Station, take #13A bus toward Haltestelle to Kellermanngasse stop.

PANDA HOSTEL

Nummer 7, Third Floor

Kaiserstrasse 77, A-1070 Vienna

Telephone Number: 01–522–5353

Rates: €8.00–12.00 (about $8.00–$12.00 US) per person; doubles €35–62 (about $37–$65 US)

Credit cards: No

Beds: Number varies

Private/family rooms: Yes

Kitchen available: Yes

Office hours: 8:00 A.M. to 1:00 P.M.

Affiliation: None

Extras: TV, lockers

Associated with the Pension Lauria in the same building, this hostel is kind of the same deal as Believe It or Not Hostel—this one's also in an apartment building and doesn't hold too many folks.

Best bet for a bite:
Supermarkets in neighborhood

Insiders' tip:
Bring earplugs

What hostellers say:
"Stop drilling!"

Gestalt:
Demolition derby

The building was in the serious process of being refurbished and was under the incessant whine of buzzsaws and jackhammers when we dropped by. The elevator didn't even work. But reports from our hostel snoops say the expensive doubles here are quite good, as was a large dorm. There are lockers to stash your stuff, although you'll have to supply your own lock. If you stay in the off-season, which runs from November to Easter, you'll be pleased with the reduced rate of about €50 per person.

The street the hostel is located on is full of restaurants and other diversions. It's somewhat of an extension of the Neubaugasse/Burggasse area, only slightly closer to the Westbahnof Station.

Just make sure the place isn't a pile of rubble before you arrive.

How to get there:

By bus: From Westbahnhof Station, take #5 tram to Burggasse. From Sudbahnhof, take #18 tram to Westbahnhof then change to #5 to Burggasse.

By car: Call hostel for directions.

By train: From Westbahnhof Station, take #5 tram to Burggasse. From Sudbahnhof, take #18 tram to Westbahnhof then change to #5 to Burggasse.

Safety: 👍

Hospitality: 👍

Cleanliness: 👍👎

Party index:

TURMHERBERGE DON BOSCO

Lechnerstrasse 12, A-1030 Vienna

Telephone Number: 01–713–1494

Rates: €7.00 (about $7.00 US) per HI member
Credit cards: No
Beds: 53
Private/family rooms: No
Kitchen available: Yes
Season: March 1–November 30
Office hours: 7:30 A.M. to noon; 5:00 to 11:45 P.M.
Curfew: 11:30 P.M.
Affiliation: Hostelling International-ÖJHW
Extras: Bugs, breakfast ($)

Reports about this former church tower vary—from "run-down but cheap" to downright "grim." This may be one of the worst hostels in Europe, and we've got proof.

The building itself does have an interesting layout, occupying several stories of the tower, but it lacks caring management. The kitchen's dirty and underequipped; dorms are cramped and contain old wooden beds and flimsy mattresses. Bugs appear to run rampant—our hostel reviewer showed us his marked-up limbs as proof. The poor guy also had all his money stolen from him as he slept. The clientele are sleazy characters who appear to have taken up permanent residence in search of a job.

Overlook this place despite the fact that it's really cheap. (They charge for sheets, so that's an extra hidden cost.) Do yourself a favor and seek other accommodations.

Best bet for a bite:
Fleas

Insiders' tip:
Don't do it

What hostellers say:
"Ouch, ooch, ouch!"

Gestalt:
Flea circus

Safety: 👎

Hospitality: 👎

Cleanliness: 👎

Party index:

How to get there:

By bus: Call hostel for transit route.

By car: Call hostel for directions.

By train: From Westbahnhof and Sudbahnhof, take the U3 line to Kardinal-Nagl Platz stop and walk toward Erdbergstrasse; take right until you reach Lechnerstrasse.

WOMBAT'S BACKPACKERS

Grangasse 6, A-1150 Vienna

Telephone Number: 01–897–2336

Fax Number: 01–897–2577
E-mail: wombats@chello.at
Rates: €14 (about $14 US) per person; doubles €36 (about $35 US)
Credit cards: No
Beds: 164
Private/family rooms: Yes
Kitchen available: No
Season: Open year-round
Office hours: Twenty-four hours
Affiliation: None
Extras: Breakfast ($), Internet access, laundry, bike rentals, in-line skate rentals, bar, bicycle tours, lockers, games, darts, movies, terrace

You get a free drink when you walk into this place, and that should tell you something—but not everything—about it. There's more to this cool new independent entry than just booze, and it's conveniently located almost right behind the city's main international train station.

Best bet for a bite:
Schwejk (Bohemian cuisine)

What hostellers say:
"Let's rock it."

Gestalt:
Wombatmobile

Safety: 👍

Hospitality: 👍

Cleanliness: 👍

Party index:
🎉🎉🎉🎉

Room arrangements consist of twelve doubles, twenty quads, and ten six-bedded dorms—with a shower and bathroom inside every room. People frequently write in the guestbook that the rooms are clean and the beds comfy, so it must be true, right?

The pub with the sun terrace is the most popular place, of course, even though it's only open from 8:00 P.M. to 2:00 A.M. It's one great party spot, that's for sure. But they do other stuff, too. Breakfast costs about $2.50 US; they've got four Internet terminals (about $4.00 US per hour) and a laundromat (about $4.00 US to do a load). Even better, they rent bikes and in-line skates for about $7.00 US per day. Reception also helps arrange local bike tours from May through October for around $16 US each, possibly less in

Wombat's Backpackers

Vienna (Wien)

(courtesy of Wombat's Backpackers)

2002. The hostel also continues to be a stop on the Busabout backpacker bus route around Europe, a bonus if you're using this service.

The train-station neighborhood may not be the most posh (or safest) in town, but it certainly does provide a selection of ethnic eateries to pick from. And the hostel's close to Vienna's great city transit. Its buzz is really spreading, though, so try to arrive before noon—or, better yet, call ahead to reserve your bunk.

How to get there:

By bus: Contact hostel for transit details.

By car: Contact hostel for directions.

By train: From Westbahnof, exit station and turn right onto Mariahilfer Strasse. Follow to #152 (at the corner of Rosinagasse); bear right at Rosinagasse and continue to Grangasse, then make a left and continue to hostel on right.

EASTERN AUSTRIA

Neu-Nagelberg 16
Drosendorf 4
3 Bad Grosspertholz
5 Freistadt
10 Krems an der Donau
9 Klosterneuburg
★ Wien/Vienna
Melk an der Donau 13
18 Oberndorf an der Melk
Ulmerfeld-Hausmening 25
Lackenhof am Ötscher 11
2 Annaberg
St. Sebastian 22
19 Pernitz
Neusiedl am See 17
26
Wiener Neustadt
7 Grundlsee
1 Admont
Neuberg an der Mürz 15
24 Ternitz
21 Rust
23 Schladming
Rechnitz 20
Judenburg 8
Maria Lankowitz
12
6 Graz
14 Murau

Page numbers follow town names.

Eastern Austria contains a tremendous variety of scenery and lifestyles—everything from strictly industrial cities and towns to the kind of emerald-green meadows for which Austria is famous, from gentle apple orchards and fields of pumpkin to genuinely big mountains set aside in national parks that haven't been given over to ski resorts.

The hostels here, too, are something special; this is the best group of hostels you'll find concentrated in one place in Austria or Switzerland. Not always as fun or personal as you might like, but if you need a clean, modern, professionally run—almost hotel-like—bed in a pinch, these are the folks to help you out. Remember, however, that they are almost all closed during November.

JUGENDGÄSTEHAUS SCHLÖSS RÖTHELSTEIN

(Admont Röthelstein Castle Guest House)

A-8911 Admont, Styria

Telephone Number: 03–613–2432

Fax Number: 03–613–279–583
E-mail: jgh.admont@jgh.at
Rates: €17–20 (about $19 US) per person; doubles €50 (about $50 US)
Credit cards: Yes
Private/family rooms: Yes
Kitchen available: No
Beds: 104
Season: May 1–September 30
Office hours: 7:00 A.M. to midnight
Affiliation: Hostelling International-ÖJHV and Hostelling International-ÖJHW
Extras: Meals ($), sauna, breakfast, bike rentals, table tennis, TV, VCR, library, foosball, tennis, basketball, handball, volleyball, playground

Here's how you get here. You walk up a hill amidst pastoral surroundings, staring in awe at the seventeeth-century castle towering above you. You glance down at your guidebook, then back up again. You can't believe this is the place.

But yes. That's it. You've found the hostel.

This is one of Europe's castle hostels, and though you've gotta strap on the hiking shoes to get here, it's quite a place once you arrive. Everything from a sauna and lots of sports facilities (including a track in front) to bikes for rent and a TV lounge. All inside a castle.

Let's back up a minute to get the big picture. There are ten special double rooms with bathrooms, radios, and hair dryers; six more double rooms have the bathroom, although no hair dryer. Ah, well. Three five-bedded rooms, nine six-bedded rooms, and an eight-bedded dorm complete the picture—all with en-suite bathrooms.

Meals are served in the amazing medieval feasting hall—okay, dining room—and there are five more lounges or common areas (one with a television and VCR, of course) to relax in. Amazingly, there are two ski lifts directly in front of the hostel, an ice-skating rink, the track, and more.

Admont's on a rather minor train line, but if you can get out here there's a local abbey with a very good library to visit. Think lots of old books and decorative fresco work. The abbey's an old one, dating back to the 1000s; the exterior has been renovated and replaced any number of times, so it isn't too special, but that library is a winner. Cough up the €4.00 (about $5.00 US) to get in, and savor the experience.

Best bet for a bite:
Eat here now!

Insiders' tip:
Check out abbey library

What hostellers say:
"I dub thee knight . . ."

Gestalt:
King-size

Hospitality:

Cleanliness:

Party index:

How to get there:

By bus: Call hostel for transit route.

By car: From Salzburg or Munich, take Highway A10 to Eben im Pongau, continue to Schladming and Admont. From Vienna or Linz, take A1 highway to Knoten; switch to A9 and continue to Admont.

By train: From Admont Station, walk left down Hauptbahnofstrasse and turn left at the post office. Keep going. Up. Another mile. To the castle. That's it.

JUGENDHERBERGE ANNABERG

(Annaberg Hostel)

Annarotte 77, A-3222 Annaberg, Lower Austria

Telephone Number: 02–728–8496

Fax Number: 02–728–8442
E-mail: jugendherberge-annaberg@aon.at
Rates: €8.00–11.00 (about $9.00–$12.00 US) per HI member
Credit cards: No
Private/family rooms: Yes
Kitchen available: No
Beds: 116
Office hours: 8:00 A.M. to 1:00 P.M.; 5:00 to 10:00 P.M.

Affiliation: Hostelling International-ÖJHW
Extras: Disco, meals ($), breakfast, TV, sauna, ski lift, playground, volleyball, fireplace, terrace, bike rentals

In two attached chalets set in green fields and woods, this is a good hostel—nicely balanced among families, groups, and individual hostellers.

The beds come in twenty-six quads (just eight with bathrooms, but all with sinks) plus one twelve-bedded room. There's a huge lounge and several smaller ones, plus a game room, terrace with fireplace and—yes—a disco. The sauna is popular, and sports facilities and a playground mean kids and jocks are well taken care of, too. Heck, there's even a ski lift owned by the hostel right outside.

The drawback here is that you're pretty close to beautiful little Mariazell, which has its own hostel—so you're probably gonna stay there if you can get in. If you can't, this is a fine second choice.

How to get there:

By bus: Call hostel for transit route.

By car: From Vienna or Linz, take Highway A1 to St. Pölten and then take Bundesstrasse B20 to Richtung Mariazell. Continue to Annaberg.

By train: Call hostel for transit route.

Best bet for a bite:
On-site
(but reserve ahead)

Insiders' tip:
Bring the kids
and the skis

What hostellers say:
"Hey, it's like a
sauna in here."

Gestalt:
Annaberger helper

Hospitality:

Cleanliness:

Party index:

JUGENDHERBERGE BAD GROSSPERTHOLZ

(Bad Grosspertholz Hostel)

Nummer 177, A-3972 Bad Grosspertholz, Lower Austria

Telephone Number: 02–857–2965

Fax Number: 02–857–2965
E-mail: oejhw-wien-noe@telecom.at
Rates: €9.00 (about $11 US) per HI member
Credit cards: No
Private/family rooms: Yes
Kitchen available: No
Beds: 52
Season: April 15–October 15
Office hours: 8:00 A.M. to 2:00 P.M; 5:00 to 7:00 P.M.
Affiliation: Hostelling International-ÖJHW
Extras: Meals ($), breakfast, bike rentals, TV

A two-story, functional hostel, this place is fine if smallish. It's got one single room, two double rooms with full bathrooms, seven four-bedded rooms with bathrooms, a six-bedded dorm with bathroom, and then a quad and four triples that share hallway bathrooms. In fact that's the watchword here: share. You'll have to share your personal space with the multitudes of groups that routinely book the place out.

In the dining room, staff serve meals and breakfast; there is also a television area, and bikes can be rented from reception.

There's little to do in this village, but you're pretty close to the bigger town of Gmund, where a huge organ in the village church is interesting and several clean lakes in the area offer good swimming. If you need personal space, though, we'd suggest you find a hostel that caters more to the individual traveler than this one does.

Best bet for a bite:
All three meals served
(book ahead)

Insiders' tip:
Lookout tower at Nordwald
nature reserve

Gestalt:
Organ donor

Hospitality:

Cleanliness::

Party index:

How to get there:

By bus: Call hostel for transit route.

By car: From Wien, drive through Horn to Zettle and continue to Bad Grosspertholz; total drive about 100 miles.

By train: Call hostel for transit route.

JUGDENDHERBERGE DROSENDORF

(Drosendorf Hostel)

Badstrasse 25, A-2095 Drosendorf, Lower Austria

Telephone Number: 02–915–2257

Fax Number: 02–915–2257
E-mail: oejhw-wien.noe@telecom.at
Rates: €9.00–10.00 (about $9.00–$11.00 US) per HI member
Credit cards: No
Private/family rooms: Yes
Kitchen available: No
Beds: 63
Season: April 1–October 15
Office hours: 7:30 to 9:30 A.M.; 5:00 to 9:00 P.M.
Affiliation: Hostelling International-ÖJHW
Extras: Meals ($), breakfast, bike rentals, solarium, sauna, TV, pool, grill, VCR, table tennis

A two-story, rectangular structure with an attached annex, this hostel is most useful if you're back-roading it by car or cycle on your way to Czech out the Czech Republic.

The main building contains a lone single room, two doubles, a four-bedded room, three six-bedded rooms, and three eight-bedded dorms. All have sinks and showers; none have private toilets. The annex has three more family-style rooms, two with four beds each, and one with only three beds. Common space consists of a dining room for breakfast and meals; a sauna; a TV lounge with VCR; and an outdoor section with table tennis, sunning area, and grill. You get a discount at the heated pool out front, and there are sports facilities scattered about—tennis courts, a soccer field, a miniature golf course, and bikes for rent right at the front desk.

A medieval town close to the Czech border, Drosendorf can actually be a nice place to hang for an afternoon—even if it is quiet and not really stuffed with great museums or culture. Cafes and such on the main squares could occupy you for a while.

Best bet for a bite:
Cafes in town

Insiders' tip:
Good fishing in Thaya River

What hostellers say:
"I need a lift to Prague."

Gestalt:
Czech mate

Hospitality:

Cleanliness:

Party index:

How to get there:

By bus: Call hostel for transit route.
By car: Call hostel for directions.
By train: Call hostel for transit route.

FREISTADT HOSTEL

Schlosshof 3, A-4240 Freistadt
Telephone Number: 07–942–743–65

Rates: €12 (about $13 US) per HI member
Credit cards: No
Private/family rooms: No
Kitchen available: Yes
Beds: 20
Season: June 1–November 30
Office hours: 7:30 to 9:30 A.M.; 5:00 to 9:00 P.M.
Affiliation: Hostelling International-ÖJHW
Extras: Breakfast ($), roller skating, sheets

Incredibly small in a tiny town, this hostel's probably not gonna be in your plans. They've got only twenty beds in two big dorms, with breakfast the only extra—that and a roller skating (?!) area. The availabil-

Best bet for a bite:
Goldenen Hirschen inn

ity of a kitchen is another big plus, but there are no family rooms, which is unusual in Austria. At least the place enjoys excellent position, steps from an old castle on the town's main square.

The town does have some nice medieval churches and buildings. The small Heimathaus museum is a worthy peek at local culture, with guided tours sometimes given; a music festival also hits town more than a week each mid-July.

How to get there:

By bus: Call hostel for transit route.
By car: Call hostel for directions.
By train: Call hostel for transit route.

JUGEND & FAMILIENGÄSTEHAUS GRAZ

(Graz Family Guest House Hostel)
Idlhofgasse 74, A-8020 Graz, Styria
Telephone Number: 03–167–148–76

Fax Number: 03–167–148–7688
E-mail: jgh.graz@jgh.at
Rates: €17–18 (about $18–$20 US) per HI member; doubles €40-45 (about $42–$47 US)
Credit cards: Yes
Beds: 96
Private/family rooms: Yes
Kitchen available: No
Office hours: 7:00 A.M. to 11:00 P.M.
Curfew: Variable
Affiliation: Hostelling International-ÖJHV and Hostelling International-ÖJHW
Extras: Garden, grill, table tennis, meals ($), sauna, Internet access, TV, laundry, lockers, key deposit (€22), breakfast

Flagship hostel of Steiermark's stellar, privately owned chain of hostels, this four-story block of soap in an undiscovered corner of the country conceals one of the best urban hostels in Austria: professionally run with hotel-quality beds, staff, and facilities. It may be a little on the bland side, but it's a mile or less from the center of this fairly large city—and spotless, too.

They've got eleven singles or doubles, fifteen quads, and eight six-bedded dorms, almost all with good private bathrooms. The grounds are nice, and the hostel now has Internet access, a sauna, a game room, a laundry, and grilling capabilities. Families seem to like it best, but it's the only hostel in town and fine for backpackers, too.

Usually overlooked on a tour of Austria, Graz—second-biggest city in Austria—in fact makes a pretty good stop for several reasons. First, it's as Austrian as you can get. The architecture—dating back to the twelfth-century digs of various Hapsburg hotshots—is great. Then there's a vibrant nightlife of mostly-locals bars, clubs, and restaurants, thanks to three universities here. All those red-tiled roofs might even make you think you're in Florence for a second. And there are the usual summer music festivals and lots of green parks to check out.

Oh, it's Ah-nold's hometown, too. In fact the rest of his family is said to still live in town.

The city sprawls, but the old core is compact and central. A 1,500-foot hill known as Schlossberg rises above the red roofs; it was once home to a fort but now is just a place to stroll up for romantic views and occasional stage performances. A small-gauge train carries wimps to the summit, but we prefer taking winding Sporgasse by foot and catching our breath at the top instead. The clock tower up here is also cool; its bell was raised in 1382, and the passage to the top is covered with ivy. Local lovers use it as a make-out spot.

Down below, check out the Landhaus' Italian Renaissance architecture and peek inside the city armory if you're into old weapons. We'd also recommend hitting Eggenberg castle, not far from the train station by streetcar.

Outside the city, at the stop and town called Stübing, a big open-air folk museum re-creates and preserves houses and buildings from around Austria. It's strongest on old huts and farms and is worth a

Best bet for a bite:
Mangolds

Insiders' tip:
Open-air folk museum

What hostellers say:
"Like a hotel."

Gestalt:
Green Graz

Hospitality:

Cleanliness:

Party index:

KEY TO ICONS

Attractive natural setting	Comfortable beds	Especially well suited for families
Ecologically aware hostel	Among our very favorite hostels	Good for active travelers
Superior kitchen facilities or cafe	A particularly good value	Visual arts at hostel or nearby
Offbeat or eccentric place	Handicapped-accessible	Music at hostel or nearby
Superior bathroom facilities	Good for business travelers	Great hostel for skiers
Romantic private rooms		Bar or pub at hostel or nearby

look; admission costs €5.50 (about $6.00 US) and the indispensable guide another €2.00 (about $2.30 US), well worth it in our opinion.

How to get there:

By bus: Take #50 bus to hostel.

By car: From Vienna, take Highway A2 to Graz West exit; from Salzburg, take Highway A9.

By train: Call hostel for transit route.

JUGENDHERBERGE & FAMILIENGÄSTEHAUS GRUNDLSEE

(Grundlsee Family Guest House Hostel)

Wienern-Gössl 49, A-8990 Grundlsee, Styria

Telephone Number: 03–622–8629

Fax Number: 03–622–862–94

E-mail: bookingcenter@jgh.at

Rates: €15 (about $15 US) per HI member

Credit cards: MC, VISA, Diner's Club

Private/family rooms: Yes

Kitchen available: No

Beds: 60

Season: May 1–October 31

Office hours: 7:00 to 9:00 A.M.; 5:00 to 10:00 P.M.

Affiliation: Hostelling International-ÖJHV and Hostelling International-ÖJHW

Extras: Meals ($), table tennis, bike rentals, breakfast, campground

A yellow farmhouse a bit outside the lake resort town of Grundlsee, this place gets points for good facilities, rustic atmosphere, and access to the local lake.

Best bet for a bite:
Evening meal at hostel

Insiders' tip:
Boat trip

What hostellers say:
"Last one in is a rotten egg."

Gestalt:
Lake break

There are four single rooms, thirteen doubles, nine quads, and three six-bedded dorms—none with private bathrooms though. They include breakfast, serve dinner, maintain a small recreation room, and rent out mountain bikes. This is also one of the few hostels in Austria to include a campground, a pretty big one, too—sixty spaces.

Most hostellers hit the hiking trail around skinny Grundlsee lake. One of the most interesting excursions around involves taking a sequence of boats around three local lakes; inquire at the hostel or head for the pier at the edge of Grundlsee proper. The trip costs around €10 (about $11 US) per person and a nice combination of scenic ferry riding and walking.

Hospitality:

Cleanliness:

Party index:

How to get there:

By bus: Call hostel for transit route.

By car: From Germany, take Bundestrasse 158 through Bad Ischl toward Bad Aussee; continue toward Grundlsee to Wienern. From Vienna, take Highway A1. From Graz, take Highway A9.

By train: Bad Aussee Station, 7½ miles away, is closest train station; call hostel for transit route.

JUGEND & FAMILIENGÄSTEHAUS JUDENBURG

(Judenburg Guest House Hostel)

Kaserngasse 22, A-8750 Judenburg, Styria

Telephone Number: 03–572–87355

Fax Number: 03–572–87355–88
E-mail: jgh.judenburg@jgh.at
Rates: €15–16 (about $15.00–$16.50 US) per HI member
Credit cards: Diner's Club, MC, VISA
Private/family rooms: Yes
Kitchen available: No
Beds: 98
Season: January 1–October 31; December 25–31
Office hours: 8:00 A.M. to 10:00 P.M.
Affiliation: Hostelling International-ÖJHV and Hostelling International-ÖJHW
Extras: Meals ($), breakfast, bike rentals, sauna, gym, table tennis

This three-story old red building is set on top of a hill; consequently, from the train station you have to hike up to town and the hostel. Once you're here, though, the place is amazingly close to everything—set your pack down, and in about three minutes of walking you are in the center of the action.

A handsome, if big, place, it's stuffed with small-size rooms: There's one double, five triples, five quads, and ten six-bedded dorms—all with their own private bathroom and shower. They have a sauna inside, a small gymnasium, table tennis, meals and breakfast in a dining room, and bikes for hire—all professionally run. They can

Best bet for a bite:
Willy's Place

Insiders' tip:
Hauptplatz for people watching

What hostellers say:
"Pinch me. I'm in Judenberg."

Gestalt:
Close quarters

Hospitality:

Cleanliness:

Party index:

direct you to attractions and stuff to do in downtown Judenburg, although all you really need to know is that the central square called Hauptplatz is the focus of eating and hanging out.

How to get there:

By bus: Call hostel for transit route.

By car: From Vienna or Graz, take Highway S36 to east Judenburg; from Klagenfurt, take Highway B77 to Judenburg.

By train: Call hostel for transit route.

KLOSTERNEUBURG–MARIA GUGGING HOSTEL

Hüttersteig 8, A-3400 Klosterneuburg, Lower Austria

Telephone Number: 02–243–83501

Rates: €14 (about $14 US) per HI member
Credit cards: No
Private/family rooms: Yes
Kitchen available: Yes
Beds: 65
Season: May 1–September 1
Office hours: 7:30 to 9:30 A.M.; 5:00 to 9:00 P.M.
Affiliation: Hostelling International-ÖJHW
Extras: Meals ($), bike rentals

Achtung! Only German is spoken here.

Best bet for a bite:
Bring yer own

Insiders' tip:
Check out the abbey

What hostellers say:
"This is nowheresville."

Gestalt:
Kloster-phobia

Hospitality:

Cleanliness:

Party index:

A medium-size place with many kinds of bed configurations, this hostel isn't really all that great . . . just a functional, unremarkable place to bunk down. Why stay when Vienna is so close? Well, maybe as a quiet break from the city. OK. But we could find better rural hostels around than this one. Heck, they don't even include breakfast for free, which is normally a given in Austria.

The hostel isn't close at all to the town, which is itself just a short hop from the big city of Vienna. You can't miss the central feature—an amazing twelfth-century abbey—once you've arrived, which features a spectacular altar crafted back in the same day and age. And when they say the museum has old books, they do mean *old.* Interesting historical footnote: Duke (later St.) Leopold had this church built.

How to get there:

By bus: Call hostel for transit route.
By car: Call hostel for directions.
By train: From Vienna's Franz-Josefs Station, take #40 S-train to Klosterneuberg-Kierling stop, then change to bus for Gugging or walk 2 miles to hostel.

RADFAHRERJUGENDHERBERGE KREMS

(Krems Hostel)

Ringstrasse 77, A-3500 Krems an der Donau, Lower Austria

Telephone Number: 02–732–83452

Fax Number: 02–732–83452
E-mail: oejhv-noe@oejhv.or.at
Rates: €15 (about $15 US) per HI member
Credit cards: No
Beds: 52
Private/family rooms: Yes
Kitchen available: No
Season: April 1–October 31
Office hours: 7:00 to 9:30 A.M., 5:00 to 8:00 P.M.
Affiliation: Hostelling International-ÖJHV
Extras: Meals ($), breakfast, TV, lockers, bike storage, bike repair shop, sauna

This plain but central place is wildly popular with cyclists doing the pretty Danube River trail to or from Vienna, which is at its very best around here. And the hostel is also a good pick if you want to see vineyards or quaint towns because it's close by bike (or foot) to an older section of town called Stein—the area to find old, old houses and cobblestoned streets and squares right on the river.

Rooms consist of four quads (which they'll happily make into family rooms whenever possible) plus six six-bedded rooms, all with ensuite bathrooms. They have bikes for rent, a place to store bikes, and a bike repair shop on premises in case you've got a flat. Heck, a bike sculpture even greets you outside the entrance. A television lounge, dinner service, free breakfast, and lockers are just some of the other perks here. Families really like the place.

Folks have been making wine in these parts since Celtic times—the Austrians are just the

Best bet for a bite:
Heurigen (wine cellars) in Stein

Insiders' tip:
Enroll in Wine College

What hostellers say:
"Got any spare . . . tires?"

Gestalt:
Wheel deal

Hospitality:

Cleanliness:

Party index:

latest to perfect the art of viticulture. At one point there were almost three dozen monasteries crowding along one strip of the river, each making its own distinctive wine; a 1784 law change allowed private winemakers to sell their products, and that's when the industry really exploded. The Weinstadt museum is literally a museum of wine, and there's also a Wine College (sign us up!!) at the local monastery and the campus of Danube University to check out.

Dürnstein, upriver (away from Vienna), is our pick for best day trip on the Danube. Richard the Lion-Heart was once thrown into a prison there, and the wine cellars and monastery—as well as the old twisting streets—make for a fine excursion.

How to get there:

By bus: Call hostel for transit route.
By car: Take Highway A1 to Melk exit, continue along Donau River to Krems.
By train: Call hostel for transit route.

JUGENDHERBERGE LACKENHOF AM ÖTSCHER

(Lackenhof am Ötscher Hostel)

Ötscherweg 3, A-3295 Lackenhof am Ötscher, Lower Austria

Telephone Number: 07–480–5251

Fax Number: 07–480–5338
E-mail: oejhw-wien-noe@telecom.at
Rates: €18–23 (about $19–$24 US) per HI member
Credit cards: No
Beds: 137
Private/family rooms: Yes
Kitchen available: No
Office hours: 7:30 to 9:30 A.M.; 5:00 to 9:00 P.M.
Affiliation: Hostelling International-ÖJHW
Extras: Meals ($), breakfast, TV, VCR, grill, bike rentals, game room, terrace, indoor pool, ski rentals, snowboard rentals, fireplace

Up on a hill, this hostel really caters to hardbody hostellers who want to get out and stay out. You start by hiking up to the place, and the fun never stops. With Lackenhof being such a small town, the hostel isn't hard to find or use, only a couple minutes' walk from everything.

Rooms consist of a single, seven doubles, one quad, five sixes, and nine eight-bedded dorms; none has a private bathroom. The common space includes a dining room with seating for 140, a big conference room, a game room warmed by a real fireplace, and an outdoor terrace with grills and two open fireplaces.

There are plenty of concessions to the sports-minded here: Try an indoor swimming pool, two table tennis tables, a badminton court, bikes for hire, and lots of ski equipment. Staff will lend you slalom poles and racing numbers and rent you cross-country skis and snowboards—everything you need to have your own mini-Olympics.

Lackenhof's a small town, but a pretty one; though dominated by tourists—most coming to ski, plus others who come to hike the hills—you can find some agreeable corners. A cable car will pull you up to within striking distance of the Ötscher's 5,700-foot-high summit.

A pretty nearby town, Waidhofen, has its own train station and an impressive castle of Orthodox domes, too. Though it isn't used or showcased as a castle anymore—it's actually a university—you can gawk awhile, then walk the cute old streets in the center of the village. There's good swimming in nearby Lake Lunzer, as well.

How to get there:

By bus: Call hostel for transit route.
By car: Call hostel for directions.
By train: Call hostel for transit route.

Best bet for a bite:
Slap some chow on the grill

Insiders' tip:
Check out the Carthusian Monastery

What hostellers say:
"Play ball!"

Gestalt:
Hardbody paradise

Hospitality:

Cleanliness:

Party index:

JUGEND & FAMILIENGÄSTEHAUS MARIA LANKOWITZ
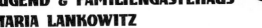

(Maria Lankowitz Guesthouse Hostel)

Am See 2, A-8591 Maria Lankowitz

Telephone Number: 03–144–71700

Fax Number: 03–144–717–0088
E-mail: jgh.marialankowitz@jgh.at
Rates: €15–17 (about $16.00 to $17.30 US) per HI member
Credit cards: Yes
Beds: 124
Family/private rooms: Yes
Kitchen available: No
Season: January 1–October 31; December 25–31
Office hours: Twenty-four hours
Affiliation: Hostelling International-ÖJHV
Extras: Meals ($), breakfast, sauna, bike rentals, TV, gym

A three-story yellow hostel, this is as well run as any other Styrian hostel. Rooms are mostly quads, with eight singles or doubles, twenty-one three-to-four-bedded dorms, and six five-to-six-bedded dorms—all with private en-suite bathrooms.

Insiders' tip:
Rent a bike

Gestalt:
Ave Maria

Hospitality:

Cleanliness:

Party index:

There are a bunch of common areas, including a TV room, a sauna, and a gym. Outdoor diversions include bikes for hire. You're up in a range of little-known mountains called the Stubalpe, halfway between Judenburg and Graz, and if you're tiring of the stimulation in Graz, you might like it up here even more.

How to get there:

By bus: Call hostel for transit route.
By car: Call hostel for directions.
By train: Call hostel for transit route.

JUGENDHERBERGE MELK AN DER DONAU

(Melk an der Donau Hostel)

Abt Karl-Strasse 42, A-3390 Melk an der Donau, Lower Austria
Telephone Number: 02–752–52681

Fax Number: 02–752–54257
E-mail: jugendherberge.melk@aon.at
Rates: €10–13 (about $11.00–$13.50 US) per HI member
Credit cards: No
Beds: 104
Private/family rooms: Yes
Kitchen available: No
Season: March 15–October 31
Office hours: 8:00 to 10:00 A.M.; 5:00 to 9:00 P.M.
Lockout: 10:00 A.M. to 5:00 P.M.
Affiliation: Hostelling International-ÖJHW
Extras: Meals ($), sauna, TV, breakfast, bike rentals, garden, grill, disco, bike storage, volleyball, table tennis

This good and attractive hostel—painted green and pink—is nice, and if it weren't for the all-day lockout we'd call it stellar. You can still reserve a bunk if you show up midday, using the clever envelope-drop reservation system; you just can't rest your feet until they open back up at 5:00 P.M.

It's almost all quad rooms here, twenty-four of 'em, which means families will have no trouble at all; there's also one eight-bedded dorm, usually for groups. Bathrooms and showers are all shared. Everything is spotless inside, and the grounds outside are well kept, too. There's a dining room with breakfast and dinners, a small disco, a TV lounge, table tennis, and (outdoors) a grill and volleyball area—all potential spots for meeting other traveling backpackers who've come down the same road you have. The big garden with picnic tables is especially popular. You're close to the train station—quite close, actually—and near a soccer field, as well.

The big yellow wedding-cake Benediktinerstift monastery, one of Austria's best sights to see, is unmissable from anywhere in town. Although there has been an abbey on the site for more than nine centuries, the present showy building was actually only built in the early 1700s; it's a pretty small monastery today, with only about a dozen monks living on the site, but hundreds of religious students still come annually to take instruction. Parts of the complex are free, but the central interior section costs 3 to 7 euros (about $3.00 to $7.00 US). Spring for it; the hand-copied books alone are worth it.

More bits of abbey trivia: Umberto Eco based his novel *The Name of the Rose* largely on the place; they hold summertime concerts of classical music on the grounds; Napoleon was here (for a little while).

Melk also has a pretty old town, with a grandly decorated old post office, for instance, on Linzerstrasse. One of the best trips out of Melk, once you've seen the abbey, is to grab a bike (well, rent one) and pedal 3 miles outside town to Schallaburg Castle so that you can gawk at its picturesque carved-clay decorations. As with much else here in Melk, you're sure to expend lots of film on the place, though it does cost about 7 euros (about $7.00 US) to get in.

If you're really going whole hog on this sight-seeing thing, take a tip from us and economize by picking up a combination ticket to

Best bet for a bite:
Pizza La Casa

Insiders' tip:
Buy sightseeing combo ticket

What hostellers say:
"Fantastic abbey!"

Gestalt:
Cookies and Melk

Hospitality:

Cleanliness:

Party index:

KEY TO ICONS

Attractive natural setting

Ecologically aware hostel

Superior kitchen facilities or cafe

Offbeat or eccentric place

Superior bathroom facilities

Romantic private rooms

Comfortable beds

Among our very favorite hostels

S A particularly good value

Handicapped-accessible

Good for business travelers

Especially well suited for families

Good for active travelers

Visual arts at hostel or nearby

Music at hostel or nearby

Great hostel for skiers

Bar or pub at hostel or nearby

both the castle and the abbey. That saves you a couple bucks on the combined entry fees—for about $14 US it's a great investment if you've got the time to hit both sights.

Finally, Melk's on the boat line that cruises up and down the Danube daily. Your Eurail pass gets you a ride all the way to Vienna or just to the pretty town and good hostel at Krems if you want to get off there.

How to get there:

By bus: Call hostel for transit route.

By car: Take Highway A1 from Vienna or Linz to Melk.

By train: From Linz or Vienna, take train to Melk and walk ½ mile to hostel.

JUGENDHERBERGE ZUM DEUTSCHEN RITTER

(Murau Hostel)

St.-Leonhard-Platz 4, A-8850 Murau, Styria

Telephone Number: 03–532–2395

Fax Number: 03–532–2395
E-mail: jgh.murau@jgh.at
Rates: €14 (about $15 US) per HI member
Credit cards: Diner's Club, MC, VISA
Private/family rooms: Yes
Kitchen available: No
Beds: 126
Season: May 1–December 31
Office hours: 8:00 A.M. to 10:00 P.M.
Affiliation: Hostelling International-ÖJHW
Extras: Meals ($), breakfast, TV, VCR, table tennis, bike rentals, tennis, sauna, Internet access

A nice two-story house with a lawn and attached annex, this place exemplifies the community spirit that's supposed to be what hostelling is all about. It's also quite close to everything central you'll need and, surprisingly, open most of the year.

The original wing of the hostel contains a single room, a double room, two triple rooms, a quad, and eight larger dorms, all sharing bathrooms and toilets. In the newer (and handicapped-accessible) annex, you've got sixteen quad rooms, all with private bathrooms, so if you're in a family, this is where you wanna be. Common facilities include a TV lounge, a sauna, bikes for hire, a tennis court, and meal service.They sometimes run language camps or other worthy programs here, so beds might be more full than usual during those times.

This is an extremely pretty town, with a bunch of pretty churches and abbeys and graveyards—just take your pick, they're all quite pleasant. Oh, and don't forget the thirteenth-century castle that looms above town. It's not at all contradictory, either (we feel), to follow up a tour of the churches with a visit to the town's brewery museum—followed once more, of course, with a beer. We believe the monks would have approved. Word to the quaffing wise: The museum and the dark local beer are *both* good.

It can be a little expensive to get to Murau without a car, however; you take a tourist-train, which Eurail passes won't cover, from Tamsweg or maybe Unzmarkt. There's a second, even more touristy train that comes more slowly from Tamsweg but provides the atmosphere of chugging up mountains on a hunk of steaming steel.

Best bet for a bite:
On Schwarzenberggasse

Insiders' tip:
Local beer

What hostellers say:
"Internet bitte."

Gestalt:
Murau majority

Hospitality:

Cleanliness:

Party index:

How to get there:

By bus: Call hostel for transit route.
By car: Call hostel for directions.
By train: From Murau Station, walk ⅔ mile to hostel.

NEUBERG AN DER MÜRZ HOSTEL

Kaplanweg 8, A-8692 Neuberg an der Mürz, Styria

Telephone Number: 03–857–8495

Fax Number: 03–857–84954
E-mail: bookingcenter@jgh.at
Rates: €12 (about $13 US) per HI member
Credit cards: Diner's Club, MC, VISA
Beds: 50
Private/family rooms: Yes
Kitchen available: No
Season: January 1–March 31; May 1–October 31; December 12–25
Office hours: 7:00 to 10:00 A.M.; 5:00 to 10:00 P.M.
Affiliation: Hostelling International-ÖJHV
Extras: Breakfast, sauna, bike rentals, TV, VCR, tennis

A quiet rural place, this looks like some-one's house—or maybe someone's rural schoolhouse. Inside, though, it's a very good little hostel. There are three double rooms, three quads, four six-bedded dormi-

Best bet for a bite:
Forage on yer own

Insiders' tip:
Steamy sauna

Gestalt:
Neu deal

Hospitality:

Cleanliness:

Party index:

tories, and one big one. Extras include a television room with VCR, a sauna, tennis, and meal service.

Tucked among mountains, you're not really close to any major towns, cities, or transit points—so getting here will take a little work, or a car that likes hills.

How to get there:

By bus: Call hostel for transit route.
By car: Call hostel for directions.
By train: Call hostel for transit route.

HANZ CZETTEL JUGENDHERBERGE NEU–NAGELBERG

(Neu Nagelberg Hostel)

Nummer 114, A-3871 Neu-Nagelberg, Lower Austria

Telephone Number: 02–859–7476

Fax Number: 02–859–7476
E-mail: oejhv-noe@oejhv.or.at
Rates: €16–19 (about $16.30–$20.00 US) per HI member
Credit cards: No
Beds: 39
Private/family rooms: Yes
Kitchen available: No
Season: January 11–December 23
Office hours: 7:30 to 9:30 A.M.; 5:00 to 9:00 P.M.
Affiliation: Hostelling International-ÖJHV
Extras: Breakfast, meals ($), bike rentals

S 👪 👤

Almost literally on the Czech border, this small place is surprisingly well equipped even if it's out of your way. As a bonus, it's got a lovely, quiet, lakeside location amidst the trees.

Insiders' tip:
Town of Budweis isn't far

Gestalt:
Czech point

Hospitality:

Cleanliness:

Party index:

The thirty-nine beds include one double room, eight quads, and a six-bedded dormitory. We're talking standard bunks, but in nice rooms of wood with plenty of skylights; the peaked roof means some top-bunkers are near the ceiling. You eat meals in a long dining hall, and they rent bikes and serve meals, too.

This is a good stop if you've brought your own wheels and are driving onward to Prague.

If you're coming by train, though, this is only useful if you're stopping in Gmünd, which is still a good 3 or 4 miles away. This Gmünd, between Vienna and Prague—Eurailers who bought an extra ticket to get to the Czech Republic will pass right through it—is one of two Gmünds in the country. (The other one's down by Italy, in Carinthia.) As picturesque as any other town in these parts, maybe a little more so, Gmünd has a quiet wooded park for whiling away the time. You can walk through a gate across the border into the Czech Republic, even if what's on the other side isn't exactly Thrillsville.

How to get there:

By bus: Call hostel for transit route.
By car: Call hostel for directions.
By train: Call hostel for transit route.

JUGENDHERBERGE NEUSIEDL AM SEE

(Neusiedl am See Hostel)

Herbergsgasse 1, A-7100 Neusiedl am See, Burgenland

Telephone Number: 02–167–2252

Fax Number: 02–167–2252
Rates: €11–12 (about $12–$13 US) per person
Credit cards: No
Beds: 86
Private/family rooms: Yes
Kitchen available: No
Season: March 1–November 20
Office hours: 8:00 A.M. to 2:00 P.M.; 5:00 to 10:00 P.M.
Affiliation: Hostelling International-ÖJHW
Extras: Breakfast, meals ($), groups, bike storage

This hostel is not particularly central nor close to Lake Neusiedl, but it is well equipped. They've got twenty-one four-bedded rooms and a double, every single one of 'em with a private shower. Toilets are shared and are on the hall. The great terrace here is especially popular with hostellers.

Best bet for a bite:
Tittler

Insiders' tip:
Walk or bike to
the border

What hostellers say:
"I forgot my towel."

Gestalt:
See-saw

Hospitality:

Cleanliness:

Party index:

You get here in less than an hour by direct trains from Vienna's South Station. The town itself isn't so great, but it is a quick train ride from Vienna—and once here you've got full access to the See itself, a big shallow lake, part of which lies within Hungary. Sure, you can bike around it, but let's be honest: There are much more scenic lakes in Austria than this one. Still, plenty of ferries run around the lake, and little Rust is a genuinely cute town with vineyards, storks on the rooftops, and such, albeit diametrically opposite Neusiedl town; you have to take a ferry that circles the lake carefully, making many stops, to get there from here.

If you've come on a bike, it's easy to cross into Hungary and continue the circuit; there's even a special border point south of Morbisch, feet and bikes only.

How to get there:

By bus: Call hostel for transit route.
By car: Call hostel for directions.
By train: Call hostel for transit route.

OBERNDORF AN DER MELK HOSTEL

Unterhub 5, Rauschof, A-3281 Oberndorf an der Melk, Lower Austria

Telephone Number: 07–483–267

Rates: €14 (about $15 US) per HI member
Credit cards: No
Beds: 60
Private/family rooms: Yes
Kitchen available: No
Season: May 1–November 30
Office hours: 7:30 to 9:30 A.M.; 5:00 to 9:00 P.M.
Affiliation: Hostelling International-ÖJHW
Extras: Breakfast, bike rentals, camping

Achtung! Only German is spoken here.

Out in the county, not far from the monastery city of Melk, this one's yet another simple place that's good enough if you need it.

The sixty beds here are divvied up into two doubles, four six-bedded rooms, and four eight-bedded dormitories. They don't serve dinners, don't do much of anything extra. So consider yourself warned.

How to get there:

By bus: Call hostel for transit route.
By car: Call hostel for directions.
By train: Call hostel for transit route.

Best bet for a bite:
In town

Gestalt:
Independence Day

Hospitality:

Cleanliness:

Party index:

PERNITZ HOSTEL

Hauptstrasse 79, A-2763 Pernitz, Lower Austria
Telephone Number: 02–632–72373

Rates: €14 (about $15 US) per HI member
Credit cards: No
Beds: 45
Private/family rooms: No
Kitchen available: Yes
Season: April 1–October 31
Office hours: 7:30 to 9:30 A.M.; 5:00 to 9:00 P.M.
Affiliation: Hostelling International-ÖJHW

Not to be confused with the hostel just down the road in similar-sounding Ternitz, this place isn't anything great for the backpacking hosteller, since it's mostly inundated with schoolchildren.

Its forty-five beds are contained in three big dorms, and they don't serve any meals or breakfast. There is a kitchen—that's it. Expect tons of groups, if you come at all.

How to get there:

By bus: Call hostel for transit route.
By car: Call hostel for directions.
By train: Call hostel for transit route.

Best bet for a bite:
Supermarket in town

Insiders' tip:
Learn how to say "shut up!" in German

What hostellers say:
"Giggle, shriek, scream."

Gestalt:
Rugrats

Hospitality:

Cleanliness:

Party index:

RECHNITZ HOSTEL

Hochstrasse 1, A-7471 Rechnitz, Burgenland
Telephone Number: 03–363–79245

Fax Number: 03–363–79245
Rates: €15–23 (about $15–$22 US) per HI member
Credit cards: No
Beds: 58
Private/family rooms: Yes
Kitchen available: No
Office hours: 8:00 A.M. to 10:00 P.M.
Affiliation: Hostelling International-ÖJHV
Extras: Meals ($), bike rentals, breakfast

Just off the Hungarian border, this hostel is run by the Lutheran church, but they don't serve religion to you with your breakfast. They've got three double rooms, five five-to-six-bedded dorms, and three eight-bedded dorms, administered by a hardworking and friendly female pastor.

Best bet for a bite:
Vineyard Mandl Koch

Insiders' tip:
Bike, bike, bike

What hostellers say:
"Nicest people."

Gestalt:
Church chat

Hospitality:

Cleanliness:

Party index:

Meals are either easy or hard to come by if you plan on eating at the hostel. Breakfast is included with your stay, but you might luck out on lunch or dinner if a group is staying there—you'll have to order the meal in advance. Otherwise, hit the road for some grub: Grab a bike and seek out some of the many vineyards in the surrounding area that sell cheap meals for about €4.00.

The town of Rechnitz isn't much to look at, but it's in nice countryside. It's really only a useful pit stop if you're back-roading it on the way to Hungary or Slovakia, and in that case you'll be happy to find a rare Burgenland hostel. But this is some of the most unspoiled (by industry) area in all of Austria. There are many castles in the nearby area, five are a twenty-minute drive if you have a car, and three are a two-hour journey by bike.

How to get there:

By bus: Call hostel for transit route.
By car: Call hostel for directions.
By train: Call hostel for transit route.

JUGENDGÄSTEHAUS RUST

(Rust Guest House Hostel)
Conradplatz 1, A-7071 Rust, Burgenland
Phone Number: 02–685–591
Fax Number: 02–685–5914

Rates: €12–14 (about $11-$13 US) per HI member
Credit cards: Yes
Beds: 58
Private/family rooms: Yes
Kitchen available: No
Season: Open year-round
Office hours: 8:00 A.M. to 2:00 P.M.; 4:00 P.M. to 10:00 P.M.
Affiliation: Hostelling International-ÖJHW
Extras: Parking, meals ($), cafe

Rust is probably the prettiest town in often-overlooked Burgenland, so it's a major bonus that a new hostel has opened here. Even better, it's right by a lakeside beach. (The address listed above is the booking office in town, not the actual hostel location—a ten-minute hoof away.)

There's nothing spectacular about this place, just the usual dorm rooms and family-sized quads, but the meal service and quiet location might win you over.

Rust itself is the kind of town that Germanic tourists love: heavy on the wine, wine gardens, and quaint houses—plus the added attraction of mondo water sports taking place right at the town's doorstep. It's like combining two vacations in one.

Best bet for a bite:
Romerzeche

What hostellers say:
"Good location."

Gestalt:
Rust never sleeps

Hospitality:

Cleanliness:

Party index:

How to get there:

By bus: Contact hostel for transit details.
By car: Contact hostel for directions.
By train: Contact hostel for transit details.

JUGENDHERBERGE MARIAZELLERLAND NR

(St. Sebastian Hostel)

Erlaufseestrasse 49, A-8630 St. Sebastian, Styria

Telephone Number: 03–882–2669

Fax Number: 03–882–266–988
E-mail: jgh.mariazellerland@jgh.at
Rates: €17 (about $17 US) per HI member
Credit cards: Diner's Club, MC, VISA
Beds: 136
Private/family rooms: Yes
Kitchen available: No
Office hours: 8:00 A.M. to 10:00 P.M.
Affiliation: Hostelling International-ÖJHV
Extras: Meals ($), breakfast, sauna

This hostel is set in gorgeous territory, near Mariazell—in fact, it was meant to replace the existing hostel in that must-see little town.

The 136 beds in the place include four double rooms, a dozen quad rooms, and eight six-bedded dorms. There are also family apartments. The chief draw in the area remains water sports, but as for the hostel, we'll have to see it to let you know the skinny. Till then, chances are that it's a decent place.

How to get there:

By bus: Call hostel for transit route.
By car: Call hostel for directions.
By train: Call hostel for transit route.

JUGEND & FAMILIENGÄSTEHAUS SCHLADMING

Coburgstrasse 253, A-8970 Schladming, Styria

Telephone Number: 03–687–24531

Fax Number: 03–687–245–3188
E-mail: jgh.schladming@jgh.at
Rates: €15–19 (about $15–$19 US) per HI member
Credit cards: MC, VISA, Diner's Club
Beds: 215
Private/family rooms: Yes
Kitchen available: No
Season: January 1–October 31; December 25–31
Office hours: 8:00 A.M. to 1:00 P.M.; 5:00 to 10:00 P.M.
Affiliation: Hostelling International-ÖJHW and Hostelling International-ÖJHV
Extras: Breakfast, bike rentals, meals ($), table tennis, TV, garden, lockers, Internet access, store, volleyball, playground

A big four-story building snuggled up against a hillside with its own big lawn, this one's nice—and it's good and close to the center of town for a change.

Rooms consist of two singles, ten doubles with private bathrooms, three triples, twenty quads, and seventeen larger dormitories. There are ten—count 'em—common areas in all, including a TV lounge, game room, garden, and Internet area. They rent bikes, serve meals, and maintain a playground—everything you need, basically.

Schladming itself is nice for a resort town, actually, if uninspiring. Gondolas climb and descend the surrounding peaks for about $8.00 to $12.00 round-trip, where you can ski or hike to your heart's content.

How to get there:

By bus: From Schladming Station, take bus to Zad Hausplatz and walk 100 yards to hostel.

By car: From Salzburg, take Highway A10 through Eben im Pongau and then Bundessstrasse 146 to Schladming. From Vienna, take Highway S6 through Bruck an der Mur to Highway A9, then change to Highway B146 and continue to Schladming.

By train: From Schladming Station, take bus to Zad Hausplatz and walk 100 yards to hostel.

Gestalt:
Gonzo gondola

Hospitality:

Cleanliness:

Party index:

TERNITZ HOSTEL

Strasse des 12, Februar 38, A-2630 Ternitz, Lower Austria
Telephone Number: 02–630–38483

Fax Number: 02–630–384–834
Rates: €13 (about $14 US) per HI member
Credit cards: No
Beds: 30
Private/family rooms: No
Kitchen available: No
Season: January 1–31; February 15–October 15; November 15–December 31
Office hours: 7:30 to 9:30 A.M.; 5:00 to 9:00 P.M.
Affiliation: Hostelling International-ÖJHV
Extras: Meals, breakfast ($), sauna

Achtung! Only German is spoken here.

Practically nobody finds his or her way out here to this hostel, though it's actually not all that far from Vienna.

Quite simple, it's wedged among hills south of the big city and consists of just five dorm rooms—a quad, a six-bedded dorm, and three eight-bedded rooms. One nice touch here is the inclusion of a hostel sauna. They include breakfast, serve meals, and are close to a number of sports facilities.

Best bet for a bite:
Stock up at a grocery store

Insiders' tip:
Steam in the sauna

What hostellers say:
"Lots of peace and quiet."

Gestalt:
Good Ternitz

Hospitality:

Cleanliness:

Party index:

How to get there:

By bus: Call hostel for transit route.
By car: Call hostel for directions.
By train: Call hostel for transit route.

JUGENDHERBERGE SCHLÖSS ULMERFELD

(Ulmerfeld Castle Hostel)

Burgweg 1, A-3363 Ulmerfeld-Hausmening, Lower Austria

Telephone Number: 07–475–54080

E-mail: oejhv-noe@oejhv.or.at
Rates: €20–22 (about $20–$23 US) per HI member
Credit cards: No
Beds: 62
Private/family rooms: Yes
Kitchen available: No
Office hours: 7:30 to 9:30 A.M.; 5:00 to 9:00 P.M.
Season: April 1–October 31
Affiliation: Hostelling International-ÖJHV
Extras: Meeting room, meals ($), TV, table tennis, breakfast, laundry

Complete with its own turret, this hostel really is castlelike. The inside features basic and slightly tight dorms of four beds each, plus a handful of single and double rooms; all have their own private bathrooms. Arched entryways make for nice atmosphere in the dining hall and elsewhere inside the place.

Best bet for a bite:
You can eat meals here

Insiders' tip:
Check out the Austrian TV stations

What hostellers say:
"You wascally wabbit."
Gestalt:
Ulmer Fudd

Hospitality:

Cleanliness:

Party index:

You're in a castle, but don't expect luxury. The extras here are minimal, if useful: a television room, a game room, meal service, and a conference room. Breakfast is included, too. Unique as a hostel experience, certainly, but not superluxurious.

How to get there:

By bus: Call hostel for transit route.
By car: From Salzburg, take Highway A1 to Amstetten-West exit, follow B121 to Weisses Kreuz and continue to Ulmerfeld.
By train: Call hostel for transit route.

WIENER NEUSTADT HOSTEL

Promenade 1, A-2700 Wiener Neustadt, Lower Austria

Telephone Number: 02–622–29695

Fax Number: 02–622–29695
E-mail: oejhv-noe@oejhv.or.at
Rates: €14 (about $14 US) per HI member
Credit cards: No
Beds: 36
Private/family rooms: Yes
Kitchen available: Yes
Office hours: 7:00 to 10:00 A.M.; 5:00 to 8:00 P.M.
Affiliation: Hostelling International-ÖJHV
Extras: Breakfast ($)

Located in a park, this place is certainly quiet but kinda far south from whatever action there is in the center of the city. The place also tends to get booked up early with overnighters or school groups from Vienna.

They've got nine singles or doubles, six three-to-four-bedded rooms, and a lounge; and breakfast is served for a fee. Still, it's a little too simple to be useful for some hostellers who need a kitchen, meal service, or a laundry.

Wiener Neustadt's old town is decent, though World War II bombs destroyed a good part of it. It is interesting to think that this was once briefly the center of the Western world, when Emperor Friedrich III moved his digs here for a short time during the late 1400s. Definitely take a tour for a slice of Austrian history.

Best bet for a bite:
Pizza delivery to hostel

Insiders' tip:
Big music concerts in summer

What hostellers say:
"I'd rather be in Vienna."

Gestalt:
Park place

Hospitality: 👍

Cleanliness: 👍

Party index: 🎉 🎉

To get here, take one of the trains that run about twice an hour from Vienna's Südbahnof.

How to get there:

By bus: Call hostel for transit route.
By car: Call hostel for directions.
By train: Call hostel for transit route.

SALZBURG AND CENTRAL AUSTRIA

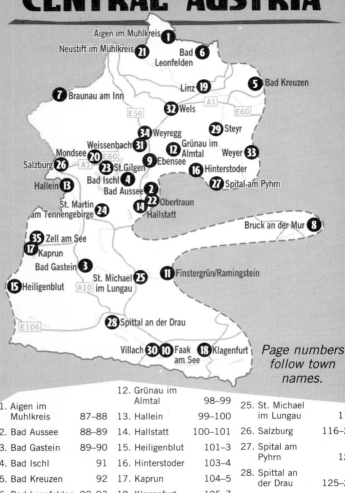

Aigen im Muhlkreis **1**

Neustift im Muhlkreis **21**

Bad Leonfelden **6**

5 Bad Kreuzen

7 Braunau am Inn

Linz **19**

32 Wels

29 Steyr

34 Weyregg

Weissenbach **31**

12 Grünau im Almtal

Weyer **33**

Mondsee **20**

23 St.Gilgen

9 Ebensee

Salzburg **26**

16 Hinterstoder

Bad Ischl **4**

27 Spital am Pyhrn

Hallein **13**

Bad Aussee **2**

St. Martin am Tennengebirge **24**

14 Hallstatt

22 Obertraun

Bruck an der Mur **8**

Zell am See **35**

17 Kaprun

Bad Gastein **3**

11 Finstergrün/Ramingstein

Heiligenblut **15**

St. Michael im Lungau **25**

28 Spittal an der Drau

Villach **30** **10** Faak am See

18 Klagenfurt

Page numbers follow town names.

SALZBURG AND CENTRAL AUSTRIA

Austria's center might be its most pastoral region, a combination of Alpy edges and soft, lakeside meadows.

Salzburg is the chief destination in these parts, with tremendous culture and sights for such a small city. Not to mention the chocolate. We'll go into more detail about the city in the introduction to the city's hostels below.

Most folks, though, just come for the *Sound of Music* tours and then head out to the pretty surrounding countryside called the Salzkammergut. A region of blue lakes, fringed with pointy mountains and bright fields of wildflowers, the area offers some of this country's prettiest walking and can be surprisingly untouristed in the right places.

Farther to the south, the district of Carinthia (Kärnten to locals) is extremely well known by those who need to know such things—Europeans, that is. Its good summertime weather, lakes, and hills make it a popular vacation spot. The fact that Americans and English bent for Salzburg and Vienna haven't really discovered Carinthia yet also makes it more attractive to the hordes of Germans, Austrians, and Italians who come. Once arrived in Carinthia, we'd head first to Klagenfurt for big-city fun, later ambling over to Villach—smaller in scale and very attractive. In between we'd hit huge Lake Wörther for watery fun.

Other stops on our central Austrian itinerary would include Feldkirchen and, way to the west, the beginnings of Tirol, where some seriously big mountains begin to show up on your radar.

Getting around in the region takes a bit of doing, as with anywhere else in Austria. Major train lines connect Salzburg, Zell am See, Villach, and Klagenfurt. But to get to smaller towns, and many of the hostels in this chapter, you'll need to take a Bundesbus from one of the larger centers. Salzburg has a good bus network that leaves from its main downtown shopping street and fans out across Salzburgerland, often several times a day.

ADALBERT-STIFTER- 👍 👎 LANDESJUGENDHERBERGE

(Aigen Hostel)
Berghäus 32, A-4160 Aigen im Muhlkreis, Upper Austria
Telephone Number: 07–281–6283
Fax Number: 07–281–62834

E-mail: ljh-aigen.post@ooe.gv.at
Rates: €13–20 (about $14–$21 US) per HI member
Credit cards: No
Beds: 80
Private/family rooms: Yes
Kitchen available: No
Season: January 1–September 6; September 21–December 31
Office hours: 7:00 to 9:00 A.M.; 5:00 to 10:00 P.M.
Affiliation: Hostelling International-ÖJHV
Extras: Dinner ($)

What hostellers say:
"Boring."

Gestalt:
Oh my Aigen head

Hospitality:

Cleanliness:

Party index:

Remote and barely in Austria, this place wasn't too popular with our hostellers, since it lacks many facilities they wanted—a laundry and a kitchen, for instance. There are, however, six double rooms in addition to two quads, six five-to-six-bedded dorms, and three larger ones.

Practically surrounded by German and Czech territory, the town doesn't make a useful stop unless you're en route to one of those other two countries and can't find a bed there. Big Moldaustau Lake does beckon across the Czech border.

How to get there:

By bus: Call hostel for transit route.
By car: Call hostel for directions.
By train: Call hostel for transit route.

JUGEND & FAMILIENGÄSTEHAUS BAD AUSSEE

(Bad Aussee Family Guest House Hostel)

Jugendherbergsstrasse 148, A-8990 Bad Aussee, Styria

Telephone Number: 03–622–52238

Fax Number: 03–622–522–3888
E-mail: oejhv@chello.at
Rates: €18–25 (about $19–$25 US) per HI member
Credit cards: Yes
Beds: 158
Private/family rooms: Yes
Kitchen available: No
Season: January 1–October 31; December 25–31
Office hours: 8:00 A.M. to 1:00 P.M.; 5:00 to 7:00 P.M.
Affiliation: Hostelling International-ÖJHV
Extras: Laundry, meals ($), sauna, gym, TV, disco, breakfast

On a hillside above town, this hostel's made up of bland white buildings—but it turns out to be more comfortable than the usual hostel.

There's one single room, about a dozen doubles with private bathrooms, and quads—mostly the latter, about half of those containing bathrooms. The place has almost everything you'd need, like a laundry, breakfast, meal service, a small gym, a television lounge, and even a tiny disco. No kitchen, though.

Bad Aussee isn't named for some criminal Australian; instead, it's a spa town where some interesting folk festivals come through.

Best bet for a bite:
On Meranplatz

What hostellers say:
"Good location."

Gestalt:
Bad boys

Hospitality:

Cleanliness:

Party index:

How to get there:

By bus: Call hostel for transit route.

By car: From Germany, take Bundesstrasse 158 past Bad Ischl to Bad Aussee; from Wien, take A1; from Graz, take A9 toward St. Michael.

By train: Call hostel for transit route.

JUGENDHERBERGE BAD GASTEIN

(Bad Gastein Hostel)

Ederplatz 2, A-5640 Bad Gastein

Telephone Number: 06–434–2080

Fax Number: 06–434–50688
E-mail: hostel.badgastein@salzburg.co.at
Rates: €16–23 (about $16–$24 US) per HI member
Credit cards: Yes
Beds: 150
Private/family rooms: Yes
Private bathrooms: All
Office hours: 7:00 to 11:00 A.M.; 5:00 to 10:00 P.M.
Affiliation: Hostelling International-ÖJHW
Extras: Playground, Internet access, volleyball, garden, information desk, sauna, table tennis, bike rentals, TV, VCR, laundry, lockers, library, gym, fireplace, grill, terrace

This hostel is one of central Austria's best decked-out places, featuring a sauna, television lounge with VCR, laundry, and lots of other comfy extras that elevate it to a great family hostel. It's quite central, too, in this resort town.

The big, fairly bland buildings in a very pretty setting—they're in a field beneath mountains—reminded us of a standard cookie-cutter hotel. Except there's no fast food outlet next door. Inside, they've

Jugendherberge Bad Gastein

Bad Gastein

(courtesy of Österreichisches Jugendherbergswerk)

got eleven double rooms, ten triples, thirty-two quads—and every darned *one* of 'em has its own private bathroom. Not to mention some rooms with television and phones, although they seem to reserve these for the dreaded teachers and group leaders who accompany kiddies. Shoot!

Common space is nice, too, consisting of two dining rooms—where breakfast is included and meals are served—the TV room, a lounge with a real fireplace, a grilling deck, and a patio. What else could you ask for? Maybe a little more atmosphere in the building, but that's about it.

This is both a summer and winter playground, but winter is higher season; some fifty area ski lifts and cable cars get going. You can do anything from snowboarding and telemarking to ice-climbing to curling (to take two opposite extremes), and more.

As is so often the case in this part of the country, you don't come for the nightlife but the quiet. The town's streets wind quaintly up and down the one hill, but the main attractions here are the radon-rich mineral baths and springs that are almost everywhere. Radon? Hmmm. You just might glow in the dark after a glass of this stuff. But they say you'll feel better. Anyway . . .

Best bet for a bite:
Jägerhäusl

Insiders' tip:
Toboggan runs nearby

Gestalt:
Radon love

Hospitality: 👍

Cleanliness:: 👍

Party index:

How to get there:

By bus: Call hostel for transit route.
By car: Call hostel for directions.
By train: From Badgastein Station, walk ½ mile to hostel.

JUGENDGÄSTEHAUS BAD ISCHL

Am Rechensteg 5, A-4820 Bad Ischl, Upper Austria

Telephone Number: 06–132–26577

Fax Number: 06–132–265–7775
E-mail: jgh.badischl@oejhv.or.at
Rates: €11–14 (about $11 US) per person;
doubles €23–29 (about $23–$29 US)
Credit cards: No
Beds: 122
Private bathrooms: Some
Private/family rooms: Yes
Kitchen available: No
Season: January 24–December 5
Office hours: 8:00 A.M. to 1:00 P.M.; 5:00 to 7:00 P.M.
Lockout: 9:00 A.M. to 5:00 P.M.
Curfew: 10:00 P.M.
Affiliation: Hostelling International-ÖJHV
Extras: Bike rentals, table tennis, garden, breakfast, dinner ($)

This big blocky building is unlikely to inspire you but is easily reached, at least, from Bad Ischl's train station. And it's got unusually private private rooms, if you know what we mean. As a result, it gets quite full in the summer.

The rooms break out this way: two singles, four double rooms (two with private bathrooms), three triples (two with bathrooms), seventeen quads—about half with bathrooms—and seven six-bedded dorms. That's a lot of showers and toilets for a hostel, some kind of a record, maybe. Also, your breakfast and sheets are included with your overnight rate. They will rent you a bike and serve you dinner; they maintain a garden and are close to walking trails in the woods. The whole place is wheelchair-accessible, and there's a small rec room with the ubiquitous table tennis table.

The town is enclosed by a horseshoe bend of the Ischl River, but there isn't much here; it's not a hopping place at all, just a salt-mining town turned spa town where people soak their way back to health or recover from ski trips. There is one extremely significant sight in the area, however, the Kaiservilla—Emperor Franz Joseph I's getaway pad, and the place from which he declared war on Serbia and thus kicked off the First World War.

Best bet for a bite:
Amigos

Insiders' tip:
Woods are full of deer

What hostellers say:
"Unimpressive outside but fine inside."

Gestalt:
Not Bad

Hospitality:

Cleanliness:

Party index:

How to get there:

By bus: From bus stop, walk ½ mile to hostel.
By car: Call hostel for directions.
By train: From Bad Ischl Station, walk ½ mile to hostel.

BAD KREUZEN HOSTEL

Neuaigen 14, Burg, A-4362 Bad Kreuzen, Upper Austria

Telephone Number: 07–266–6686 or 07–266–625–578

Rates: €14–15 (about $16 US) per HI member
Credit cards: No
Beds: 45
Private/family rooms: Yes
Kitchen available: Yes
Season: April 1–October 31
Office hours: 2:00 P.M. to midnight
Affiliation: Hostelling International-ÖJHW
Extras: Sauna, bike rentals, camping, breakfast ($), meals ($), laundry, campground

A fairly simple if bigger-than-necessary place, this hostel scores by adding some nice extra touches. It's out of the way, though, so you gotta work some to get here—and once arrived, you might find that school groups have taken over. Ah, well.

There are two double rooms, seven quads, and four dorms of various larger sizes; the private rooms are nicest here. And the equipment—a laundry machine, a hosteller kitchen, bikes for rent, a sauna—just might entice you to bring the family. There's also a campground on-site if you've brought a tent and want to save some bucks.

The town is nondescript, another spa town in the hills, but you're fairly close to noisy Linz if you get bored, and you're not far from the Danube River, either.

Best bet for a bite:
Supermarket in town

Insiders' tip:
Camping area

What hostellers say:
"Well-equipped."

Gestalt:
Kreuzen down main street

Hospitality:

Cleanliness:

Party index:

How to get there:

By bus: Call hostel for transit route.
By car: Call hostel for directions.
By train: Call hostel for transit route.

JUGENDHERBERGE BAD LEONFELDEN

Passauer Strasse 3, A-4190 Bad Leonfelden

Telephone Number: 07–213–8109

Rates: €9.00 (about $9.00 US) per HI member
Credit cards: No
Beds: 44
Private/family rooms: Yes
Kitchen available: Yes

Office hours: 7:00 to 10:00 A.M.; 5:00 to 9:00 P.M.
Affiliation: Hostelling International-ÖJHW
Extras: Bike rentals, sauna, laundry

North of Linz, practically in the Czech Republic in fact, Bad Leonfelden isn't going to be a major stop for you. But the hostel here's got just enough to keep you interested if you do.

There are two quad rooms, both potentially family or private rooms, plus a lounge and—sigh—only three showers for the whole place. There's a sauna at the hostel, and they rent bikes, but the presence of a kitchen is counterbalanced by the rural location. This is one case where we wished they'd serve meals to hostellers.

Adequate, though.

How to get there:

By bus: Call hostel for transit route.
By car: Call hostel for directions
By train: Call hostel for transit route.

Best bet for a bite:
Stock up at Euro Spar

Insiders' tip:
Bring some food

What hostellers say:
"I'm starvin'"

Gestalt:
Bad manor

Hospitality:

Cleanliness:

Party index:

BRAUNAU AM INN HOSTEL

Osternbergerstrasse 57, A-5280 Braunau am Inn, Upper Austria

Telephone Number: 07–722–81638

Fax Number: 07–722–81638 or 07–722–63136–14
Rates: €15 (about $15 US) per HI member
Credit cards: No
Beds: 54
Private/family rooms: Yes
Kitchen available: Yes
Season: January 7–December 22
Office hours: 7:00 to 10:00 A.M.; 5:00 to 9:00 P.M.
Affiliation: Hostelling International-ÖJHV
Extras: Bike rentals, breakfast

Inside a wing attached to a church, this simple facility contains all triples or quad rooms, which makes it nice if you're looking for a German-Austrian border town with history and closeness to both Salzburg and Munich. They have a kitchen, make you breakfast, and rent bikes, too.

Braunau turns out to have been Hitler's actual birthplace, under a different last name, though

Best bet for a bite:
Bogner

Insiders' tip:
Mexican bar in town

they don't exactly tout it as such in the tourist office. Smart people.

Though he lived here two years, you'll have to hunt to even find his childhood house today. It's at #15 Salzburger Vorstadt; ignore the urge to spit, and come instead for the town's fifteenth-century domed church and fine old quarter. The rectangular Stadtplatz, in particular, has some attractive buildings. Bring a camera.

Better still, come in fall—just before Oktoberfest—when locals get the jump on Munich by putting on their own minibeer fest.

What hostellers say:
"WHO was from here?!"

Gestalt:
Return of Braunau

Hospitality:

Cleanliness:

Party index:

How to get there:

By bus: Call hostel for transit route.
By car: Call hostel for directions
By train: Call hostel for transit route.

JUGENDGÄSTEHAUS BRUCK AN DER MUR

(Bruck an der Mur Guesthouse Hostel)

Stadtwaldstrasse 1, A-8600 Bruck an der Mur, Styria

Telephone Number: 03–862–58448

Fax Number: 03–862–584–4888
E-mail: jgh.bruck@jgh.at
Rates: €16 (about $15 US) per HI member; doubles €35 (about $40 US)
Credit cards: Diner's Club, MC, VISA
Beds: 92
Private/family rooms: Yes
Kitchen available: No
Season: Closed April
Office hours: 7:00 A.M. to 10:00 P.M.
Affiliation: Hostelling International-ÖJHW and Hostelling International-ÖJHV
Extras: Meals ($), breakfast, sauna, bike rentals, TV, gym

Another good hostel in the Steiermark chain of "guesthouse-style" places, this hostel is well equipped with amazing plumbing. The structure is a little blah, though—that's what you get for recycling a former hospital. You mean babies were being born in these very rooms? Yeeeesh . . .

Best bet for a bite: Along Mittlergasse

What hostellers say:
"Better than I thought it would be."

Anyhow, they've got eight quad-size rooms that can be made private and twelve five-to-six-bedded rooms—all with bathrooms. There are also seven

Jugendgästehaus Bruck an der Mur
Bruck an der Mur
(courtesy of Österreichisches Jugendherbergswerk)

common areas, including a sauna, a television lounging area, a small gym, and more. Meals, breakfast, bikes for hire—it all helps.

Only one problem: The town isn't any great shakes. The main reason for coming here, in fact, is just to change for a spectacular bus ride up to the town and hostel at Mariazell; if they're full up top, though, and you're waiting out the night, this hostel is fine as a stop.

How to get there:

By bus: Call hostel for transit route.
By car: Call hostel for directions.
By train: Call hostel for transit route.

Gestalt:
Bruck 'em, Danno

Hospitality:

Cleanliness:

Party index:

JUGENDHERBERGE EBENSEE

(Ebensee Hostel)

Rindbachstrasse 15, A-4802 Ebensee, Upper Austria

Telephone Number: 06–133–6698

Fax Number: 06–133–669–885
E-mail: ebensee@jutel.at
Rates: €15 (about $15 US) per HI member
Credit cards: No
Beds: 80
Private bathrooms: All
Private/family rooms: Yes

Kitchen available: No
Season: April 1–October 31
Office hours: 7:00 A.M. to 8:00 P.M.
Affiliation: HI-ÖJHW
Extras: TV, VCR, table tennis, bike rentals, breakfast, meals ($), camping, game rooms

This is a pretty good hostel, surprisingly comfortable for a small Austrian deal, and in a cool-looking building that seems like something out of the Addams Family—a tall, narrow, spooky-looking thing surrounded by trees.

Rooms are three quads, three six-bedded rooms, five eight-bedded dorms, and a larger one, each with its own bathroom; no hall showers here. There are two dining rooms in which to eat breakfast and dinner, several lounges, a couple of game rooms with table tennis and such, and a cellar hangout area that's even been made wheelchair-accessible. Kudos for that.

This is yet another Austrian town on a lake, not as spectacular or pretty as some. There's also the usual gondola service up into some rather nice scenery above; most hit the gondola and go up to Feuerkogel, with hikes, cross-country skiing tracks, and better views. There are tons of water sports on the Ebensee lake itself, as well as hiking, biking (they rent 'em here), and more.

Insiders' tip:
Hit local history museum

What hostellers say:
"Decent."

Gestalt:
East of Ebensee

Hospitality:

Cleanliness:

Party index:

How to get there:

By bus: From Ebensee Station, walk ¾ mile around lake to hostel.

By car: From Highway A1, take Regau exit, and drive toward Gmunden to Ebensee.

By train: From bus stop, walk ¾ mile around lake to hostel.

KEY TO ICONS

Attractive natural setting

Ecologically aware hostel

Superior kitchen facilities or cafe

Offbeat or eccentric place

Superior bathroom facilities

Romantic private rooms

Comfortable beds

Among our very favorite hostels

S A particularly good value

Handicapped-accessible

Good for business travelers

Especially well suited for families

Good for active travelers

Visual arts at hostel or nearby

Music at hostel or nearby

Great hostel for skiers

Bar or pub at hostel or nearby

FAAK AM SEE HOSTEL

Nummer 12, A-9583 Faak am See, Carinthia
Telephone Number: 04–254–2301

Fax Number: 04–254–46464
Rates: €11 (about $11.50 US) per HI member
Credit cards: No
Beds: 50
Private/family rooms: No
Kitchen available: Yes
Office hours: 8:00 A.M. to 9:00 P.M.
Affiliation: Hostelling International-ÖJHW

This place is always open and is a potential stop on the fairly untouristed Faakersee. (Say that with a smile on your face.) As a bonus there are ten double rooms at this place, plus a few quads, and some bigger rooms. The family who runs this place asks that you call a day or two ahead, though, since family members work during the day and won't be here unless otherwise notified.

There are two kitchens in which to whip something up—a big one for large groups and a small one for, you guessed it, small groups and individuals like yourself. Those are the chief benefits.

This lake town isn't actually on the lake, but close enough. A big local railway mock-up is fun, but hardly reason to hang out for a long while.

Best bet for a bite:
Euro Spar (small);
motorists can stop at Billa

Insiders' tip:
Check out the village of
(yes) Egg

What hostellers say:
"Thanks for the kitchen."

Gestalt:
See-side

Hospitality:

Cleanliness:

Party index:

How to get there:

By bus: Call hostel for transit route.
By car: Call hostel for directions.
By train: Call hostel for transit route.

RAMINGSTEIN HOSTEL NR

Wald 65, Burg Finstergrün, A-5591 Ramingstein (Finstergrün),
Salzburgerland
Telephone Number: 06–475–228

Fax Number: 06–475–2284
E-mail: ejoe@gmx.at
Rates: €23 (about $23 US) per HI member
Credit cards: No
Beds: 160

Private/family rooms: Yes
Kitchen available: No
Season: May 1–October 15
Office hours: 7:00 A.M. to 10:00 P.M.
Affiliation: Hostelling International-ÖJHV
Extras: Meals ($), breakfast

This rarely found hostel is in the hamlet of Finstergrün, just outside St. Michael im Lungau. The place sports six double rooms, seven four-bedded rooms for families when needed, four five-to-six-bedded dorms, seven rooms with seven to eight beds each, and six more dorms containing nine or more beds.

It's a historic old building, but they've kept things simple inside—a kitchen that serves meals and breakfast is about it. There isn't a whole lot of privacy due to a lack of showers per hosteller, so if they're full you're probably going to wait in line. Be sure to check out the local church in Burg Finstergrün.

Best bet for a bite:
Here, but call to reserve dinner

Insiders' tip:
Take a shower at night

What hostellers say:
"What am I doing here?"

Gestalt:
Bride of Ramingstein

Hospitality: NR

Cleanliness: NR

Party index:

How to get there:

By bus: Call hostel for transit route.
By car: Call hostel for directions.
By train: Call hostel for transit route.

TREEHOUSE BACKPACKER HOTEL

Schindlbachstrasse 525, 4645 Grünau im Almtal, Salzburgerland
Telephone Number: 07–616–8499

Fax Number: 07–616–8599
E-mail: treehousehotel@hotmail.com
Web site: www.oenet.at/user/treehouse
Rates: €14–16 (about $15–$17 US) per person; doubles €35 (about $37 US)
Credit cards: MC, VISA
Beds: 41
Private/family rooms: Yes
Kitchen available: No
Office hours: 8:00 A.M. to 10:00 P.M.
Affiliation: None
Extras: Meals ($), Internet access ($), TV, movies, bars, pickups, ski rentals, bike rentals ($), snowboard rentals ($), tennis court, basketball, tours, sauna

This backpacker-style hostel, way up in the hills of Austria and off the beaten track for sure—but still reachable by train—gets rave reviews for its nice rooms, meals, laid-back atmosphere, and facilities. Plus a slice of true rural Austrian life.

The rooms here come in doubles, triples, quads, and six-bedded dorms, all with bathrooms and showers; most of 'em have balconies, too! They serve dinner for €7.00 (about $7.00 US), and it's pretty good.

Best bet for a bite:
Seehaus

Insiders' tip:
Be here during big American holidays

What hostellers say:
"Like staying at a friend's."

Gestalt:
Tree-for-all

Hospitality:

Cleanliness:

Party index:

Management offers an amazing array of activities here—everything from skiing and snowboarding to horseback riding and a hoops court—and will even lend you free ski togs if you didn't bring any. An Internet terminal is also popular. They also rent snowboards and mountain bikes; maintain two (count 'em) bars plus a sauna; and all rooms have their own bathrooms and showers. You drift to sleep under down comforters. In winter, the curious phenomenon of people jumping into the sauna and then jumping into an icy-cold river takes hold.

The bars are open late. And here's one bonus for American guests: a huge Halloween party, plus celebrations of Thanksgiving, Christmas, New Year's, and the Austrian Fasching (Carnival).

How to get there:

By bus: Call hostel for transit route.

By car: Call hostel for directions.

By train: From Salzburg or Vienna, take train to Wels and change to regional train (track 11) for Grünau. Take to end of line, then call hostel for pickup.

SCHLÖSS WISPACH–ESTERHAZY

(Hallein Hostel)

Wispachstrasse 7, A-5400 Hallein, Salzburgerland

Telephone Number: 06–245–80397

Fax Number: 06+245–803–973
E-mail: jgh.hallein@jgh.at
Rates: €19–20 (about $20–$21 US) per HI
Credit cards: No
Beds: 112
Private/family rooms: Yes
Season: April 1–September 30
Office hours: 7:00 to 10:00 A.M.; 5:00 to 10:00 P.M.
Affiliation: Hostelling International-ÖJHV
Extras: Bike rentals, table tennis, breakfast, meals ($)

A beautiful building, in a nice area, but this castlelike structure is often completely booked up with school or tour groups—on purpose, we mean—who have rented the whole place out. That means you'd better not show up late at night expecting a bed, 'cause it might be Shutout City.

Best bet for a bite:
Stadtkrug Inn

Insiders' tip:
Use the pool

What hostellers say:
"The hills are alive . . ."

Gestalt:
Study Hallein

Hospitality:

Cleanliness:

Party index:

If you do snag a bed here, however, it's okay—less than a mile from the station, not central, but in a really nice house and next to the town's nice public swimming pool. Facilities are so-so, with some double rooms and quads but mostly a bunch of bigger ones occupying a five-story structure with a grand door and true character. They serve breakfast and meals in the dining hall, rent bikes, and have a game area with table tennis.

Hallein has some really attractive streets, squares, and buildings downtown, owing their prosperity to years of salt mining in the hills. The town museum (about $4.00 US) focuses largely on the old Celtic encampments here, and obviously there's also a lot of material dealing with salt mining and trading. You also get a big discount at that pool, too.

Get here by taking a bus 10 miles or so south from Salzburg; the ride takes maybe half an hour.

How to get there:

By bus: Call hostel for transit route.
By car: Call hostel for directions.
By train: From Hallein Station, walk ¾ mile to hostel.

GÄSTEHAUS ZUR MUHLE

Kirchenweg 36, A-5400 Hallstatt, Salzburgerland

Telephone Number: 06–134–8318

Fax Number: 06–134–8318
Rates: €8.00 (about $9.00 US) per person
Credit cards: No
Beds: 57
Private/family rooms: Yes
Kitchen available: No
Season: January 1–October 31; December 15–31
Office hours: 8:00 A.M. to 2:00 P.M.; 4:00 to 10:00 P.M.
Affiliation: None
Extras: Lockers (€15), meals ($), breakfast ($), sheets (€3.00)

Still the only hostel in what's probably Austria's most attractive town, you're probably gonna end up here at some point, with about a thousand other tourists. The restaurant here serves pizza, pasta, and Austrian food and is good and cheap; and the bed is lots cheaper than other options around, but it's just your usual friendly hostel. No greater, no worse.

The place isn't in downtown Hallstatt but on the outskirts, through a tunnel. Beds come in doubles and triples and then in big- gish dorms that are really a bit too tight a fit, but you might not care. Sheets cost extra here, so the low price isn't quite as low as it might appear.

Because, as we said, Hallstatt is Austria's prettiest town, clinging to a strip of land between cliffs and a lake; even locals call it a jewel. There's an interesting annual ritual here—locals take to the lake and cross it for services in a small church across the way— but even if you miss that you'll love the views and the local hikes above the town.

Best bet for a bite:
In-house pizza

Insiders' tip:
Be here at the end of May

What hostellers say:
"Beauty, eh?"

Gestalt:
Kids in the Hallstatt

Hospitality:

Cleanliness:

Party index:

How to get there:

By bus: Call hostel for transit route.
By car: Call hostel for directions.
By train: From Hallstatt Station, take ferry across lake to town and walk to hostel.

JUGENDHERBERGE HEILIGENBLUT

(Heiligenblut Hostel)

Hof 36, A-9844 Heiligenblut, Carinthia

Telephone Number: 04–824–2259

Fax Number: 04–824–2259
E-mail: jgh.heiligenblut@oejhv.or.at
Rates: €14 (about $15 US) per HI member
Credit cards: No
Beds: 93
Private bathrooms: Yes
Private/family rooms: Yes
Kitchen available: No
Season: Mid-December–mid-October
Office hours: 7:00 to 10:00 A.M.; 5:00 to 10:00 P.M.
Curfew: 10:00 P.M.
Affiliation: Hostelling International-ÖJHV
Extras: Sauna, solarium, TV, parking, breakfast, dinner ($)

Sitting in a tiny valley with a pointy 1400s-ish church, this is one of the prettier places you'll stop for the night in Austria; they were

Jugendherberge Heiligenblut

Heiligenblut

(courtesy of JHV)

smart to build a hostel here. The hostel is on the way down to the bottom of the valley from the bus stop—a valley with the 10,000-plus-foot peak of the Grossglockner overhanging it for effect.

There are three double rooms, all with bathrooms, so couples will especially like the place. For bigger families there are five triples—some with bathrooms—seven quads, a six-bedded dorm, and four eight-bedded rooms. Those larger ones don't come with private bathrooms. The extra facilities here are good, with a sauna, sunning area, television lounge, and such.

The nicest thing to see is literally right next door, a handsome old fifteenth-century church. A local network of several gondolas and lifts can get you to various hiking or skiing points in the smaller mountains. This is also the jumping-off point for the splendiferous (though expensive) Grossglockner toll highway, which winds in white-knuckle fashion through just incredible scenery—think of this curvy 30-mile ride as a Blue Ridge Parkway . . . on steroids.

Remember that it's cheaper (and possibly less stressful, if you're a nervous driver) to take one of the buses that come through several times daily in summertime rather than pay for a car and then again for the steep toll. However, a car would give you the freedom to explore the fantastic wilderness surrounding Hohe Tauern park.

Best bet for a bite:
ADEG

Insiders' tip:
Hop on Hochalpenstrasse bus ($) for great views

What hostellers say:
"Excellent church next door!"

Gestalt:
Park place

Hospitality:

Cleanliness:

Party index:

How to get there:

By bus: From Mallnitz or Lienz Station, take postbus to Heiligenblut.

By car: Drive A10 to Spittal area and take Lendorf exit, then follow Bundestrasse B100 to Mollbrucke; continue to Heiligenblut.

By train: From Mallnitz or Lienz Station, take postbus to Heiligenblut.

JUGENDHERBERGE HINTERSTODER

(Hinterstoder Hostel)

Mitterstoder 137, A-4573 Hinterstoder, Upper Austria

Telephone Number: 07–564–5227

Fax Number: 07–564–5227–1711
E-mail: hinterstoder@jutel.at
Rates: €12 (about $14 US) per HI member
Credit cards: No
Beds: 96
Private bathroom: Yes
Private/family rooms: Yes
Kitchen available: No
Season: Year-round
Office hours: 8:00 A.M. to 10:00 P.M.
Affiliation: Hostelling International-ÖJHW
Extras: Garden, TV, VCR, caving equipment, meeting room, table tennis, library, foosball, campfire, playground, ski rentals, bike rentals, meals ($), breakfast

Hinsterstoder's hostel is a very sports-oriented place. How much so? Well, this is probably the only place in the world where they keep *caving gear* on hand in case you suddenly get the urge to go spelunking. Add in skiing lessons in the winter and hiking trips in the summer, and you certainly won't get bored if you like the outdoors.

Rooms consist of four doubles with showers, two quads with their own bathrooms (families will like these a lot), ten more quads with just showers, and six eight-bedded rooms. There's a dining room, lounge with TV and VCR, a game room with table tennis and foosball, a reading room, plus all that caving equipment—boots, jackets, lamps, the whole deal.

In summer this is a great hiking area. In winter skiers hit the slopes on a World

Best bet for a bite:
On-site half or full pension

Insiders' tip:
Watch out for stalagmites

What hostellers say:
"Who wants to belay me?"

Gestalt:
Hinterland

Hospitality:

Cleanliness:

Party index:

Cup–caliber run and also find the cross-country tracks in the area nice. Expect plenty of groups and families if you come—not a party atmosphere, but it's definitely a place to get lots of fresh air.

How to get there:

By bus: Call hostel for transit route.

By car: From Highway A1, take Sattledt exit and go to A9; continue to B138, going toward Kirchdorf to Hinterstoder.

By train: Call hostel for transit route.

JUGENDGÄSTEHAUS KAPRUN

Nikolaus Gassnerstrasse 448, A-5710 Kaprun, Salzburgerland

Telephone Number: 06–547–8507

Fax Number: 06–547–8507–3
E-mail: jgh.kaprun@jgh.at
Rates: €15–23 (about $15–$23 US) per HI member
Credit cards: Yes
Beds: 150
Private/family rooms: Yes
Kitchen available: No
Office hours: 7:00 to 10:00 A.M.; 5:00 to 10:00 P.M.
Affiliation: Hostelling International-ÖJHV
Extras: Bike rentals, TV, disco, volleyball, information desk, garden, meeting rooms, playground, breakfast, dinner ($)

You come here for one reason, pretty much: to ski. There's some hiking above this town, sure, but not as spectacular as in some other nearby towns.

Best bet for a bite:
Dorfstadl

Insiders' tip:
Check out snowboard park in Zell

What hostellers say:
"Wax me."

Gestalt:
Kaprun crunch

Hospitality:

Cleanliness:

Party index:

The three-story, blocky hostel includes two single rooms, four doubles, four triples, nine quads, thirteen sixes, and two bigger ones; it's a big place, designed for hordes of ski-tripping groups in winter. The facilities cater to a young bunch too—there's a small disco, believe it or not (well, a dance area), a playground, volleyball net, garden, and television lounge. They rent bikes, serve meals, and include breakfast, too.

The small town of Kaprun is really just a satellite of better-known Zell am See, about 4 miles off, which is good to know if Zell's hostel is full to the rafters. And this one's closer to ski lifts, too—the gondola actually carries you right over a glacier. Which is so coooool. Literally.

How to get there:

By bus: Call hostel for transit route.

By car: Call hostel for directions.
By train: From Zell am See Station, 4 miles away, take postbus to Kaprun.

KLAGENFURT

Klagenfurt's the capital of Carinthia, a south-central Austrian region where you'll find more than a few resort towns—but also some substantial cities with actual people (as opposed to tourism officials and T-shirt vendors) living in them. The region's proximity to Italy means the food is even better than usual, and its closeness to the Slovakian border adds additional interest for those who like to stamp their passports with odd destinations. You might even hear a bit of Slovakian if you're lucky.

If you're sticking around the city and the area for a long time, buy a regional card like the Kärnten Card, a summer-only deal that gets you three weeks' worth of free transportation—that's buses, gondolas, lake ferries, the whole deal—and museum entry in Carinthia for €25 (about $26 US). Other tourist areas have similar setups. Heckuva deal, though you've gotta stick around a little while to make it worth its while.

JUGENDGÄSTEHAUS KLAGENFURT

(Klagenfurt Guesthouse Hostel)

Universitatsviertel, Neckheimgasse 6, A-9020 Klagenfurt, Carinthia

Telephone Number: 04–632–30020

Fax Number: 04–632–300–2020
E-mail: jgh.klagenfurt@oejhv.or.at
Rates: €15–18 (about $16.50–$18.50 US) per HI member; singles €23–26 (about $23–$26 US); doubles €33–39 (about $35–$40 US)
Credit cards: Yes
Beds: 146
Private bathrooms: Yes
Private/family rooms: Yes
Kitchen available: Yes
Office hours: 7:00 to 9:00 A.M.; 5:00 to 10:00 P.M.
Curfew: 10:00 P.M.
Affiliation: Hostelling International-ÖJHV
Extras: Sauna, solarium, information desk, lockers, garden, TV, laundry, meeting rooms, meals ($), breakfast, bike rentals

Right by the Wörther See lake, this very nice looking hostel has the double fortune of being near the city of Klagenfurt's university district—which means inexpensive food and fun abounds on the main strips nearby. You won't mind, for once, the fact that you're far from town.

Rooms in this rambling complex are almost all quads with en-suite bathrooms, plus there are also two double rooms, so you're virtually guaranteed a private sleep. The inside is very interestingly decorated; all is kept clean and tidy, and there are just a ton of facilities—the sauna, laundry, and television lounge are the ones you'll probably appreciate most. Breakfast is included, meals are served, and they actually have a kitchen for you to cook your own meals if you want.

Most folks here just want to laze by the water or else hit the bars in the area, and we agree with 'em—that's probably the best use of your time here.

Best bet for a bite:
SPAR

Insiders' tip:
Nude sunbathing at
Europapark

What hostellers say:
"Friendly and well
located."

Gestalt:
Rugrats

Top bunk:

Cleanliness:

Party index:

How to get there:

By bus: Take 40, 41, or 42 bus and get off at Heiligengeistpl. Switch to 10 or 11 bus and stop at Neckheimg from platform #2. At night, buses run hourly until 11:30 P.M.

By car: Take Highway A10 to Klagenfurt and take Klagenfurt-West–Minimundus exit; continue to hostel.

By train: Klagenfurt Station, 2½ miles away, is closest; call hostel for transit route.

JUGENDGÄSTEHAUS KOLPING

Enzenbergstrasse 26, A-9020 Klagenfurt

Telephone Number: 04–635–6965

Fax Number: 04–635–696–532
Rates: €20–24 (about $21–$25 US) per person; singles €26 (about $27 US)
Credit cards: No
Beds: 200
Private/family rooms: Yes
Kitchen available: No
Season: July 10–September 10
Office hours: Twenty-four hours
Affiliation: Hostelling International-ÖJHW
Extras: Breakfast ($)

This is the most central of the city's hostels, and it's very well equipped if kinda drab.

Every single room in this place has two beds, all one hundred of 'em, and each comes with private bathrooms or showers, too—so it's basically a hotel. Unfortunately it's open only for three months in the summer.

The staffers are helpful, and you've gotta like the six common areas—plenty of room to stretch out and/or meet others. Also, the hostel's close to corny but fun Europa park, with its zoo, minigolf course, and planetarium—enough to satisfy any lingering craving for Euro-kitsch.

How to get there:

By bus: Call hostel for transit route.

By car: Call hostel for directions.

By train: From Klagenfurt Station, walk down Bahnofstrasse to 8 Mai Strasse, then turn slightly right.

Best bet for a bite:
Zum Augustin, near Pfarrkirche church

Insiders' tip:
Nude (but not coed) beach on lake

What hostellers say:
"Wish it was open year-round."

Gestalt:
Klagenfurtive

Hospitality:

Cleanliness: 👍

Party index:
🎉🎉

LINZ

Linz gets a bad rap. Yes, Hitler lived here for a while, sure, but check this out: so did Johannes Kepler. (They both rocked the world in their respective ways.) And although this city is primarily industrial, which is what you see coming in by car or train, the old city center is quite attractive. There are many intriguing museums here—Ars Electronica, the best of 'em, ranks among Austria's very best thanks to its cool virtual-reality room in the basement.

The train station here is inconveniently situated, so take a city streetcar to the old town, which itself centers around a central square that's one of the country's best—amazing considering the industrial sprawl reaching in concentric rings around the city for great distances. Around this central area (called the Hauptplatz) stand a few interesting buildings, but it's not far across the river and uphill to the more interesting eighth-century castle ("schloss"), which includes a good museum.

Ars Electronica, as we said, features as its star attraction the virtual-reality room (good luck getting into that one) but also other cool stuff; there's an Internet cafe up top with splendid views. It might be among the best €6.00 (about $7 US) you spend in Austria.

Don't forget to try the ubiquitous Linzer torte, a jelly-filled cake invented here and still good today.

JUGENDGÄSTEHAUS LINZ

(Linz Guest House Hostel)

Stanglhofweg 3, A-4020 Linz

Telephone Number: 07–326–64434

Fax Number: 07–326–644–3475 or 07–326–646–02164

E-mail: jgh.linz@oejhv.or.at

Rates: €13–26 (about $13–$26 US) per HI member; doubles €35 (about $37 US)

Credit cards: No

Beds: 172

Private/family rooms: 24

Season: January 8–December 21

Office hours: 8:00 A.M. to 4:00 P.M.; 6:00 to 9:00 P.M. Monday to Thursday; 8:00 A.M. to 1:00 P.M. Friday; 6:00 to 9:00 P.M. Saturday and Sunday

Curfew: 11:00 P.M.

Affiliation: Hostelling International-ÖJHV

Extras: Table tennis, TV, terrace, bar, lockers, information desk, playground, garden, volleyball, tennis, breakfast, bike rentals

About a mile south of the city's old core, this place is roomy, clean, and damned boring. It's a safe, adequate bed with zero atmosphere, so if that's what you need, it's just fine—especially if you're traveling with a sweetie or little one. If you want fun, go elsewhere in town.

The modern slab of a building contains six single rooms, twelve doubles, four triples, and thirty-four quads—all of them with en-suite bathrooms. As it's near the city's sports stadium complex, it tends to get very booked up with Austrian schoolkids or families, not exactly your recipe for excitement. In fact it might even be full when you call.

Other facilities include group-friendly stuff like a game room, bar, volleyball net, and so forth.

Best bet for a bite:
Mangolds (veggie)

Insiders' tip:
Call wayyy ahead

What hostellers say:
"Achtung, baby"

Gestalt:
Full house

Hospitality:

Cleanliness: 👍

Party index:

How to get there:

By bus: From Linz Station, take #27 bus to Blaumauerstrasse, then walk down Roseggerstrasse to hostel.

By car: From Highway A1, take Linz Zentrum (downtown Linz) exit and follow signs to Richtung Stadium.

By train: From Linz Station, take #27 bus to Blaumauerstrasse, then walk down Roseggerstrasse to hostel.

LANDESJUGENDHERBERGE LINZ IM LENTIA 2000

(Linz Hostel in Lentia 2000)

Blütenstrasse 23, A-4040 Linz, Upper Austria

Telephone Number: 07–327–37078

Fax Number: 07–327–370–7815
E-mail: jgh.linz@oejhv.or.at
Rates: €11–13 (about $11.50–$13.50 US) per person
Credit cards: No
Beds: 106
Private/family rooms: Yes
Kitchen available: No
Office hours: 7:30 to 9:30 A.M.; 5:00 to 9:00 P.M.
Affiliation: None
Extras: Breakfast

This hostel is pretty blah—it's basically a high-rise in a shopping mall, let's put it that way. At least it's on the same side of the Danube as the city's train station, but it's still not our first or even second pick here.

Rooms in the fifteen-story monstrosity are broken up into six doubles, six quads, and fourteen larger dorms that in summer are full with kiddies. They serve breakfast here, and the place is wheelchair-accessible—hey, we just said something positive about it. All in all, though, it's still a piece of Eastern Bloc architecture, and you'll no doubt want to call the other two hostels first.

Best bet for a bite:
Wein Fassl

Insiders' tip:
Try the other hostel first

What hostellers say:
"It's like an Eastern Bloc party."

Gestalt:
2002, a Space Odyssey

Hospitality:

Cleanliness:

Party index:

How to get there:

By bus: From Linz Station, take #3 streetcar across river to Reindlstrasse, then walk to next street on right.

By car: Call hostel for directions.

By train: From Linz Station, take #3 streetcar across river to Reindlstrasse, then walk to next street on right.

JUGENDGÄSTEHAUS MONDSEE

(Mondsee Hostel)

Krankenhausstrasse 9, A-5310 Mondsee, Upper Austria

Telephone Number: 06–232–2418

Fax Number: 06–232–241–875
E-mail: jgh.mondsee@oejhv.or.at
Rates: €10 (about $10 US) per HI member;
doubles €27–34 ($28–$36 US)
Credit cards: No
Beds: 80
Private/family rooms: Yes
Kitchen available: No
Season: February 1–December 15
Office hours: 8:00 A.M. to 1:00 P.M.; 5:00 to 7:00 P.M. Monday to
Friday; 5:00 to 7:00 P.M. Saturday and Sunday
Curfew: 10:00 P.M.
Affiliation: Hostelling International-ÖJHV
Extras: Meals ($), breakfast, bike rentals, terrace

This tidy and comfortable hostel near the center of Mondsee village makes a fine stop. Unfortunately, it's often full of school groups—but if you can snag a bed it's pretty good. We'll tell you why it's so popular in a moment.

Best bet for a bite:
On the lake

Insiders' tip:
Go ahead, check out
the church!

What hostellers say:
"Isn't that the church
where . . ."

Gestalt:
Rodgers and Hammerstein

Hospitality: 👍 👎

Cleanliness: 👍

Party index:

Beds come mostly in doubles or quad rooms, meaning families and couples have got it made, plus one big ten-bedded dorm. Meals are served, there's a terrace for hanging out, and they'll rent you a bike if you want to get around Mondsee lake. The surrounding grounds are nice and green.

This town is one of the nicest in the region, and its lake is among Austria's prettiest, but that's not why it's popular; it's popular because the producers of the film *The Sound of Music* used the village church for the film's emotional wedding scene, making it a perpetual attraction for hordes of Americans ever since. The little museum next door to the church—in former abbey buildings—is also pretty good, easily worth the €2.00 (about $2.00 US) admission fee.

Not much farther away, just above town on a slight rise, an outdoor folk museum gives another idea of what it was like to live here long ago. Finally there's good swimming in that lake as well as plenty of other water sports to occupy you.

Though this is very close to Salzburg, you can't get here by train. Regular buses leave from Salzburg's main street several times daily and make the ride.

How to Get There:

By bus: From Salzburg, 20 miles away, take Bundesbus to Mondsee.

By car: From Highway A1, take Mondsee exit and continue to Bundestrasse (B154), then follow B154 to Mondsee.

By train: From Salzburg, 20 miles away, take Bundesbus to Mondsee.

NEUSTIFT IM MUHLKREIS HOSTEL

Nummer 71 Rannahof, A-4143 Neustift im Muhlkreis, Upper Austria

Telephone Number: 07–284–8196

Fax Number: 07–284–8396
E-mail: jugendherberge@vpn.at
Rates: €13 (about $14 US) per HI member
Credit cards: No
Beds: 100
Private/family rooms: Yes
Kitchen available: No
Office hours: 8:00 A.M. to 10:00 P.M.
Affiliation: Hostelling International-ÖJHW
Extras: Meals ($), breakfast, bike rentals

Not much to this place, just four doubles, sixteen five-and-six-bedded dorms, and three common areas. They serve breakfast for free, add dinner for an extra charge, and rent you bikes.

The hostel's situated off the beaten track in a tiny corner of Austria up near Germany, the Czech Republic—and two other similar hostels. Groups tend to fill it up, but with the Aigen hostel nearby, you might not care.

How to get there:

By bus: Call hostel for transit route.
By car: Call hostel for directions.
By train: Call hostel for transit route.

Best bet for a bite:
On-site

Insiders' tip:
Load up at breakfast

What hostellers say:
"Anyone going to Prague?"

Gestalt:
Neustift on the block

Hospitality:

Cleanliness:

Party index:

JUGENDHERBERGE OBERTRAUN

(Obertraun Hostel)

Winkl 26, A-4831 Obertraun, Upper Austria

Telephone Number: 06–131–360

Fax Number: 06–131–3604
E-mail: obertraun@jutel.at

Rates: €10–12 (about $11–$12 US) per HI member
Credit cards: No
Beds: 160
Private/family rooms: Yes
Kitchen available: No
Office hours: 8:00 A.M. to 1:00 P.M.; 5:00 to 7:30 P.M.
Curfew: 10:00 P.M.
Lockout: 2:00 to 5:00 P.M.
Affiliation: Hostelling International-ÖJHW
Extras: Meals ($), breakfast, bike rentals, garden, library, TV, VCR, table tennis, ski rentals, campfire, playground

You can't miss this building when in Obertraun; it's very yellow and very popular if you can get out here. Families in particular like it, probably because of the playground and special rooms for families. Then again, so do school group leaders and outdoorsy types. The town is not as beautiful as nearby Hallstatt, but this hostel is more likely to have room than that town's joint.

There are four double rooms in a freaky chalet-concrete job—all with bathrooms—plus ten four-bedded dorms (half with bathrooms); two five-bedded rooms; fourteen six-bedded rooms; and two larger, ten-bedded rooms. The kitchen serves breakfast and dinners. People hang in one of several common areas, including a game room, a television lounge, a reading room, and a garden.

The hostel's well placed on the way to a gondola that leads up to the Dachstein ice cave complex. These amazing ice caves are the main reason to get out to Obertraun—interesting if you can put up with the tacky promotions along the way. Cradled by peaks, hiking trails

Best bet for a bite:
Restaurants near the train station

Insiders' tip:
Check out the ice caves

What hostellers say:
"Worth the trek."

Gestalt:
Obertraun unit

Hospitality:

Cleanliness:

Party index:

in the area are also nice. In winter there are ski schools in the area, when the hostel gets even more full.

How to get there:

By bus: From Hallstatt, take local bus to Obertraun. Walk ¾ mile from station, cross river, and take first left; continue to hostel.

By car: Take Highway A1 to Regau exit and continue through Gmunden, Ebensee, and Bad Ischl to Obertraun.

By train: From Hallstatt Station, take local bus to Obertraun. Walk ¾ mile from station, cross river, and take first left; continue to hostel.

JUGENDGÄSTEHAUS ST. GILGEN

(St. Gilgen Guest House)

Mondseerstrasse 7–9, A-5340 St. Gilgen, Salzburgerland

Telephone Number: 06–227–2365

Fax Number: 06–227–236–575
Rates: €13–15 (about $13.50–$15.00 US) per HI member
Credit cards: No
Beds: 128
Private/family rooms: Yes
Kitchen available: No
Season: January 25–December 18
Office hours: 8:00 to 9:00 A.M.; noon to 1:00 P.M.; 5:00 to 7:00 P.M.
Curfew: 11:00 P.M.
Affiliation: Hostelling International-ÖJHV
Extras: Meals ($), breakfast, sauna, bike rentals, table tennis, solarium, TV, garden, gym, lockers, garden, playground, information desk

A half-timbered building on a lake, tucked among much higher-priced villas and cottages, this is probably one of Austria's best deals. It's in a great little village, with tiny streets and old-faced buildings, but people around Austria know about it. So *book ahead.*

The rooms consist of twelve singles and doubles and then twenty-six quads, almost all of them with bathrooms, and dorms as well. Nice. The problem is, schools have gotten wind of the place and sometimes book the dorms and smaller rooms to the rafters. They come because of tremendous extras such as a sauna, bikes for hire, a game room, television lounge, small gymasium, playground for kids, and meal service. Some rooms even come with stellar windows looking out onto the lake.

Best bet for a bite:
K and K

Insiders' tip:
Bring a towel for the lake

What hostellers say:
"I was first in line!"
. . . "No, I was!"

Gestalt:
Gilgen's Island

St. Gilgen, a resort town close to Salzburg, is chiefly famous for the lake and the house where Mozart's momma was born. It isn't anything superspecial, but it's perfectly fine as a stop—larger and more commercial than others in the Salzgammergut, maybe, but still not too bad. A nearby gondola leads up the side of a 4,500-foot-tall mountain, which you could hike back down in several enjoyable hours. And the lake is a base for summertime fun—surfing, swimming, boating and the like.

Hospitality:

Cleanliness:

Party index:

How to get there:

By bus: From Salzburg Station, 20 miles away, take postbus to St. Gilgen and walk ⅓ mile to hostel.

By car: Call hostel for directions.

By train: From Salzburg Station, 20 miles away, take postbus to St. Gilgen and walk ⅓ mile to hostel.

JUGENDHERBERGE SONNRAIN

(St. Martin am Tennengebirge Hostel)

Nummer 100, A-5522 St. Martin am Tennengebirge, Salzburgerland

Telephone Number: 06–463–7318

Fax Number: 06–463–73183
E-mail: jgh.stmartin@jgh.at
Rates: €10–24 (about $15–$25 US) per HI member
Credit cards: No
Beds: 126
Private/family rooms: Yes
Kitchen available: Yes
Season: January 1–mid-April; mid-May–September 30; December 16–31
Office hours: 8:00 to 9:00 A.M.; 5:00 to 7:00 P.M.
Affiliation: Hostelling International-ÖJHV
Extras: Meals ($), breakfast

Best bet for a bite:
Eat here!

Insiders' tip:
Practice your German with the locals.

What hostellers say:
"Dude, let's shred"

Hospitality:

A four-story warehouse for hostellers, this place manages to spread out the beds. They've got a bunch of quads and triples rooms, some with bathroom, and then some quads—again, some with bathroom, some with just a sink—two six-bedded dorms, and ten still larger dorms. They serve meals and include breakfast, but overall it's pretty simple pickings here.

St. Martin lies in a range of hills called the Tennengau, just south of Salzburg and just southwest of the famous lakes where tourists go. You'll find yourself among fewer travelers and more locals when you go wandering around the village streets. And that can be a nice change. Just don't expect lots of character at the hostel itself, 'cause you likely won't find it.

Cleanliness:

Party index:

How to get there:

By bus: Call hostel for transit route.
By car: Call hostel for directions.
By train: Call hostel for transit route.

JUGENDHERBERGE ST. MICHAEL

(St. Michael Hostel)

Herbergsgasse 348, A-5582 St. Michael im Lungau, Salzburgerland

Telephone Number: 06–477–630

Fax Number: 06–477–6303
E-mail: jgh.stmichael@jgh.at
Rates: €15–24 (about $15–$25 US) per HI member
Credit cards: No
Beds: 188
Private/family rooms: Yes
Kitchen available: Yes
Season: January 1–mid-April; mid-May–September 30; December 16–31
Office hours: 8:00 to 9:00 A.M.; 5:00 to 7:00 P.M.
Affiliation: Hostelling International-ÖJHV
Extras: Meals ($), table tennis, TV, VCR, disco, breakfast

This complex of long, barnlike (or maybe chaletlike) buildings conceals a decent, though huge, hostel.

There are at least a dozen double rooms, all with bathrooms, plus four quad rooms with bathrooms and about twenty-five six-bedded dorms sharing bathrooms—yeah, that's where the kiddies stay. In fact, tons of sports groups come here, but there's a separate floor and section for families and travelers—a nice touch, and the happy inclusion of a kitchen makes this place doubly desirable.

Other features include meal service, included breakfast, a TV room with a VCR, a rec room with table tennis, and—this being Europe and all—a disco.

Best bet for a bite:
Go with the pension plan

Insiders' tip:
Ask if a school group has reserved before you book.

What hostellers say:
"Will you shut up?"

Gestalt:
Michael from mountains

Hospitality:

Cleanliness:

Party index:

How to get there:

By bus: Call hostel for transit route.
By car: Call hostel for directions.
By train: Call hostel for transit route.

SALZBURG

You'll see the likeness of Mozart and hear his music everywhere around here, in one of Europe's most distinctive small cities, but take time to explore the actual life of the cafes, eateries, and bars, too. It's a friendly, well-heeled place that never fails to impress, whether you've come as a *Sound of Music* tourist or just dropped by on a lark from Munich.

Get around using the efficient bus and tram system, which stops anywhere you need it to—although things close early in this town, so get where you're going before too, too late. Everyone hits the Augustiner brewhouse, a fun place where they tap kegs of good beer. Others climb or ride to the Monschberg hill that looms above town for a better view on the domes, squares, and Alps.

A few of the many scenic highlights include the Mirabell garden, with good views of the Fortress Hohensalzburg; several castles; and Mozart Square, where you hear the famous Salzburger Glockenspiel (chimes) from the clock tower of the bishop's palace. And festival time, of course, is just nuts around here: Thousands of locals and foreigners—and their kids—descend for an orgy of classical music that leaves no bunk unfilled. So book ahead.

Among the cool things to do outside the town itself are a bunch of different bike trips, each taking a few days but well worth it in terms of scenery. One takes you along the Salzach River and the edge of Hohe Tauern National Park, with several deep gorges just off the road en route; you can bike all the way to the salt-mining town of Hallein on this route, in fact—a town with its own good hostel. Another journey might take you off on a circuit of the Salzgammergut lakes and caves, again passing through a number of resort towns with good little hostels en route.

Finally you could try heading along Austria's newest bicycling path, the Enns Path, over to Steiermark (Styria)—a region that boasts the best collected regional group of hostels in the land; on the way you'd pass through Enns, an old and attractive town.

SALZBURG HOSTELS at a glance

	RATING	PRICE	IN A WORD	PAGE
HI Josef-Preis-Allee	👍	€13–17	functional	p.120
Institut St. Sebastian	👍	€14–29	holy	p.119
Gästhaus Burgerwehr	👍	€9.00–10.00	lofty	p.117
YO-HO Hostel	👍	€12	gonzo	p.123
HI Eduard-Heinrich-Haus	👍	€14	equipped	p.121
HI Haunspergstrasse	👍👎	€12	drab	p.122
Aigner Strasse	👍👎	€13–15	grouchy	p.117

AIGNER STRASSE HOSTEL

Aigner Strasse 34, A-5026 Aigen (Salzburg)

Telephone Number: 06–626–23248

Fax Number: 06–626–232–484
E-mail: hostel.aigen@salzburg.co.at
Rates: €13–15 (about $14–$15 US) per HI member;
doubles €41 (about $43 US)
Credit cards: No
Beds: 105
Private/family rooms: Yes
Kitchen available: No
Office hours: 7:00 to 9:00 A.M.; 5:00 P.M. to midnight
Curfew: Midnight
Affiliation: Hostelling International-ÖJHW
Extras: Bike rentals, breakfast, lockers, table tennis, TV

A big, boring place in an admittedly nice villa-type of setup, this is a summer-only place that offers you a potential bed in high Salzburg season, sure. But the staff isn't great—we found them to be grumpy and disorganized when we checked in—and there are closer hostels to the central action. Finally, the midnight curfew makes it tough to hang downtown.

Beds come in five doubles, six quads, and ten six-bedded dorms. There's a recreation room with gym equipment and table tennis and a television lounge, and they rent bikes. But that's about it. No meals, no kitchen, no fun.

Not the best in town, nope.

Best bet for a bite:
Wine bar at Moostrasse

Insiders' tip:
Buy the five-ride bus
ticket at the station

What hostellers say:
"Yawn."

Gestalt:
Grumpy old men

Hospitality: 👎

Cleanliness: 👍👎

Party index:

How to get there:

By bus: From Salzburg Station, take #5 bus to Rudolfskai, then change to #49 bus and continue to hostel.

By car: Call hostel for directions.

By train: From Salzburg Station, take #5 bus to Rudolfskai, then change to #49 bus and continue to hostel.

GÄSTHAUS BURGERWEHR HOSTEL 👍

Monchsberg 19, Salzburg

Telephone Number: 06–628–41729

Rates: €9.00–10.00 (about $9.00–$10.00 US) per person;
doubles €20 (about $20 US)
Credit cards: No
Beds: 26
Private/family room: Yes

Kitchen available: No
Season: Mid-May–mid-August
Office hours: 8:00 A.M. to 9:00 P.M.
Curfew: 1:00 A.M.
Affiliation: None
Extras: Meals ($), sheets (€2.00)

The great views from this hostel more than make up for the lack of facilities. You're perched atop Salzburg with commanding views of this impressive little city—within yodeling distance of those many attractions you're in town to gawk at. Out of season it's quiet as a mouse up here, but when the place is full you might find a bunch of fellow hostellers congregating at the cafe downstairs to sip beers and watch the sun setting over the domes of Salzburg.

Best bet for a bite:
In-house

Insiders' tip:
Bring your binoculars

What hostellers say:
"I can see for miles . . ."

Gestalt:
Hillsville

Safety:

Hospitality:

Cleanliness:

Party index:

What the hostel provides is a clean bed in a simple room. There is one double, and though the other rooms are smallish four- and six-bed bunkrooms, you didn't come all the way to Salzburg to spend the entire day in your room. Didja? Shower (which you pay €1.00/four minutes) and toilet facilities are down the hall, a bit sparse in number, and there's no laundry to wash your clothes in.

Still, the friendly couple who manage the hostel run a decent cafe below that serves everything from ice cream sundaes and coffee to wiener schnitzel, so you've got some food to ease the pain of the long hike up. Breakfast is served here, but it's not free.

Getting here can be a bit of a challenge, since there are no signs pointing toward the Monchsberg lift (you know, elevator) that whisks you up top for about €2.00 (about $2.00 US) round-trip, 9:00 A.M. to 11:00 P.M. You can either use it or hoof up a really steep hill. Save yourself and take the lift, you'll thank us later; hike back down if you're into saving the bucks.

This may not be the easiest hostel to get to, but it's still pretty central to most sight-seeing areas and good for a night or two.

How to get there:

By bus: Take #29 bus and ask driver to stop at the Monchsberg lift. Take Monchsberg lift (€1.00–2.00) from A. Neumayr Platz, or walk uphill from Max Rainhardt Platz.

By car: Call hostel for directions

By train: Take #55 bus from station to F-Hanuschplatz and change to #60 bus and ask driver to stop at the Monchsberg lift.

INSTITUT ST. SEBASTIAN

Linzergasse 41, Salzburg

Telephone Number: 06–628–71386

Fax Number: 06–628–713–8685
Rates: €14–29 (about $15–$31 US) per person;
doubles €51 (about $51 US)
Credit cards: MC, VISA
Beds: 100 (summer); 40 (winter)
Private/family rooms: Yes
Kitchen available: Yes
Affiliation: None
Season: Varies; call hostel for season
Office hours: 7:30 A.M. to noon and 1:00 to 10:00 P.M. (summer);
8:00 A.M. to noon and 3:00 to 9:00 P.M. (winter)
Extras: Terrace, laundry (€3.00), breakfast, pianos, sheets (€2.00),
lockers

This place, set adjacent to a pretty church with an interesting grave-yard and mausoleum, is one of the nicest hostels in a town that's already full of decent options. But the management sometimes gets disorganized, and that could skew your stay. Here's what happened to us.

We booked ahead and confirmed twice (they don't take credit cards), told 'em we'd arrive in the morning, then strolled in at 11:00—only to learn that they had given our room away by mistake. Big boo-boo. They scrounged around and found room for us in the student dormitory wing, which was considerably more beat-up than the beautiful room we lost out on, and that didn't make us happy.

If you do manage to get the right room, however, you'll probably get a good one—nice upper-floor views in the case of the doubles. They are close to the terrace, which offers a stunning overview of Salzburg, much like the view seen on postcards with church spires, domes, and other architectural goodies. The rooms come with closets and desks and chairs, obviously used as dorm rooms when school is in session and so a little worn.

Each floor comes with its own kitchenette, complete with fridge and hotplate as well as a lounge in which to eat. Supermarkets like Spar and Julius Meinl are within close range, as well as smaller fruit and vegetable markets that line pedestrian-only Linzer Gasse.

Best bet for a bite:
Spar supermarket

Insiders' tip:
You need an appointment
for laundry

What hostellers say:
"Rock me, Amadeus!"

Gestalt:
Saint in the city

Safety:

Hospitality:

Cleanliness:

Party index:

Be sure that you get a key, because the reception desk closes fairly early, and if locked out you'll have to wait for a guest or resident to let you in—a problem if (as it often is here) it's raining cats and dogs. Also take note that the fire station next door gets calls at all hours of the night, so it's possible you'll be awakened by the blare of sirens.

How to get there:

By bus: Terminal for Bundes buses is on Linzer Gasse, a few blocks north of the hostel; walk down Linzer Gasse to hostel on right, at arch, a block or two before the river.

By car: Call hostel for directions.

By plane: From Salzburg Airport, take #77 bus to train station. Then take #29 bus to stop near corner of Franz-Josef Strasse and Linzer Gasse. Walk down Linzer Gasse to arch; hostel is through arch.

By train: From Salzburg Station, take #29 bus to stop near corner of Franz-Josef Strasse and Linzer Gasse. Walk down Linzer Gasse to arch; hostel is through arch.

JUGENDGÄSTEHAUS SALZBURG

(Salzburg Guest House Hostel)

Josef-Preis Allee 18, A-5020 Salzburg

Telephone Number: 06–628–426–700

Fax Number: 06–628–4110
E-mail: jgh.salzburg@jgh.at
Rates: €13–17 (about $13.50–$18.00 US) per HI member; doubles €42 (about $44 US)
Credit cards: Yes
Beds: 390
Private/family rooms: Yes
Kitchen available: Yes
Office hours: 7:00 A.M. to midnight (but closed periodically)
Curfew: Midnight
Affiliation: Hostelling International-ÖJHV
Extras: Bar, bike rentals, breakfast, cafeteria ($), Internet access, library, garden, playground, meeting rooms, laundry, lockers, store, information desk, volleyball, table tennis, TV, VCR, disco, movies

A big but nice facility, this is one of your top picks in town because it's close to town and well equipped despite the bland exterior. It's a little more hopping than the usual Hostelling International joint, thanks to a small disco and an entryway that looks like something out of a movie. That midnight curfew sure is a bummer, though.

In a massive building just south of the river that divides Salzburg in two, they've installed twenty-one doubles and five triples with private bathrooms, nineteen four-bedded rooms (some with bathrooms, some sharing them), and thirty-two eight-bedded dorms—yeah, that's where the groups stay, in two single-sex, color-coded wings, no less.

Trying to get in on the *Sound of Music* stuff, they're a pickup point for *SOM* tours of the area and also show the film sometimes in the hostel. The facilities include the bar and disco, a television lounge with VCR, green grounds and playground, a restaurant, and the all-important laundry machines. Remember to book ahead because this place gets *very* popular with the groups and Austrian families vacationing in Salzburg.

The architecture sucks, but ignore it—this is one of your best choices. Just expect rules, rules, rules.

How to get there:

By bus: From Salzburg Station, take #5 bus to Justizgebaude. Or take #5 streetcar and walk 150 yards to hostel.

By car: Call hostel for directions.

By train: From Salzburg Station, take #5 bus to Justizgebaude. Or take #5 streetcar and walk 150 yards to hostel.

Best bet for a bite:
St. Paul's Stuben

Insiders' tip:
Buy one cafe coffee, sit all afternoon

What hostellers say:
"If I hear 'do, a deer,' again I'll scream!"

Gestalt:
Preis is right

Safety:

Hospitality:

Cleanliness:

Party index:

JUGENDHERBERGE EDUARD– HEINRICH-HAUS

(Eduard-Heinrich House Hostel)

Eduard Heinrich Strasse 2, A-5020 Salzburg

Telephone Number: 06–626–25976

Fax Number: 06–626–27980
E-mail: hostel.eduard-heinrich@salzburg.co.at
Rates: €14 (about $14 US) per HI member
Credit cards: MC, VISA
Beds: 120
Private/family rooms: Yes
Kitchen available: Yes
Office hours: 7:00 to 10:00 A.M.; 5:00 P.M. to midnight
Lockout: 9:00 A.M. to 5:00 P.M.
Curfew: Midnight (summer); 11:00 P.M. (winter)
Affiliation: Hostelling International-ÖJHW
Extras: Lockers, information desk, meals ($), breakfast, TV, VCR, gym, laundry, library, Internet access, table tennis, playground, garden

Despite being a fairly huge and drab complex, this is one of the better outfitted hostels in town and you might end up here. We hate the curfew and noncentral location, but it's got enough stuff to keep families happy at least. And the surrounding greenery is nice.

They've got just four doubles, four triples, one quad, and then the bulk of the beds in sixteen six-bedded dorm rooms. There's everything from a playground and a small gym to a laundry and a kitchen. Don't forget the new Internet terminals, meal service, or lockers. Not thrilling at all, and night owls will no doubt want to look elsewhere first.

The location is a couple miles southwest of town, in a quiet section close to the Salzach Forest.

How to get there:

By bus: From Salzburg Station, 2½ miles away, take #51 or #95 bus to Polizeidirektion stop and walk ⅔ mile to hostel.

By car: Call hostel for directions.

By train: From Salzburg Station, 2½ miles away, take #51 or #95 bus to Polizeidirektion stop and walk ⅔ mile to hostel.

Best bet for a bite:
Julius Meinl supermarket

Insiders' tip:
Change is king!

What hostellers say:
"Can I go on-line?"

Gestalt:
Heinrich maneuver

Safety:

Hospitality:

Cleanliness:

Party index:

JUGENDHERBERGE
HAUNSPERGSTRASSE

(Haunspergstrasse Hostel)

Haunspergstrasse 27, A-5020 Salzburg

Telephone Number: 06–628–75030

Fax Number: 06–628–83477
Rates: €12 (about $13 US) per HI member
Beds: 105
Private/family rooms: Yes
Kitchen available: No
Season: July 1–August 26
Office hours: 7:00 A.M. to 2:00 P.M.; 5:00 P.M. to midnight
Curfew: 11:00 P.M.
Affiliation: Hostelling International-ÖJHW
Extras: Bike rentals, breakfast, TV, laundry (€6.00), table tennis, foosball

Our first impression of this hostel was that staying here was like being in the army: They give you only an hour for breakfast (and you'd better be up between 7:00 and 8:00 to get it), they kick you out all day in the morning, and the building itself is quite plain. Make that drab. (The ten thousand dollar question: Was this place a Catholic boys' school or a prison in another life? Or both?)

Rooms are four-bedded, and they're actually halfway decent—two sets of double bunk beds in a spacious room, with a kind of combination table-desk surrounded by two chairs and a sort of bench. We don't know what garage sale the managers got this stuff at, but the airy rooms were certainly a breather from the usual cram job.

The neighborhood is so-so, safe enough but not really exciting enough to keep you around for long. Main attractions include the historic downtown, just a five- to ten-minute walk straight down the road or along the river. Your joy at the proximity to Salzburg might be dampened somewhat, though.

A least it's very close to the city of Salzburg's train station, probably the closest of all of them in fact—3 or 4 blocks at most. Yippee.

But this still doesn't overcome the serious limitations of this place, which have to do with all those rules, rules, rules. Yikes.

Best bet for a bite:
Fred's Vegy
(two locations)

Insiders' tip:
Train station is close by
for early departure

What hostellers say:
"Good beds, but these
rules suck."

Gestalt:
Preis is right

Safety:

Hospitality:

Cleanliness:

Party index:

How to get there:

By bus: Call hostel for transit route.
By car: Call hostel for directions.
By train: Call hostel for transit route.

YO-HO HOSTEL

(International Youth Hotel Hostel)
Paracelsusstrasse 9, A-5020 Salzburg
Telephone Number: 06–628–79649
Fax Number: 06–628–78810
Rates: €12 (about $13 US) per person; doubles €32 (about $34 US)
Credit cards: No
Beds: 148
Private/family rooms: Yes
Kitchen available: No
Office hours: 6:00 A.M. to 1:00 A.M.
Curfew: 1:00 A.M.
Affiliation: None

Extras: Laundry, lockers, bar, meals ($), snack shop, movies, breakfast ($), TV

This place is so central it's amazing, and so social that you might never wanna leave. But it's also so Anglicized that you might wanna throw up after a day or two of all the "like, cool!"s and such.

Anyhow, the place has one of the most interesting interior designs we've seen in a Euro-hostel—multicolored doors, a cool look. Up wooden stairs, the dorm rooms contain from two to eight bunks each, with generic bunks—mattresses on wooden shelves, really—plus a sink in each room. Shared showers in the hall work on a token system (boo!), whereby you pay €1.00 (about 80 cents US) per six minutes of time. And lockers *also* cost, €1.00 (about 80 cents US), to use. All these add-on charges just plain suck.

Best bet for a bite:
Euro-Spar near
train station

Insiders' tip:
Free *SOM* showing

What hostellers say:
"Didn't we meet at
Balmer's?"

Gestalt:
Preis is right

Safety:

Hospitality:

Cleanliness:

Party index:

The big common room is one of the most popular places to hang, with a TV tuned to CNN most of the time and *The Sound of Music* supposedly playing daily. A basement laundry was only so-so—lots of stupid American graffiti down there, too—but at least they have one. There's no kitchen, and they won't let you bring your own beer or food into the dining areas, so you've got to eat out or belly up to the bar during mealtimes. A vendor opens up shop at odd hours inside the lobby to vend snacks from a cart, and the convenience market next door provides access to actual fruit and other snacks in a pinch.

The bar looks suitably barlike, paneled in cozy wood, with steins stacked up at the ready. It's the most popular hangout spot, and the meals are pretty good. (It's also hectic, since the barkeep doubles as the receptionist.) People tend to get a little wasted later at night, though it's all in good fun certainly. Again, though, the 80 percent American/Aussie crowd mars the experience of getting to know Austria and Europe.

What else? Well, a message board is useful for getting out the word. (Typical post: "Going to Budapest? Space in our car!!!") They run a ton of adventure tours and other stuff out of here, too, though we'd prefer to just walk around town and see the many sights for free. The location, so very close to the city's train station, makes it very handy for late arrivals, early departures, or even day trips to Munich (two hours away by train), *Sound of Music*–type lakes (an hour or less by bus), and so forth.

And it's certainly friendly. Yeah, this place is super-social and central, and those are all good things—but never forget that the driving motive here is pure profit, baby, and you're gonna be surprised when you add up what you spent for that good time.

How to get there:

By bus: Call hostel for transit route.
By car: Call hostel for directions.
By train: Call hostel for transit route.

JUGENDHERBERGE LINDENHOF

(Spital am Pyhrn Hostel)

Nummer 77, A-4582 Spital am Pyhrn, Upper Austria

Telephone Number: 07–563–214

Rates: €14 (about $14 US) per HI member
Credit cards: No
Beds: 140
Private/family rooms: Yes
Kitchen available: No
Season: January 1–October 31; December 1–31
Office hours: 7:30 to 9:30 A.M.; 5:00 to 9:00 P.M.
Affiliation: Hostelling International-ÖJHW
Extras: Breakfast

This supersimple place is really only appropriate for groups. They don't have a kitchen or laundry or serve meals.

Anyway, rooms consist of seven doubles, two quads, two six-bedded dorms, and thirteen huge ones. The area's scenic and features some ski trails, but this Spital—with one "t," and not to be confused with the other, more-scenic Spittal west of Villach with its own two hostels (see next two entries)—is a little tucked away. The town is pretty close to Admont, actually, which has a castlelike joint that supplies much more atmo and is probably a better choice.

Best bet for a bite:
Forage in town

Insiders' tip:
Check out castle in Admont

What hostellers say:
"I'm heading to Admont."

Gestalt:
Little spital

Party index:

How to get there:

By bus: Call hostel for transit route.
By car: Call hostel for directions.
By train: Call hostel for transit route.

JUGENDHERBERGE GOLDECK

(Spittal-Goldeck Hostel)

Mittelstation Goldeck, A-9800 Spittal an der Drau, Carinthia

Telephone Number: 04–762–2701

E-mail: goldeck@gmx.at

Rates: €15–25 (about $15–$26 US) per HI member
Credit cards: No
Beds: 45
Private/family rooms: Yes
Kitchen available: No
Season: December 26–Easter; late-June–September 20 (depends on gondola schedule)
Office hours: 8:00 to 9:00 A.M.; 5:00 to 9:00 P.M. (vary, though)
Affiliation: Hostelling International-ÖJHW
Extras: Meals ($), breakfast, table tennis

Simpler than its cousin hostel down at the base of the mountain, this one offers much better views from a tiny, cute chalet with forty-five beds somehow packed inside.

You get here by taking a gondola over the Drau River and partway up the mountain to Goldeck landing; the gondola closes in spring and fall, though, and then so does the hostel. Rooms consist of four doubles, four quads, and four six-bedded dorms—some have showers, but none has its own private bathroom. The main common area has a tiled stove, which is nice and homey (and warm); there's also table tennis. They serve meals and include breakfast.

Outside, a big Austrian meadow with views makes for green fun. Skiing is big on this mountain—it's actually possible to ski right to the hostel. In summer climbing the rocks and hills around here is a popular pasttime—mountain huts up high provide very cheap hostel-like beds indeed for those so motivated to do a couple of hard, beautiful days of hiking.

Best bet for a bite:
Eat here for all three meals (if you get full-board)

Insiders' tip:
Bring that ski wax

What hostellers say:
"Schuss."

Gestalt:
Cable guys

Hospitality: 👍

Cleanliness: 👍

Party index:

It's very important to note that you must arrive at this hostel before 4:30 P.M., because that's when the gondola stops running. Also, the hostel has two quite different personalities according to season: During winter skiers are the only people who will enjoy it because that's all there is to do. During summer Hans, the manager, offers the place mostly to families and individual travelers who want to take part in his hiking program—which includes meals.

How to Get There:

By bus: From Gmünd, take Bundesbus to Spittal; walk past post office to Ortenbugerenstrasse, turn right and cross under train tracks. Continue to gondola station, take gondola to Goldeck landing (partway up).

By train: From Spittal Station, walk past post office to Ortenbugerenstrasse, turn right and cross under train tracks. Continue to gondola station, take gondola to Goldeck landing (partway up).

JUGENDHERBERGE SPITTAL AN DER DRAU

(Spittal an der Drau Hostel)

Zur Seilbahn 2, A-9800 Spittal an der Drau, Carinthia

Telephone Number: 04–762–3252

Fax Number: 04–762–32524
Rates: €20–27 (about $21–$28 US) per HI member
Credit cards: No
Beds: 67
Private/family rooms: Yes
Kitchen available: Yes
Office hours: 8:00 to 9:00 A.M.; 5:00 to 7:00 P.M.
Affiliation: Hostelling International-ÖJHV
Extras: Meals ($), sauna, pool table, solarium, TV

A three-story chalet right at the base of Goldeck Mountain next to the cable car base station, this place is more than adequate and might entice you to come out here for a peek at another corner of Austria off your usual tourist itinerary.

It's got two single rooms, two doubles, five quad rooms, two six-bedded dorms, and four larger ones—all with en-suite bathrooms. There's a kitchen and meal service but, strangely, no breakfast included. The facilities include a sauna, a television room, and a lounge with a pool table.

The town has a couple of interesting diversions. First there's Schloss Porcia, a very nice Renaissance castle constructed for a Spanish guy who was tight with Archduke Ferdinand at the time. There's also a Spanish festival each June (same reason), and then the local Culture Museum, €3.00 (about $3.50 US), has interesting displays of local history. The gondola nearby leads up the 6,400-foot peak of the Goldeck, with another hostel partway up it (see Jugendherberge Goldeck).

Best bet for a bite:
Gösser Bräu

Insiders' tip:
Good kayaking on the river

Gestalt:
Chalet stay

Hospitality:

Cleanliness:

Party index:

How to get there:

By bus: From Gmund, take Bundesbus to Spittal; walk past post office to Ortenbugerenstrasse, turn right, and cross under train tracks. Continue to hostel on right.

By car: Take Highway A10 or A1 to Spittal an der Drau.

By train: From Spittal Station, walk past post office to Ortenbugerenstrasse, turn right, and cross under train tracks. Continue to hostel on right.

STEYR HOSTEL

Josef Hafnerstrasse 14, A-4400 Steyr, Upper Austria

Telephone Number: 07–252–45580

Fax Number: 07–252–48386
Rates: €14 (about $15 US) per HI member
Credit cards: No
Beds: 50
Private/family rooms: Yes
Kitchen available: No
Season: January 9–December 22
Office hours: 8:00 to 10:00 A.M.; 5:00 to 9:00 P.M.
Affiliation: Hostelling International-ÖJHV
Extras: Breakfast, bike rentals, TV

This hostel is in kind of a strange position, behind train tracks and separated from the main city by them. As a result it's not near anything interesting—from the train station, it's the opposite direction from the town center. So try to hang out in town before hiking out here.

The place has one double room, one quad room, four six-bedded dorms, and five eight-bedded rooms. There's no kitchen or meals; the sole concession to food concerns is the included breakfast. Mostly groups stay at the place, sapping its atmosphere, but if you come you'll find the television room useful. They also rent bikes.

Steyr is an amazingly beautiful little town, worth going quite out of your way to see, and this is doubly remarkable considering that for most of its history, the place has made a mint off such pedestrian trades as mining. The central Stadtplatz (supposed to be a square, but really a rectangle) is pretty neat. Old buildings, shops, and a castle crowd around its edges.

Best bet for a bite:
Konsum supermarket

Insiders' tip:
Check out Stadtplatz

What hostellers say:
"So pretty!"

Gestalt:
Old world

Hospitality:

Cleanliness:

Party index:

How to get there:

By bus: Call hostel for transit route.
By car: Call hostel for directions.
By train: Call hostel for transit route.

JUGENDGÄSTEHAUS VILLACH

(Villach-St. Martin Guest House Hostel)

St. Martin, Dinzlweg 34, A-9500 Villach, Carinthia

Telephone Number: 04–242–56368

Fax Number: 04–242–563–6820

E-mail: jgh.villach@oejhv.or.at
Rates: €15 (about $15 US) per HI member
Credit cards: Yes
Beds: 144
Private/family rooms: Yes
Kitchen available: No
Office hours: 7:00 to 10:00 A.M.; 5:00 to 10:00 P.M.
Curfew: Midnight
Affiliation: Hostelling International-ÖJHV
Extras: Meals ($), breakfast, sauna, bike rentals, TV, garden, playground, disco, table tennis, meeting rooms, information desk, library

About a half mile west of Villach center, near the river, this big concrete slab is just fine inside if you can ignore its drab outside.

In a building decorated in some freaky pastels, there are a handful of double rooms and then a whole bunch (like twenty-eight) of the five-bedded dorms, every one of them with en-suite bathrooms, and those fivers can usually be converted to a family or private room unless they're getting full up. Additional facilities include a disco, sauna, TV lounge, playground for kids, and reading room—among many other things.

This small city is a more interesting and lively place than Klagenfurt and more attractive, too, even though it's smaller. You can ski in the surrounding hills or check out the interesting downtown.

Best bet for a bite:
Lederergasse should do it

Insiders' tip:
Stadtmuseum a good rainy-day pick

What hostellers say:
"Great little city."

Gestalt:
Cools Villach

Hospitality:

Cleanliness:

Party index:

How to get there:

By bus: From Villach Station, take Fellach or Untere Fellach bus to Mehrzweckhalle St. Martin and walk to hostel.

By car: Take Highway A10 to Villach and take Villack-Landskron exit; continue to hostel. From the south, take Highway A2 to Villach-Maria Gail exit.

By train: From Villach Station, take Fellach or Untere Fellach bus to Mehrzweckhalle St. Martin and walk to hostel.

WEISSENBACH AM ATTERSEE

Europacamp
Franz von Schonthanallee 42, A-4854 Weissenbach, Upper Austria
Telephone Number: 07–663–220
Fax Number: 07–663–8905–14

Rates: €14 (about $14 US) per HI member
Credit cards: No
Beds: 172
Private/family rooms: Yes
Kitchen available: No
Season: June 1–August 31
Office hours: 8:00 to 9:00 A.M.; 5:00 to 9:00 P.M.
Affiliation: Hostelling International-ÖJHV
Extras: Meals ($), camping, bike rentals

This big summer-only place won't win any prizes for character, but it's okay. Groups just tend to dominate it, that's all.

Best bet for a bite:
Filling dinners here

Insiders' tip:
Bring a water noodle

What hostellers say:
"Eeek!"

Gestalt:
Camp Grenada

Hospitality: 👍

Cleanliness: 👍

Party index:

🎉 🎉 🎉

The prime reason for being here is proximity to the Attersee lake, a water-sports mecca in this part of Austria. Think diving, swimming, sailing, and just about anything else. The hostel has just two doubles and one quad room, with ten six-bedded dorms and twelve really big ones holding the bulk of the hostellers. Meals (but not breakfast) are served, bikes are rented, and the place is wheelchair-accessible.

There's also a campground. Ah, so that's where they got the name "Europacamp."

How to get there:

By bus: Call hostel for transit route.
By car: Call hostel for directions.
By train: Call hostel for transit route.

WELS HOSTEL

Dragonerstrasse 22, A-4600 Wels, Upper Austria
Telephone Number: 07–242–67284 or 07–242–235757

Fax Number: 07–242–235–756
Rates: €14 (about $14 US) per HI member
Credit cards: No
Beds: 50
Private/family rooms: Yes
Kitchen available: No
Season: January 7–December 23
Office hours: 7:30 to 9:00 A.M.; 5:00 to 9:00 P.M.
Lockout: 9:00 A.M. to 5:00 P.M.
Affiliation: Hostelling International-ÖJHV
Extras: Breakfast, roller skating, bike storage

This very central hostel is practically on top of Wels's train station, which means it's as close as can be to town—no more than a five-minute walk, certainly, from the main historic drag known as Stadtplatz.

It's the usual boring deal, unfortunately, but as the hostel's attached to a music hall (whose name translates as "The Slaughterhouse"), if you're lucky you might find something interesting going on when you show up. Rooms come as two doubles, four quads, and five six-bedded rooms; they serve breakfast.

For most Wels is merely a through-point train station on the way to somewhere else. But the compact center of town actually turns out to be nice as a short visit, with good stained-glass work, a museum containing evidence of former Roman occupations, and the Kaiserliche museum complex commemorating the place where Emperor Maximilian died, while lightening the mood considerably with exhibits and toys. Give it a shot if you're in the area and don't want to deal with bigger, more industrial Linz or the transit to that city's hostels.

Best bet for a bite:
Café Urbaan

Insiders' tip:
Bird sanctuary

What hostellers say:
"I've got to catch an early morning train."

Gestalt:
Deeper Wels

Hospitality:

Cleanliness:

Party index:

You can also catch a local train or bus to get to several interesting other places like Lambach abbey or the big Schmiding Vogelpark bird conservatory. The bird joint isn't cheap to visit (figure twelve bucks a head), but you get lots of fresh air, a gander at exotic winged things, and entry to a museum.

How to get there:

By bus: Call hostel for transit route.
By car: Call hostel for directions.
By train: Call hostel for transit route.

JUGENDHERBERGE WEYER

(Weyer Hostel)
Mühlein 56, A-3335 Weyer, Upper Austria
Telephone Number: 07–3556–284

Fax Number: 07–3556–2844
E-mail: weyer@jutel.at
Rates: €11 (about $12 US) per HI member
Credit cards: No
Beds: 136
Private/family rooms: Yes
Kitchen available: No
Office hours: 8:00 A.M. to 10:00 P.M.

Affiliation: Hostelling International-ÖJHW
Extras: Meals ($), breakfast, table tennis, ski rentals, TV, VCR, gym, playground

In an area that's not on the usual quick itinerary of central Austria, this place caters more to groups and sports teams than individuals. You can tell because they've got gymnastic equipment and mats. What's up with that?

Anyway, the hostel consists of a couple of small identical buildings adjacent to each other filled with seven doubles, twenty-four quads, and three six-bedded dorms—all rooms with a shower and some with toilets. There's the usual dining room, common areas, TV lounge, a balcony, a rec room, the gym, and a cellar that wheelchairs can get to. Outside, there are some campfire rings and a playground for kids.

The town itself is known around Austria as a health resort town, so there are plenty of hiking and ski trails in the area for getting fresh air.

Best bet for a bite:
Euro Spar

Insiders' tip:
Bring the kids

What hostellers say:
"Suit up."

Gestalt:
Weyer we here

Hospitality: 👎

Cleanliness: 👍

Party index:

How to get there:

By bus: Call hostel for transit route.
By car: Take Bundestrasse B115 from Enns toward Steyr to Weyer.
By train: Call hostel for transit route.

JUGENDHERBERGE WEYREGG

(Weyregg Hostel)

Attersee Nummer 3, A-4852 Weyregg, Upper Austria

Telephone Number: 07–664–2780

Fax Number: 07–664–27804
E-mail: weyregg@jutel.at
Rates: €13 (about $14 US) per HI member
Credit cards: No
Beds: 42
Private/family rooms: Yes
Kitchen available: No
Season: May 1–October 31
Office hours: 8:00 A.M. to 10:00 P.M.
Affiliation: Hostelling International-ÖJHW
Extras: Meals ($), breakfast, bike rentals, playground, TV, VCR, grill

Jugendherberge Weyregg

Weyregg

(courtesy of Österreichisches Jugendherbergswerk)

A pretty little building in town, this is yet another Austrian hostel set in gorgeous territory—and geared toward throngs of Austrian kids. So you might or might not like its antiseptic, school-hall feel. At least it's smaller than most.

There are four double rooms with bathrooms, four quads, and three six-bedded dorms—some with shower, some with a toilet, too. Common facilities include a dining room (for meals and free breakfast), a couple of lounges (one with TV), and a conference room. Outside there's more—table tennis, a grill, a playground, and so forth. All the usual basics.

Lake Attersee, as we've said before, has got lots of water sports on tap—you can learn to sail, dive, water-ski, or whatever. Hiking and bike trails are also easy to find.

Best bet for a bite:
Evening meal reserved in advance

Insiders' tip:
Höhenwildpark Hochkreut

What hostellers say:
"Let's hit the trails."

Gestalt:
Hill Country

Hospitality:

Cleanliness:

Party index:

How to get there:

By bus: From Linz, take train to Kammer-Schörfling; then switch to Linienbus and continue by bus to Weyregg.

By car: Call hostel for directions.

By train: From Linz, take train to Kammer-Schörfling; then switch to Linienbus and continue by bus to Weyregg.

Jugendherberge Zell am See
Zell am See
(courtesy of Österreichisches Jugendherbergswerk)

JUGENDHERBERGE ZELL AM SEE

(Zell am See Hostel)

Seespitzstrasse 13, A-5700 Zell am See, Salzburgerland

Telephone Number: 06–542–57185

Fax Number: 06–542–571–854
E-mail: hostel.zell-see@salzburg.co.at
Rates: €12 (about $13 US) per HI member
Credit cards: MC, VISA
Beds: 106
Private/family rooms: Yes
Kitchen available: No
Season: January 1–October 31; December 1–31
Office hours: 7:00 to 10:00 A.M.; 4:00 to 10:00 P.M.
Lockout: Noon to 4:00 P.M.
Curfew: 10:00 P.M.
Affiliation: Hostelling International-ÖJHW
Extras: Meals ($), breakfast, lockers, TV, VCR, Internet access, library, information desk, table tennis, garden, playground, bike rentals, balconies

Right on Zeller See, this place comes with tremendous views of towering mountain ranges plus its own little beach—and even though it's actually in a suburb, you probably won't care.

Everything is kept sparkling in the seven doubles, nineteen quad rooms, and two six-bedded dorms (all have en-suite bathrooms). There's a television lounge with a VCR, another common area, a dining room, a game area with pinball and foosball, and bikes for rent. And the meals served by the kitchen here are especially delicious.

Zell am See is well known in Austria as a beautiful spot, tucked between beaches and peaks. Near both Salzburg and Innsbruck by train, this is the closest swimming lake to Salzburg and a popular destination year-round. In winter you've got many ski hills and trails lacing the hillsides. In summer hiking is fun— or try tobogganing down the grassy slopes over in Saalfelden. With a hostel this good, you just might end up sticking around for a while.

Best bet for a bite:
Schloss Kammer
(Austrian)

Insiders' tip:
Best bet: Crazy Daisy
(bar)

What hostellers say:
"I think I'll stay a week
. . . nah, make it two."

Gestalt:
See here now

Hospitality:

Cleanliness:

Party index:

How to get there:

By bus: From Salzburg, take Bundesbus to Zell and walk ¾ mile around lake to hostel.

By car: Call hostel for directions.

By train: From Innsbruck, take train to Zell; from Salzburg, take Bundesbus to Zell and walk ¾ mile around lake to hostel.

WESTERN AUSTRIA

Page numbers follow town names.

WESTERN AUSTRIA

The star in western Austria, of course, is Tyrol. It's a magical place of soaring peaks, cute farmhouses, rugged hikes, ski resorts, and brown cows. Locals wear traditional garb (feathered hats, leather shorts, that kind of stuff). Coming in from Switzerland, you ascend the high and tight Arlberg Pass beneath huge mountains that seem even bigger than those you just left behind.

From there the tracks diverge. You can go directly to the scenery, choosing a place like Seefeld, or head for Innsbruck—the main center of activity and the largest city, a beautiful place where you'll no doubt want to hang for a few days sucking up the atmosphere and gearing up for treks into the mountains. There's a variety of places to stay here, though some open only for summer.

Bregenz, right on the Swiss border and on big Lake Konstanz, is a small resort town with a great hostel that could serve as a quieter base for area explorations before you hit Tyrol—it's served by busy regular trains going from Munich to Zurich.

JUGENDGÄSTEHAUS BREGENZ

(Bregenz Guest House Hostel)

Mehrerauerstrasse 3-5, A-6900 Bregenz, Vorarlberg

Telephone Number: 05–574–42867

Fax Number: 05–574–428–674
E-mail: jgh.bregenz@jgh.at
Rates: €20–24 (about $18–$25 US) per HI member; doubles €46 (about $46 US)
Credit cards: Yes
Beds: 142
Season: May 1–December 31
Office hours: 7:00 A.M. to midnight
Affiliation: Hostelling International-ÖJHV
Extras: Meals ($), breakfast, bar, snacks, Internet access, play area, volleyball, currency exchange, TV

This new hostel, located in a town that tickles the borders of both Germany and Switzerland, is blessed with a good facility and one of the nicest staffs we've met in all of Europe. Unfortunately, it's also indundated with bunches of very young schoolkids from time to time, so you might not get to enjoy it at all if they're booked full (summer can be especially rough). Snag a bunk, though, and you're sure to have a good time hanging out around big Lake Konstanz/Constance/Bodensee/whatever ya wanna call it.

The hostel occupies a former textile mill; it seems like just another drab brick schoolhouse-style hostel on the outside, but they've done a beautiful restoration job throughout, polishing up old wooden floors till they shine, putting in all-new windows and thick sound-muffling doors, installing brand-new pine bunks. There's lots of comfort here, bathrooms in every single room, an ultramodern key system (you wave a key before a sensor and the lock magically opens), and—for some reason—bad pop music pumping through the hallway speakers.

We loved the supercomfortable dorms, all with not just their own bathrooms but also some with amazing touches like thick comforters, airy windows, lofts, and fancy new showers. There are four doubles, four quads, sixteen nice six-bedded dorms, and one great big one. Each floor comes with a nice TV room with a new set that gets about a jillion stations—in languages including, but not limited to, French Swiss, German Swiss, German, Italian, Austrian, Turkish, Hungarian (we think), and (yes!) the Cartoon Channel in plain English. Train buffs will love some of the back rooms, which have views of the tracks and various trains going off to Innsbruck, Vienna, etc., without tooting or otherwise disturbing your slumbers.

Down by reception there's a great little bar that serves local beer on tap, ice cream sundaes, and snacks round the clock. You can cruise the Internet in the same area by popping schilling coins into one of the machines. And did we mention the neato laundry that both washes *and* dries the clothes in the same machine? We've never seen that before.

Best bet for a bite:
Bella Napoli,
downtown

Insiders' tip:
Underwear outlet store
next door

What hostellers say:
"More of everything!"

Gestalt:
Bregenz Sie Deutsch?

Hospitality:

Cleanliness:

Party index:

We'd be remiss if we didn't point out that this hostel is extremely close to Bregenz's well-connected rail station (four direct trains a day to Munich and Zurich, plus others to Innsbruck and Vienna). And we gotta give props to the really good dinners, which cost just about 5 euros (about $5.00 US—a steal); cooked by a professional chef who actually enjoys feeding the masses good stuff, they feature a vegetarian and a meat entree each night, both usually Austrian specialties. Breakfast is included, too, bread and hot chocolate and muesli. You have to pay for drinks, but the vending machines stock great mineral water and sodas.

Though it doesn't look that way today, Bregenz has actually been settled for a very, very long time. Let's put it this way: When the Romans got here right around the time B.C. was becoming A.D., there had already been Celts here for centuries. Today this is a wealthy town, and most folks come here for the upscale beach, quaint and touristed streets, or other sights. Dadgum if there isn't a casino right across the street, too, though you probably won't be blowing your dough there. A better idea: Get a bike and haul it over to pretty

Lindau, Germany, a few miles around the lake on an island. Bring that passport just in case, though the border guards rarely check or stamp.

Make a trek a few hundred yards over to Seebühne, a giant floating stage on the lake that was being used in 1999 for a giant skeleton turning the pages of a book—the backdrop for a year-long opera. That's typical of this area: Things peak each summer around August, when the month-long Bregenz Festival gets going.

The town's a bit uppity, we'll concede, but you'll find some nice shops—and friendly people—if you poke a little. Also poke into the pretty good museum of Vorarlberg history, where Celtic and Roman ruins are all carefully explained. They've got some work from local hero painter Angelika Kaufmann, too, who made a big splash in the man's world of eighteenth-century art.

How to get there:

By bus: Call hostel for transit route.

By car: Call hostel for directions.

By train: From Bregenz Station, walk up to long corridor in station crossing tracks. Follow signs toward AM SEE (away from CITY); walk to end of corridor, down stairs, and turn left. Walk past casino and through casino parking lot to main road (Meeraurergasse); cross street. Hostel entrance is just across road.

JUGENDHERBERGE ALTES SIECHENHAUS

Reichstrasse 111, A-6805 Feldkirch-Levis, Vorarlberg

Telephone Number: 05–522–73181

Fax Number: 05–522–79399

Rates: €10–12 (about $11–$12 US) per person; doubles €28 (about $30 US)

Beds: 80

Private/family rooms: Yes

Kitchen available: No

Season: January 1–November 4; December 15–31

Office hours: 7:00 A.M. to 10:00 P.M. Monday to Saturday; Sunday 7:00 to 10:00 A.M.; 5:00 to 10:00 P.M.

Curfew: 10:00 P.M.

Affiliation: Hostelling International-ÖJHW

Extras: Bike rentals, snack bar ($), table tennis, garden, laundry, sheets (€2.00)

The Feldkirch hostel is a decent enough place although, according to our hostel scouts, the staff are fairly aloof and could make you feel as though you're invisible. Dripping with wooden atmosphere in a classic old building, the hostel used to be a hospital.

The twelve rooms are broken down into a variety of bed combinations, with plenty of quads and a couple of doubles. Cheaper options include rooms of seven, eight, nine, ten, and eleven beds. Communing with your bunkmates is made easy with five common rooms—although you might find yourself not talking at all with them, since each room is equipped with a television and a VCR. One of the rooms is actually pretty gigantic, with seating for about one hundred warm bodies. Speaking of warm: In winter you pay a little extra for heat here. Oh, well.

Best bet for a bite:
Pizza on the go

Insiders' tip:
Summer music festival

What hostellers say:
"Where shall I go today?"

Gestalt:
Captain Feldkirch

Hospitality:

Cleanliness:

Party index:

The reservation system is pretty outdated and not very reliable. Instead of accepting reservations over the phone, if you show up while reception is closed, you'll have to write down your name and the number of people in your party, indicating your gender. You gotta wait until they open again to even learn if you've got a bunk.

Non—couch potatoes are well catered to here, though, with a wide variety of games as well as bike rentals—among them a bicycle built for two! You can also avail yourself of nearby swimming pools as well as a tennis court for a fee.

The most obvious local landmark is the Schattenburg Castle, a thirteenth-century structure with the obligatory museum, cellar, knights' room, and more. Insiders' tip for Sherlock Holmes's fans: Arthur Conan Doyle, creator of the Holmes series, attended Jesuit school in this town; it didn't appear on Holmes's itinerary, but it did make its way into one of Thomas Mann's novels. Various festivals and events happen here year-round, but the most fun one must be the international clown festival, which fills the town with yucks once annually.

If you're into classical music, there's an annual summer festival of Schubert music. If you're going to Liechtenstein to pay for that obscure passport stamp, you're probably going through Feldkirch. (Feldkirch used to be part of Liechtenstein and once served as its capital.) Other cool day trips include a zoolike park just outside town; the tree of St. Corneli (a thousand-year-old oak), and bike trips to Lindau, Mainau, and the Flower Islands. As this is the Vorarlberg, giant mountains are looming nearby and winter attracts serious powder hounds to the various peaks of Montafon, Klostertal, and Arlberg.

Also make a detour up to the Bregenzerwald, the wooded hill towns that cover the slopes above and behind Bregenz; get there via bus.

How to get there:

By bus: Call hostel for transit route.
By car: Call hostel for directions.
By train: From Feldkirch Station, take #2 bus to hostel.

HARD HOSTEL

Allmendstrasse 87, A-6971 Hard, Vorarlberg

Telephone Number: 05–574–79716

Fax Number: 05–574–79716
Rates: €15 (about $15 US) per HI member
Credit cards: No
Beds: 22
Private/family rooms: Yes
Kitchen available: No
Office hours: 6:00 to 9:00 A.M.; 5:00 to 8:00 P.M.
Affiliation: Hostelling International-ÖJHV
Extras: Restaurant ($)

This place is fine but geared almost exclusively to groups, making it a must-miss in our book—especially with the terrific Bregenz hostel just a few miles away. We can't imagine why you'd come, unless you were shut out of the other place.

There are five dorm rooms here, four quads and one six-bedded room. There's no kitchen, no laundry, not much of anything except a decent restaurant serving various eclectic cuisines. You can get around the curfew by asking for a key. But we'd frankly head for the Bregenz joint instead.

Best bet for a bite:
Gastehaussternen

Gestalt:
Hard day's night

Hospitality:

Cleanliness:

Party index:

How to get there:

By bus: From Bregenz, take #15 Bundesbus to Hard and get off at Gastehaussternen restaurant.

By car: Call hostel for directions.

By train: From Bregenz Station, take #15 Bundesbus to Hard and get off at Gastehaussternen restaurant.

HOLZGAU HOSTEL

Nummer 66, A-6654 Holzgauer Hof, Tirol

Telephone Number: 05–633–5250

Fax Number: 05–633–52504
E-mail: holzgauer-hof@aon.at
Rates: €16 (about $17 US) per HI member
Credit cards: No
Beds: 50
Private/family rooms: Yes
Kitchen available: No
Season: December 15–May 15; June 15–November 30

> **Office hours:** 8:00 A.M. to 10:00 P.M.
> **Affiliation:** Hostelling International-ÖJHW
> **Extras:** Bike rentals, in-line skating, breakfast, dinner ($), game room

This place is specially designed for families, with nothing but double, triple, and quad rooms—all with en-suite bathrooms, thank goodness. Breakfast is always included in the price, and dinner is available, too, for extra money. However, you are nearly within spitting distance of the Schloss Neuschwanstein—a.k.a. Mad Ludwig's castle in Bavaria, Germany.

Best bet for a bite:
Austrian specialties on-site

Gestalt:
Holz up

Hospitality: 👎

Cleanliness: 👎

Party index: 🎉 🎉

There are two common rooms in the hostel. Staff rent bikes, serve breakfast, and can point you to an in-line skating area outside. For a fee, kind staff will serve you an evening meal in a jiffy if you arrive during the dinner hour. Off the beaten track, sure, but nevertheless a good pick if you're out this way.

How to get there:

By bus: Call hostel for transit route.
By car: Call hostel for directions.
By train: Call hostel for transit route.

INNSBRUCK

Twice an Olympic village, Innsbruck is our favorite little Austrian city: It's got everything you could want in a place, and more—a medium size, incredibly scenic peaks, halfway decent weather, an attractive old town, a superb local Alpine club that leads frequent walks and tours, and tons of nightlife and just plain vibrancy.

Austrian cities are great for public transit, and Innsbruck's no exception: An easy-to-use twenty-four–hour transit ticket costs about 3.00 euros (about $3.00 US), just a little bit more than a single bus or streetcar ride does. Get it instead of a regular ticket, stamp it the first time you use it and travel carefree. A weeklong pass costs about 9.00 euros (about $9.00 US).

Or look into the Innsbruck card, 17–27 euros (about $17–$27 US) for one to three days, which gets you free entry to almost all museums and free public transit, too, in one package.

You can't miss the old town, a series of museums, churches, and old buildings compressed into a walkably small area. Also very close to town and reached by either streetcar or foot is the city's Amgras castle, 5.00 euros (about $5.00 US) to get in. If you're hungry or thirsty, there are loads of cafes, eateries, discos, tourist-menu restaurants . . . you won't go hungry in Austria, so don't worry.

INNSBRUCK HOSTELS at a glance

	RATING	PRICE	IN A WORD	PAGE
Fritz Prior	👍	€14	adequate	p.143
St. Paulus	👍	€11–14	good	p.146
Innsbruck Hostel	👍	€11–14	modern	p.144
Volkshaus	👍	€15	quiet	p.147
St. Nikolaus	👍👎	€13–14	iffy	p.145

FRITZ PRIOR SCHWEDENHAUS HOSTEL

Rennweg 17b, A-6020 Innsbruck, Tirol

Telephone Number: 05–125–85814

Fax Number: 05–125–858–144
E-mail: youth.hostel@tirol.com
Web site: www.tirol.com/youth-hostel
Rates: €14 (about $14 US) per HI member ;
doubles €44 (about $46 US)
Credit cards: No
Beds: 75
Private/family rooms: Yes
Season: July 1–August 31; December 27–January 5
Office hours: 7:00 to 9:00 A.M.; 5:00 to 10:30 P.M.
Lockout: 9:00 A.M. to 5:00 P.M.
Curfew: 10:30 P.M.
Affiliation: Hostelling International-ÖJHW
Extras: Meals ($), sheets (€2.00), laundry ($)

This converted university dorm sits just north of Innsbruck's old town and comes with good views of the towering mountains; it's also close to the Inn River.

Dorms are three- to four-bedded and very nice, all containing their own en-suite bathrooms and all quite clean. A recent change in policy permits hostellers to make reservations, which are held until 6:00 P.M. But the 10:30 P.M. curfew's a real bummer. Ask for a key (your deposit is your passport) to avoid it.

Best bet for a bite:
University Mensa

What hostellers say:
"Bland but well located."

Gestalt:
Fritz the cool cat

Hospitality:

Cleanliness:

Party index:

How to get there:

By bus: Take #4 or C bus to Handelsakademie stop and walk to hostel. Or take D or E bus to Hungerburg-Talstation stop and walk to hostel.

By car: Call hostel for directions.

By train: Call hostel for transit route.

JUGENDHERBERGE INNSBRUCK

(Innsbruck Hostel)

Reichenauerstrasse 147, A-6020 Innsbruck, Tirol

Telephone Number: 05–123–46179 or 05–124–346180

Fax Number: 05–123–461–7912

E-mail: yhibk@tirol.com

Rates: €11–14 (about $12–$15 US) per HI member; doubles €32 (about $32 US)

Credit cards: No

Beds: 178

Private/family rooms: Yes

Kitchen available: Yes

Season: January 1–December 23; December 27–31

Office hours: 7:00 to 10:00 A.M.; 5:00 to 11:00 P.M.

Curfew: 10:30 P.M.

Affiliation: Hostelling International-ÖJHW

Extras: Laundry, lockers, garden, disco, volleyball, table tennis, information desk, TV, breakfast, bike rentals, shuttles

This unimpressive concrete structure, plunked down about a mile from Innsbruck's city center, is decent enough but could still do better. It clearly caters to groups, given its location—you have to take two buses to get here from the train station—and the high proportion of "group leader rooms" (translation: rooms that have their own facilities for leaders of school groups). Still, they are some of the nicest institutional rooms in town and are certainly fine if the more central bunks have all filled up. And the rate for your stay goes down the more nights you're here.

Best bet for a bite:
Buzi-Hütte

What hostellers say:
"Modern and good."

Gestalt:
Inn luck

Hospitality:

Cleanliness:

Party index:

Staff are decent and efficient, administering a complex of twenty-four two-to-six-bedded rooms, six four-bedded dorms, five doubles, and a television lounge. Some have their own bathrooms; some have shared.

There are also several dining and conference spaces and a ton of other facilities—try a laundry, a disco, a volleyball court, a game room, and more. The kitchen is a nice bonus, especially since they don't always serve meals here.

This is modern, warehouse hostelling, but it's not a problem as Innsbruck is interesting enough to get you out of here plenty. Summertime activities include hikes and ski trips led by the Club Innsbruck, and you can even get free bus transfers from the hostel to the mountain! They lend equipment for outings and are good at directing you to the loads of attractions in and out of town.

How to get there:

By bus: From Innsbruck Station, take O bus toward Konig Laurinstrasse to Studentenheim and walk to hostel. Or take R bus to Camping Platz stop and walk to hostel.

By car: Call hostel for directions.

By train: From Innsbruck Station, take O bus toward Konig Laurinstrasse to Studentenheim and walk to hostel. Or take R bus to Camping Platz stop and walk to hostel.

JUGENDHERBERGE ST. NIKOLAUS

Innstrasse 95, A-6020 Innsbruck

Telephone Number: 05–122–86515

Fax Number: 05–122–865–1514

E-mail: yhnikolaus@tirol.com

Rates: €13-14 (about $13–$14 US) per person; private rooms €36 (about $38.50 US)

Credit cards: No

Beds: 100

Private/family rooms: Yes

Kitchen available: No

Office hours: 8:00 to 10:00 A.M.; 5:00 to 10:00 P.M.

Lockout: 10:00 A.M. to 5:00 P.M.

Curfew: 11:00 P.M.

Affiliation: None

Extras: Restaurant ($), bar, Internet access, bike rentals, tours, breakfast, conference rooms, TV

Quite central, this place is not super—just serviceable. At least it's close to town and reasonably cheap.

The dorms here contain two-to-eight beds and while no great shakes, they have worked on the common spaces. Internet access, a TV lounge, and a bar are all quite popular, as is the small patio with its tiny restaurant. Breakfast is included.

Best bet for a bite:
Würst stands

Gestalt:
Grumpy ol' St. Nick

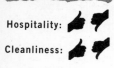

Hospitality:

Cleanliness:

Party index:

Some complaints surfaced, however. Reception can be chilly, say our snoops, and you have to pay for showers. Boo. In fact the best tip we can give ya is this one: The same owners run a pension (a small European-style hotel) nearby. Psst. You heard it here first.

How to get there:

By bus: From Innsbruck Station, take K bus toward Schmelzergasse to St. Nikolaus, then walk across street to hostel.

By car: Call hostel for directions.

By train: From Innsbruck Station, take K bus toward Schmelzergasse to St. Nikolaus, then walk across street to hostel.

JUGENDZENTRUM ST. PAULUS

Reichenauerstrasse 72, A-6020 Innsbruck, Tirol
Telephone Number: 05–123–44291

Fax Number: 05–123–442–9120
Rates: €11–14 (about $12–$15 US) per person
Credit cards: No
Beds: 150
Family/private rooms: No
Kitchen available: Yes
Season: June 15–August 15
Office hours: 7:00 to 11:00 A.M.; 5:00 to 10:00 P.M.
Curfew: 11:00 P.M.
Affiliation: None
Extras: Breakfast ($), TV

Best bet for a bite:
Pizza on the go
Gestalt:
Summer in the city
Hospitality:
Cleanliness:
Party index:

This is yet another summer-only joint, with lotsa beds in dorms that are mostly eight to a room; there are some larger ones, too. The price is right, and the staff are laid-back. Comfort suffers a bit, though, especially in some eighteen-bedded dorms. Expect groups to invade.

Other perks include breakfast service, though you must pay extra for it, and the usual television lounge with bored hostellers hanging around watching the tube.

How to get there:

By bus: Take R bus to Paula Kirche and walk to hostel.

By car: Call hostel for directions.

By train: Call hostel for transit route.

VOLKSHAUS INNSBRUCK

Radetzkystrasse 47, A-6020 Innsbruck, Tirol
Telephone Number: 05–123–95882

Fax Number: 05–123–958–824
Rates: €15 (about $15 US) per HI member
Credit cards: No
Beds: 52
Private/family rooms: Yes
Kitchen available: No
Office hours: 8:00 A.M. to 6:00 P.M.
Affiliation: Hostelling International-ÖJHV
Extras: Meals ($), TV, conference room

Located near several of the other big hostels in town, this one's not quite as good but it is an option if you're in the neighborhood.

Rooms consist of seven doubles, seven quads, and two six-bedded rooms, all fine. Meals are served, though breakfast—for some reason—isn't offered at all. Other amenities include a television lounge and a meeting room for groups.

Best bet for a bite:
Restaurant on site

Gestalt:
Volks wagon

Hospitality:

Cleanliness:

Party index:

How to get there:

By bus: Call hostel for transit route.
By car: Call hostel for directions.
By train: Call hostel for transit route.

JUGENDHEIM LECH–STUBENBACH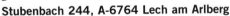

Stubenbach 244, A-6764 Lech am Arlberg
Telephone Number: 05–583–2419

Fax Number: 05–583–24194
E-mail: holger.schatzmann@cable.vol.at
Rates: €13–22 (about $14–$23 US) per HI member; doubles €41 (about $43 US)
Credit cards: No
Beds: 72
Private/family rooms: Yes
Kitchen available: No
Season: January 1–April 26; July 1–August 30
Office hours: 8:00 A.M. to 10:00 P.M.
Affiliation: Hostelling International-ÖJHW
Extras: Bike rentals, breakfast, dinner ($)

Best bet for a bite:
Pizza places

Gestalt:
Ski whacks

Hospitality: 👍

Cleanliness: 👍

Party index:

🎉🎉🎉

The dorm rates vary wildly according to season at this hostel, located in a too-hip ski town; they're *much* higher in winter, so bear this in mind when planning your visit.

They've got three doubles, five quads, one six-bedded room, and three big dorms on a hilltop with good views. Breakfast is free, dinner is served for a charge, and they rent bikes to the hordes of hardbodies in summer. As we've noted, this is a ski town all the way, not at all a town to get a taste of real Austrian rural life. But the hostel is certainly acceptable.

How to get there:

By bus: Call hostel for transit route.
By car: Call hostel for directions.
By train: Call hostel for transit route.

LECH HOSTEL

Arlberger Taxizentrale (Selbstversorger)

Nummer 428, A-6764 Lech am Arlberg, Vorarlberg

Telephone Number: 05–583–2501

Fax Number: 05–583–32586
E-mail: info@taxi-lech.at
Rates: €15 (about $15 US) per HI member
Credit cards: No
Beds: 50
Private/family rooms: Yes
Kitchen available: Yes
Season: June 20–September 20
Office hours: Vary; call hostel for hours
Affiliation: Hostelling International-ÖJHV
Extras: Breakfast ($)

Gestalt:
Ski bunnies

Hospitality: NR

Cleanliness: 👍

Party index:

Achtung! The management here speaks only German. And it's run by a taxi collective and not by the hostel association. So when you arrive in Hard, just ring up the taxi and tell them you want the jugendherberge. And remember it's do-it-yourself all the way, with no manager to answer your questions. At least the hostel, one of two in little Lech, has plenty of double rooms—twenty-three, to be exact—so you're very likely to have your own room to yourself. That's a good thing.

However, it's a little thin on the extras: no laundry, just breakfast service (which costs) and a kitchen you can cook in. They've also got three quad rooms and one huge dormitory. There's absolutely nothing wrong with the place, but it's not a hopping destination either. Best, probably, for a family who has come to this corner of Vorarlberg for the hiking or skiing.

How to get there:

By bus: Call hostel for pickup.
By car: Call hostel for directions.
By train: Call hostel for pickup.

OBERNDORF IN TIROL HOSTEL

Niederstrasserhof, Eberhartling 1, A-6372 Oberndorf in Tirol, Tirol

Telephone Number: 05–352–63651

Fax Number: 05–352–65201
Rates: €20 (about $20 US) per HI member
Credit cards: No
Beds: 104
Private/family rooms: Yes
Kitchen available: No
Season: January 1 to October 31; December 15–31
Office hours: 9:00 A.M. to noon; 6:00 to 10:00 P.M.
Affiliation: Hostelling International-ÖJHV
Extras: Sports fields, basketball, breakfast, dinner ($)

Just west of very pretty Zell am See, this place makes an excellent base from which to visit that beautiful town—especially for families. As with most other hostels in this corner of Austria, it's overequipped with single, double, and triple rooms plus some five-to-six-bedded rooms. All come with en-suite bathrooms. Other perks here include sports fields, a hoop, good meals, and a free breakfast.

An annual downhill ski race draws the crowds to a downtown of brightly painted buildings. A number of nearby gondolas can winch you up surrounding mountains for hikes, if you're so—heh, heh—inclined.

Best bet for a bite:
Prima

Insiders' tip:
Ski race

Gestalt:
Obern the river and
through the woods . . .

Hospitality:

Cleanliness:

Party index:

How to get there:

By bus: Call hostel for transit route.
By car: Call hostel for directions.
By train: Call hostel for transit route.

JUGENDGÄSTEHAUS DANGL

(Pfunds Guest House Hostel)

Nummer 347, A-6542 Pfunds, Tirol

Telephone Number: 05–474–5244

Fax Number: 05–474–52444
E-mail: info@post-pfunds.com
Rates: €16 (about $17 US) per HI member
Credit cards: No
Beds: 55
Private/family rooms: Yes
Kitchen available: Yes
Season: May 1–October 20; December 15–April 20
Office hours: 5:00 to 7:00 P.M.
Affiliation: Hostelling International-ÖJHV
Extras: Breakfast

Best bet for a bite:
Restaurant on site

Insiders' tip:
Bring some extra wax

Gestalt:
Big Pfunds

Hospitality:

Cleanliness:

Party index:

Up the river from Innsbruck, this place is decent enough, with a small supply of private rooms and about ten five-to-six-bedded dorms, too. Breakfast is served, and you can cook dinner in the hostel kitchen if you can stock up enough food locally to do it.

If you've come here, you're sleeping in the Inn Valley. From this little ski town you can reach Switzerland by bus and even Italy farther down the line. You can also take a train from here to Innsbruck or Bregenz, so you're well connected to onward points.

How to get there:

By bus: Call hostel for transit route.
By car: Call hostel for directions.
By train: Call hostel for transit route.

JUGENDGÄSTEHAUS AM GRABEN

(Reutte Hostel)

Am Graben 1, A-6600 Reutte, Tirol

Telephone Number: 05–672–626–440

Fax Number: 05–672–626–444
E-mail: jgh-hoefen@tirol.com
Rates: €14 (about $15 US) per HI member;
doubles €34 (about $35 US)
Beds: 51
Private/family rooms: Yes

Kitchen available: No
Season: January 1–November 2; December 15–31
Office hours: 8:00 A.M. to 10:30 P.M.
Affiliation: Hostelling International-ÖJHV
Extras: TV, garden, table tennis, laundry, dinner ($), breakfast

A two-story building, this is a beautiful hostel with a good dining room, good furniture—very cozy indeed in a country not always noted for homey hostels. The friendly management adds the final touch to what we consider a super place.

Rooms consist of six very good-value doubles, one triple, four quad rooms, and three larger dormitories. There are three common areas, including a TV lounge, garden, and a game room, plus a useful laundry and some wonderful meals served nightly. Breakfast and sheets are included for free, too.

Located in the Ausserfern region, just across the border from south Germany, this town—say *ROY-ta* if you wanna pronounce it right—spreads out over a plain in a valley tucked between peaks. Visitors tend to hike the hills, ride a cable car up to the tippy-top of Mount Hanhnenkamm (a good Alpine flower garden here sports more than 600 kinds of flowers), or bask in the sun along the banks of the Lech River that splits the town from its "suburbs."

The best part about staying at this great hostel, though, is the proximity of two outstanding castles—both just across the border in Germany and both well worth seeing. You've probably already

Best bet for a bite:
Prima

What hostellers say:
"One of the best in Austria."

Gestalt:
Reutte rooter

Hospitality:

Cleanliness:

Party index:

KEY TO ICONS

 Attractive natural setting

 Ecologically aware hostel

 Superior kitchen facilities or cafe

 Offbeat or eccentric place

 Superior bathroom facilities

 Romantic private rooms

 Comfortable beds

 Among our very favorite hostels

 A particularly good value

 Handicapped-accessible

 Good for business travelers

 Especially well suited for families

 Good for active travelers

 Visual arts at hostel or nearby

 Music at hostel or nearby

 Great hostel for skiers

 Bar or pub at hostel or nearby

heard about Neuschwanstein, the castle built by "Mad Ludwig" and later used as a model by Walt Disney for Sleeping Beauty's castle. But the castle where Ludwig was born, called Hohenschwangau, is close by and—to our eye—even better, if not as grand or elaborate.

You can reach both castles by a local bus service that runs from Reutte across the border to Fussen, Germany, about six times daily; make sure you catch the last bus back to Austria, or you'll be stranded—and remember that this bus doesn't run at all on Sunday. If you'll be continuing your trip onward to anywhere in Germany, proceed from Fussen: It's much better connected than Reutte to railroad lines—just a two-hour straight shot to Munich, for instance.

How to get there:

By bus: Call hostel for transit route.
By car: Call hostel for directions.
By train: Call hostel for transit route.

JUGENDGÄSTEHAUS FINSINGERHOF

(Uderns Guest House Hostel)

Finsing 73, A-6271 Uderns, Tirol

Telephone Number: 05–288–62010

Fax Number: 05–288–62866
E-mail: finsingerhof@utanet.at
Rates: €14 (about $15 US) per HI member
Beds: 90
Private bathrooms: Yes
Private/family rooms: Yes
Kitchen available: No
Office hours: 7:00 A.M. to 9:00 P.M.
Affiliation: Hostelling International-ÖJHV
Extras: TV, games, meals ($)

Located in a big white house near a quiet town, this modern building is especially good for families. Amenities like a children's playroom, nice lawn, game collection, and TV lounge will sit well with you.

Best bet for a bite:
Euro Spar supermarket

Gestalt:
White house

Hospitality:

Cleanliness:

Most dorms are four- or six-bedded, and some are reserved for families when needed. There are also some doubles and some bigger dorms, too. You can pay half-board and be served meals; otherwise you'll have to hunt for chow in the town of Uderns, as this place doesn't open its kitchen to hostellers.

What to do locally? Not a lot, frankly, though some visitors come to surf on Achensee. There are also some discos nearby the hostel if you're into really bad music.

How to get there:

By bus: Call hostel for transit route.
By car: Call hostel for directions.
By train: From station, walk ⅓ mile to hostel.

Party index:

EASTERN SWITZERLAND AND LIECHTENSTEIN

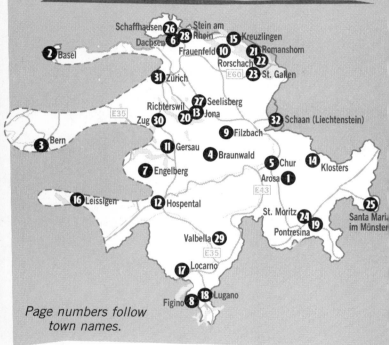

Schaffhausen 26 28 Stein am Rhein
Dachsen 6 Frauenfeld 10 15 Kreuzlingen
2 Basel 21 Romanshorn
Rorschach 22
E60 23 St. Gallen
31 Zürich

Richterswil 27 Seelisberg
E35 13 Jona
Zug 30 20 32 Schaan (Liechtenstein)
3 Bern 11 Gersau 9 Filzbach
7 Engelberg 4 Braunwald 5 Chur 14 Klosters
Arosa 1
16 Leissigen 12 Hospental E43
25 Santa Maria im Münster
St. Moritz 24 19 Pontresina
Valbella 29
E35
17 Locarno
Page numbers follow
town names.
Figino 8 18 Lugano

EASTERN SWITZERLAND

Switzerland is, quite simply, an amazing travel experience. Just don't come expecting warm fuzzies; the notoriously efficient Swiss hostel managers are hardworking, focused on cleanliness, and not really inclined to yuk it up or even show lots of emotion.

The hostels are almost all decent, if similarly devoid of character. The independent hostels of Switzerland, however, are a happy exception—homey, fun, laid-back, and tucked in quiet scenery.

Eastern Switzerland is a big place, and it includes some huge mountains and stunning lakes—not an easy place to classify, never mind break up into chapters for a book. We've included some of the country's best scenery in this chapter, where a number of hostels—including tons of independent joints—take advantage of views of huge mountains like the Jungfrau and the Eiger.

AROSA HOSTEL

Seewaldweg, CH–7050 Arosa

Phone Number: 081–377–1397

Fax Number: 081–377–1397
E-mail: arosa@youthhostel.ch
Rates: 27 SF (about $18 US) per HI member; doubles 75.50 SF (about $50.30 US)
Credit cards: No
Beds: 155
Private/family rooms: Yes
Kitchen available: No
Season: June 18–October 23; December 11–April 17
Office hours: 7:00 to 10:00 A.M.; 5:00 to 10:00 P.M.
Curfew: 10:00 P.M.
Affiliation: Hostelling International
Extras: Meeting room, breakfast, meals ($), bike storage

The hostel here's simple but fine, located in a quiet resort town. It doesn't have tons of facilities, yet if you're out this way, we'd give it a look—the gorgeous vistas of the powder-topped mountains will be enough to keep you here, gawking, awhile.

The place is all dorms: three floors' worth in the main building plus more in an annex; many come in quad rooms, though there are also some larger configurations. Breakfast is included with your tab here, and they serve meals for an additional charge. Groups tend to book it, particularly sporting groups hitting the ski hills, and that's why the place has a conference room.

Best bet for a bite:
Dinner at hostel

What hostellers say:
"By any other name . . ."

Gestalt:
Arosa's a rose

Hospitality:

Cleanliness:

Party index:

The local tourism association claims that "Arosa becomes addictive." We're not too sure about that. Still, it is just an hour away from Chur by very slow train and smack in the middle of pretty Graubünden province, bordered by big mountains.

Formerly a resort town—where older folks congregate to breathe fresh air, drink pure water, and play canasta (well, something like that)—the town's trying to make itself over lately as a hipper destination. The fact that it's at the very end of a valley means it's quiet (no through traffic), which could be a plus or a minus depending on your point of view. We say it's okay with us. If you're a skier you might be even happier, unless you need loads of nightlife with your powder.

Other good things about Arosa include a free bus that loops around the town and an annual humor festival that draws international comics and performers. Funny. Very funny.

How to get there:

By bus: Take bus to Kursaal stop and walk 100 yards to hostel.

By car: From Chur, drive 20 very slow miles into the mountains to Arosa.

By train: From Arosa Station, go right onto Poststrasse, walk downhill past tourist office, and continue ½ mile to hostel.

BASEL HOSTEL

St. Alban-Kirchrain 10, CH-4052 Basel

Telephone Number: 061–272–0572

Fax Number: 061–272–0833

E-mail: basel@youthhostel.ch

Rates: 29.00–80.60 SF (about $21.00–$53.75 US) per HI member; doubles 100 SF (about $66.70 US)

Credit cards: MC, VISA

Beds: 197

Private/family rooms: Yes

Single rooms: Yes

Kitchen available: No

Season: January 2–December 21

Office hours: 7:00 to 10:00 A.M.; 2:00 P.M. to midnight (summer); 7:00 to 10:00 A.M.; 2:00 to 11:00 P.M. (winter)

Affiliation: Hostelling International
Extras: Meeting room, breakfast, meals ($), TV, library, laundry, lockers, tourist information, garden, table tennis, snack shop, Internet access

This house, near a remaining piece of Basel's city walls, has a terrific quiet location and nice views—but the emphasis on old-fashioned rules drove us batty, to the point where we were kicking and screaming to get out of here after just one night.

You get there via a nice walk or a short tram ride from the train station (though at night it's frightfully dark and difficult to find), and everything appears pretty ducky. The river burbles below, birds twitter, and even the building's got an Old World charm. You see that it's an angled building on a street corner and that many rooms have views of greenery or something interesting. It's actually a former weaving mill, it turns out, and art in the basement illustrates some of this history.

But then you get inside and stand in line, and the line inches forward. Glacially. Staff appear confused at times. Group after group pushes past in the narrow entryway, dislodging your stuff. Some strange dude with a steel drum plays incessantly in the lobby while chain-smoking. The experience begins to sour. Ask any special favors from reception and you definitely won't be getting any smiles.

Your room won't be anything special, either. Whether it's the lone single, one of the twelve doubles and three triples with sinks, or a quad; six-bedded dorms or a great big one; they basically resemble barracks—perfectly clean, sure, but physically cold and blocky. At least some come with big windows that open up onto the rushing little St. Alban Canal, a very comforting sound that might distract you from this dreariness. You get a locker with a key and often a desk and two chairs to haggle over with your bunkmates. Bathrooms are fairly clean, not perfectly so.

Best bet for a bite:
Beer garden snacks

Insiders' tip:
Great ornate-roofed building downtown

What hostellers say:
"Enough with the rules, already . . ."

Gestalt:
Bâle game

Hospitality:

Cleanliness:

Party index:

In the morning we had to admit that the hostel breakfast was a pretty good one—yogurt, bread, cheese, actual herbal teas, and so forth. Seconds weren't discouraged at all. The common room was a popular gathering place, and the game room in the basement (think pinball and foosball) was also a big hit.

When the rules began to drive us nuts, we found a plus side in the location: It was just a five- or ten-minute walk from central Basel—a confusing city to navigate at first, but one that rewards exploration. (The hostel does give you a one-day tram ticket to get around, one of the few nice things we can say about it.)

Built on the elbow of the Rhine along the borders of France, this town is a jumping-off point for Germany's Black Forest—and one of Switzerland's most vibrant student towns. The country's oldest university, which dates from 1460, is here, so nighttime brings a slew of activity to the streets: beer gardens, museums, and pretty people trolling around to see and be seen. The most lively streets are in the areas around Barfüsserplatz, Freiestrasse, and Marktplatz, but just about anywhere's gonna turn up something. Just head for the light and noise and milling crowds and you'll be fine.

There are some mighty old buildings around, too, including an old Munster lording over the river in suitably impressive fashion and a cathedral that holds the tomb of the Dutch humanist philosopher Erasmus. That's not all, though; check out some of the many museums here in Basel, which holds more museums than any other city in the country, probably—the Caricature & Cartoons museum, the Paper Museum, a film museum, several modern art museums, and many more. Take a small ferry across the Rhine, maybe, or show up for the Autumn Fair (which has been held annually since, like, 1471). It all adds up to lots of potential side trips as you're working your way from the hostel to whichever square you finally decide to drink beer in.

Too bad about those rules. We're comin' back to Basel soon, but we won't be stayin' here. Sorry.

How to get there:

By bus: Take #2 streetcar to Kunstmuseum stop and walk ¼ mile through Alban neighborhood, down Mühleberg, and past St. Alban's church to hostel.

By car: Call hostel for directions.

By train: From Basel Station, walk ¾ mile through Aeschenplatz to hostel. Or take #2 streetcar to Kunstmuseum stop and walk ¼ mile through Alban neighborhood, down Mühleberg, and past St. Alban's church to hostel.

BERN HOSTEL 👍 👎

Weihergasse 4, CH-3005 Bern

Telephone Number: 031–311–6316

Fax Number: 031–312–5240
E-mail: bern@youthhostel.ch
Rates: 28.10–42.00 SF (about $19–$28 US) per person; doubles 73.50 SF (about $49 US)
Credit cards: MC, VISA
Beds: 186
Private/family rooms: Yes
Single rooms: Yes
Kitchen available: No
Season: January 1–9; January 25–December 31

Office hours: 7:00 to 9:30 A.M.; 3:00 P.M. to midnight
Lockout: Yes
Affiliation: Hostelling International
Extras: Meeting room, meals ($), laundry, TV

Two surprises here at the "official" Bern hostel. One, it's incredibly close to the center of the city and the train station—just downhill from the main attraction in town, in fact: Switzerland's Bundeshaus (Parliament buildings), where the government meets. We've almost never seen an official hostel that was actually in the center of the action, but this one nearly pulls it off.

Second, the hostel isn't at all what you'd expect from a Hostelling International–affiliated joint in stodgy Switzerland—it's actually pretty lively, a place where people from all over the world (Romania, when we happened to stop by) collect and interact meaningfully over pasta and salad.

But then a third, nastier surprise—not really a surprise at all, come to think of it. The hospitality here just plain sucks, as it seems to almost everywhere in German Switzerland where official hostels are concerned. Smarmy staff who adhere to rules, rules, rules and won't give you a break on curfews, laundry close-down time, checkout, or anything else.

As you enter, you're in the main gathering place, a big combination dining area/lounge with a stage for musical performances at the far end. To the side, a bistro serves three meals a day. This is likely where you'll spend most of your time when not out on the town.

Rooms are just so-so, as you'd expect from a huge hostel, a bit like prison cells really. Oh, well. Nobody we met was spending too much time in there anyway, except when they needed to bag some serious z's come bedtime. However, if you're lucky you can snag a nice private room that, unfortunately, sits above the dining room common area. If you can block out the ambient noise, you'll find a snuggly setup with in-room shower and toilet.

The staff are a mix of folks, and they do let you hang out during the daytime lockout hours *if you're staying another night*—different from most other Swiss hostels, once again. You can eat, talk, sit, do laundry (in very good facilities, though there's only one washer-dryer combo to go around), whatever you want. This is the one time they won't hassle you.

Bern itself isn't superexciting. We did find a big and good produce and crafts market operating in the Bärenplatz (Bear's Place), only a couple blocks from the hostel, during daytime hours. We'd

Best bet for a bite:
Manora,
near train station

Insiders' tip:
Coffee vending machine
works—occasionally

What hostellers say:
"Lighten up, dude . . .
it's a *hostel*, not a
prison."

Gestalt:
Crash and Bern

Hospitality:

Cleanliness:

Party index:

buy food for our dinners there—except the hostel has no kitchen. But it's easy to eat off the hoof in this area.

One caveat: The hostel touts its location on the banks of the Aare River, and indeed it can be a tranquil spot if cars aren't whizzing by; park benches and green grass add enjoyment to the picture on a sunny day. Still, we'd rather be up in the Alps, frankly. Some hostellers even reported feeling a bit spooked at night when this downtown neighborhood mostly empties out.

This town didn't thrill us as a destination anyhow. The first thing you notice, walking out of the train station, is a great big clock. That was one of the most interesting things we ever saw in town; Switzerland's capital isn't exactly Excitement City, but we did note plenty of ethnic eateries and drinkeries in the downtown area—plus a lot of posh shopping, if you've actually come here to do that—and they could keep you occupied for a night. Maybe.

How to get there:

By bus: Call hostel for transit route.

By car: Call hostel for directions.

By train: From Bern Station, walk straight across tram tracks to Bärenplatz. Bear slightly left and then turn right down Christoffelgasse, continuing to back of Parliament building. Turn left and walk along back of building, passing funicular railway, then turn right at staircase at hostel sign. Go down stairs to bottom, turn left at sign, and walk almost to river. Hostel is on left.

LANDHAUS HOTEL HOSTEL

Altenbergstrasse 4–6, CH-3013 Bern

Telephone Number: 031–331–4166

Fax Number: 031–332–6904

E-mail: landhaus@spectraweb.ch

Rates: 30–40 SF (about $21–$28 US) per person; doubles 110–160 SF (about $77–$112 US)

Credit cards: Yes

Beds: 38

Private/family rooms: Yes

Kitchen available: Yes

Office hours: Twenty-four hours

Affiliation: None

Extras: Store, restaurant ($), Internet access, laundry, lockers

The folks who run this place don't seem to understand hostellers too well—though they're all too happy to slap the "backpackers" label on their place and take your money for the night anyway. Still, it's a workable option if a little far from the action.

The hostel's situated in a former mansion above a bar and attached to the hotel that is the primary business here. Rooms are sparse if clean, with some six-bedded dorms, some doubles, and some quads for families at a special lower rate. Sure, the place's position over the Aare River gives some rooms decent views, but these rooms are really nothing special—with wooden floors, yeah, and close to a couple of tourist attractions, yet we found it all kinda boring.

They're also stingy enough here to charge you an extra $3.00 for a comforter, which we didn't like; they charge too much for breakfast as well (a whopping 7.00 SF/$5.00 US). Those double rooms are also outrageously pricey for a hostel, by the way—and some of them even lack private bathrooms or televisions, despite the high prices.

At least there's a small kitchen to fix meals in, a small supply store at reception, an Internet access terminal, and a full laundry. The good hotel restaurant is open from 11:00 A.M. to 11:00 P.M. daily, and though it's not particularly cheap, it does do takeout. Management also claims that it will provide bikes, hair dryers, and other stuff on demand, though in practice they didn't strike us as terribly hosteller-friendly.

Being primarily a hotel, most of the common-room action naturally takes place in the bar, which isn't especially great—just the usual pinball machines, chain-smoking Euros, and drunks. They do host jazz nights every Thursday, though.

If you're looking for a hotel late at night, this is a fine pick. As a hostel, though, we'd probably skip it in favor of the official Bern hostel, which is actually hip for a change and in as good or better position relative to the major sights and the station.

Best bet for a bite:
Asian takeout joint on Neuengasse

Insiders' tip:
Produce market at Barenplatz

What hostellers say:
"I wanna talk to the manager. *Now!*"

Gestalt:
Bern-Out

Hospitality:

Cleanliness:

Party index:

How to get there:

By bus: Take #12 tram toward Schlossgade to Barengraber stop, just across bridge. Hostel is on left in hotel, overlooking river.

By car: Call hostel for directions.

By train: From Bern Station, walk out front exit and cross confusing tangle of crosswalks to other side of street. Take #12 tram toward Schlossgade to Barengraber stop, just across bridge. Hostel is on left in hotel, overlooking river.

IM GYSENEGGLI HOSTEL

(Braunwald Hostel)
CH-8784 Braunwald
Telephone Number: 055–643–1356

Fax Number: 055–643–2435
E-mail: braunwald@youthhostel.ch
Rates: 26.50 SF (about $18 US) per HI member;
doubles 72.40 SF (about $48.25 US)
Credit cards: Yes
Beds: 82
Private/family rooms: Yes
Kitchen available: Yes
Season: December 18–June 4; June 18–October 25
Office hours: 7:00 to 10:00 A.M.; 5:00 to 10:00 P.M.
Affiliation: Hostelling International
Extras: Breakfast, meals ($), garden, playground, table tennis, games

A functional, schoolhouselike building tucked under shady trees and right among mountain meadows and ski trails galore, this hostel really goes the extra distance for hostelling families. Try a garden, a kids' playground, a game room and table tennis for starters—all located in a high-altitude, car-free town that's sure to fill you with the giddy joy that fresh air and quiet bring.

You can get up to the town, and the hostel, by taking a gondola from near Linthal's little train station. Once here you'll find that rooms in the wooden house-style hostel are just your average deal, four to eight beds apiece. There are five family-style rooms, each containing four beds and a sink, and there are six additional six-bedded dorms and three eight-bedded dorms. They also have a lone double room, but all bathrooms and showers here are out on the hallways; no private facilities exist. The hostel serves breakfast for free and decent dinners for a charge.

You're only steps from the local ski and sledding trails (seven ski lifts and a cross-country circuit) and other winter fun such as skating (on a natural rink, and you can rent skates on-site) and curling. Even if you come in summer there's plenty of hill walking—30 miles' worth of local trails, including a series of guided botanical tours for budding (heh, heh) naturalists—to do around here. Though Braunwald itself is certainly pretty and quaint and enjoys itself during an annual mountain festival, some hostellers prefer to make the easy walk over to the even smaller village of Nussbühl, which takes maybe an hour at most. Or they head for the Kneugrat, an overlook with great vistas.

There are two other local attractions you should know about. Europe's highest-altitude rose garden, with some 400 varieties of

Best bet for a bite:
Local Gugelhopf cake in Nussbühl

Insiders' tip:
Horse-drawn sleigh tours in winter

What hostellers say:
"Ahhhhhh, fresh air."

Gestalt:
Mountain mama

Hospitality:

Cleanliness:

Party index:

Im Gyseneggli Hostel
Braunwald
(courtesy of HI-SI, © Paul Keel)

the fragrant flower, is near here. And then, for the kiddies, there's a "Dwarf Barti" attraction. It's a Swiss thing, with a dwarf's castle, cave, and house. You kinda gotta know the story to appreciate it, but families might consider this as a day trip from the hostel.

How to get there:

By bus: Call hostel for transit route.
By car: Call hostel for directions.
By train: From Linthal Station, take gondola up to Braunwald and then walk ½ mile to hostel.

SCHWEIZERHAUS HOTEL HOSTEL

Kasernenstrasse 10, CH-7000 Chur

Telephone Number: 081–252–1096

Fax Number: 081–252–2731
Rates: 35 SF (about $23 US) per person; doubles 80–120 SF (about $56–$84 US)
Credit cards: No
Beds: Number varies
Private/family rooms: Yes
Kitchen available: No
Office hours: 7:00 A.M. to midnight
Affiliation: None
Extras: Breakfast

This hostel represents the only budget digs in Chur, the capital of Graubünden province—famous for its Romansch, a slowly disappearing regional dialect that blends elements of the other primary languages of the country (French, Italian, and German), and adds a few more local twists for good measure.

The hostel basically packs a couple rooms with quite-spare bunks, jacks up the price a lot, and charges you for sheets (or makes you sleep in your own bag)—kinda like certain other hostels, but no-frills all the way. We're talking so-so comfort and very little social interaction with your fellow hostellers unless you hit the hotel bar, maybe. It's not unclean or dangerous, just boring and way too expensive.

We're not crazy about this hostel, and though we like the city well enough, we would probably press on to the hostel in Arosa or maybe take a bus to Valbella. If you're really itching to stay in Chur, it's certainly a safe and affordable place. Just nothing special at all. Just a bed.

Chur itself offers the usual old narrow streets, big cathedral (this one's a twelfth-century job with a good altarpiece), and such. And keep your ears peeled for that distinctive, disappearing tongue.

Best bet for a bite:
Zollhaus or Falken

Insiders' tip:
"Hmmmm. Gotta think this over."

What hostellers say:
"Decent."

Gestalt:
Not so Chur

Hospitality:

Cleanliness:

Party index:

How to get there:

By bus: Call hostel for transit route.
By car: Call hostel for directions.
By train: Call hostel for transit route.

DACHSEN HOSTEL

Schloss Laufen am Rheinfalls, CH-8447 Dachsen
Telephone Number: 052–659–6152

Fax Number: 052–659–6039
E-mail: dachsen@youthhostel.ch
Rates: 24.50 SF (about $15 US) per HI member
Credit cards: Yes
Beds: 87
Private/family rooms: No
Kitchen available: Yes ($)
Season: March 19–November 15
Office hours: 8:00 to 9:30 A.M.; 5:00 to 9:00 P.M.
Affiliation: Hostelling International
Extras: Breakfast, meals ($)

This hostel sits inside two stories of stone building, topped with a third story of wood—not as nice as nearby Schaffhausen castle, no, but an interesting architectural setup nonetheless and one that takes advantage of gorgeous riverside views. What the heck. Let 'em call it a castle if they want.

This is not a fancy place. The rooms are mostly six-bedded, and there are no private rooms—it's a Swiss school–group kinda place, which might be one reason to pass on it. But there's no denying that the location is beautiful. On the plus side, they serve meals—a good thing since you're nowhere near restaurants and supermarkets. On the minus side, they charge you to use the kitchen.

The chief attraction here, by far, is the thundering falls of the Rhine River nearby—known, not surprisingly, as the Rheinfalls. This place is so damned close to the falls, you might feel like you're shooting them in a barrel; it's the only reason they put a hostel here.

A great introduction to Swiss scenery, even if the hostel isn't everything it could be.

Best bet for a bite:
Bannerstubein castle

What hostellers say:
"Beautiful river!"

Gestalt:
Rhine and dine

Hospitality:

Cleanliness:

Party index:

How to get there:

By bus: Call hostel for transit route.
By car: Call hostel for directions.
By train: From Dachsen/Neuhausen Station, walk ¾ mile to hostel.

BERGHAUS HOSTEL

(Engelberg Hostel)

Dorfstrasse 80, CH-6390 Engelberg

Telephone Number: 041–637–1292

Fax Number: 041–637–4988
E-mail: engelberg@youthhostel.ch
Rates: 30 SF (about $20 US) per HI member;
doubles 58–73 SF (about $41–$51 US)
Credit cards: No
Beds: 150
Private/family rooms: Yes
Kitchen available: No
Season: May 20–October 22; November 21–April 24
Office hours: 8:00 to 11:00 A.M.; 5:00 to 10:30 P.M.
Curfew: 10:30 P.M.
Affiliation: Hostelling International
Extras: Bike storage, breakfast, meals ($)

Not far from Luzern, this town is a good day trip or night trip up into the mountains; if we were staying in that city and wanted to spend one night up top, we might do it here. There isn't a lot to do, but the scenery is grand and there's at least one sight here worth seeing.

The hostel is a four-story wooden A-frame chalet, with lots of beds in dorms that pack eight to fourteen bodies per room plus a couple of doubles, too. They serve cheaper-than-usual meals in the dining room, include breakfast, and let you throw your bike into storage for free if you've brought one.

Engelberg's a small ski town where wintertime is high season, and if you're coming then you would be wise to make some advance reservations. Summer is just as good, though; the hiking's amazing up here, with miles of trails. Everyone seems to want to get on the Titlis Rotair, the world's first revolving cable car—though why that would be necessary, we can't imagine. Anyway, it takes you up the 9,000-foot-plus Titlis peak from 8:30 in the morning until just before 5:00 in the afternoon.

The one sight in town is mighty impressive, all the more so 'cause it's free: The Benedictus Monastery was built way back in 1120 against a stunning backdrop (and it must have taken a heck of a lotta work to do it). The beautifully decorated monastery proudly possesses the largest organ in Switzerland; a museum's attached to it.

Best bet for a bite:
Eat here,
by all means

Insiders' tip:
Great hike to
Herrenrüti

What hostellers say:
"Boy, are my legs tired."

Gestalt:
Monk-y business

Hospitality:

Cleanliness:

Party index:

How to get there:

By bus: Call hostel for transit route.

By car: Call hostel for directions.

By train: From Engelberg Station, walk down Bahnofstrasse to Dorfstrasse, turn, and continue ½ mile to hostel.

FIGINO HOSTEL

Via Casoro 2, CH-6918 Figino

Telephone Number: 091–995–1151

Fax Number: 091–995–1070

E-mail: figino@youthhostel.ch

Rates: 25.50 SF (about $17 US) per HI member; doubles 77.50 SF (about $51.70 US)

Credit cards: Yes

Beds: 160

Private/family rooms: Yes

Kitchen available: Yes

Season: February 27–October 24

Office hours: 7:00 to 10:00 A.M.; 5:00 to 10:00 P.M.

Figino Hostel

Figino

(courtesy of HI-SI)

Affiliation: Hostelling International
Extras: Breakfast, meals ($), garden, grill, bowling alley, table tennis

This hostel's set in a beautiful Italianate building—the old farmhouse is the original building—on quiet, lovely, shaded grounds. It's too bad few make it down here, even if the hostel is admittedly a ways from anything of real interest. It's best for people with cars (especially families with young'uns), groups going on retreat, or maybe the odd backpacker who has found the two great hostels in nearby Lugano to be booked up full.

The rooms are split up between two buildings, the main one and an annex with nicer rooms. All in all, you've got 160 beds doled out as follows: three double rooms, two triple rooms, nine quad rooms—two with private bathrooms—six rooms with six beds each, one with eight, then six more even larger ones.

In a third building there is a play area for children named the *casa dei bambini* (house of children). There's also a fairly rudimentary kitchen where you have to plop in a franc or two to rev up the three hotplates; a fridge (free—we think) is available for your perishables. Finding a satisfying meal is easy, too, since the staff cook up an Italian-style meal nightly. Play it on the safe side, though, and ring 'em up a few days ahead to see what's cooking and if you need to reserve a spot. You may even need to show up at a specific time, say, between 6:00 and 7:00 P.M., in order to get fed. So check before you come in order to enjoy the benefits of a decent meal.

Other stuff that makes this a likable option are the bike rentals—you'll see lots of cyclists around here—and the table tennis, foosball, and bowling alley (more like bocce than American-style bowling). What's more, there's a beach nearby on one of those beautiful lakes that adorn the area.

Nearby Figino, once a fishing village on the lake, is practically in Italy, so the weather can actually get very hot here. The palm trees look like nothing else in Switzerland, either.

Best bet for a bite:
Meals on-site

Insiders' tip:
Chocolate museum nearby in Caslano

What hostellers say:
"Goo."

Gestalt:
Family values

Hospitality:

Cleanliness:

Party index:

How to get there:

By bus: Take postbus bound for Morcote or Carabietta and get off at Casaro stop in front of hostel or at Posta Figino stop and walk 200 yards to hostel.

By car: Take highway to Lugano Sud exit and drive 3 miles (5 km) in direction of Figino. At Figino town sign, turn right and continue 100 yards to hostel.

By train: From Lugano Station, take funicular down into town center, then walk ¼ mile to bus station at Piazza Rezzonico (on the lake). Take postbus bound for Morcote or Carabietta and get off at Casaro stop in front of hostel or at Posta Figino stop and walk 200 yards to hostel.

LIHN HOSTEL [NR]

(Filzbach Hostel)

Blaukreuz Kurs und Ferienzentrum, CH-8876 Filzbach

Telephone Number: 055–614–1342

Fax Number: 055–614–1707
E-mail: filzbach@youthhostel.ch
Rates: 31–36 SF (about $20.40–$24.00 US) per HI member
Credit cards: Yes
Beds: 50
Private/family rooms: Yes
Kitchen available: No
Season: January 1–December 13; December 25–31
Office hours: 7:00 to 10:00 A.M.; 5:00 to 10:00 P.M.
Affiliation: Hostelling International
Extras: Meeting room, breakfast, meals ($)

We didn't get to this hostel, a hodgepodge three-story job with big mountains in back and a little grass yard in front. We did learn that it's largely used by groups and by vacationing families, and reports indicate that it's modern and good.

Most of the dorms at this place are quad rooms, quite suitable for families, and they serve meals at night plus an included breakfast. There's a meeting room for groups, ski trails crisscross the surrounding hils, and the hostel is wheelchair-accessible.

How to get there:

By bus: Take postbus to Filzbach and walk ¼ mile to hostel.

By car: Call hostel for directions.

By train: Nearest station is in Nafels-Mollis, 4½ miles from hostel. Take postbus to Filzbach and walk ¼ mile to hostel.

Best bet for a bite:
Evening meals here

Insiders' tip:
Bring your skis

What hostellers say:
"Bedtime, honey."

Gestalt:
Mountain Magic

Party index:

RÜEGERHOLZ HOSTEL

(Frauenfeld Hostel)

Festhüttenstrasse 22, CH-8500 Frauenfeld

Telephone Number: 054–213–680

E-mail: frauenfeld@youthhostel.ch
Rates: 12.20 SF (about $8.00 US) per HI member
Credit cards: No
Beds: 40
Private/family rooms: No
Kitchen available: Yes
Season: January 1–31; March 1–October 31; November 29–December 31
Office hours: 7:00 to 10:00 A.M.; 5:00 to 10:00 P.M.
Affiliation: Hostelling International
Extras: Parking

This very simple house on a country lane isn't much for comfort, and the fact that they've somehow packed forty beds into the tiny place isn't encouraging, either. This place is unusual in that it doesn't serve meals, something you can normally get almost anywhere in a Swiss hostel.

At least it comes with good views of the surrounding countryside.

How to get there:

By bus: Take bus to Altersheim stop, and then walk ¼ mile to hostel.

By car: Call hostel for directions.

By train: From Frauenfeld Station, walk ¾ mile to hostel.

Gestalt:
Country mouse

Hospitality:

Cleanliness:

Party index:

ROTSCHUO HOSTEL

(Gersau Hostel)

CH-6442 Gersau

Telephone Number: 041–828–1277

Fax Number: 041–828–1263
E-mail: gersau@youthhostel.ch
Rates: 23.60–36.00 SF (about $15.70–$24.00 US) per HI member; doubles 61.40 SF (about $41 US)
Credit cards: Yes
Beds: 120
Private/family rooms: Yes
Kitchen available: Yes
Season: March 1–November 30
Office hours: 7:00 to 10:00 A.M.; 5:00 to 10:00 P.M.
Affiliation: Hostelling International
Extras: Breakfast, meals ($)

An interesting-looking two-story building on huge Lake Lucerne, this simple hostel isn't a destination in and of itself. Dorms range from four-bedded (sometimes set aside for families) to eight-bedded rooms.

Best bet for a bite:
Right here, right now

Insiders' tip:
Art exhibits

What hostellers say:
"Om."

Gestalt:
Gersau packed

Hospitality:

Cleanliness:

Party index:

The hostel staff serve meals for a charge, and breakfast is included with your bunk. That's probably not enough to entice you all the way out here, but we will admit that its architecture and surroundings are a lot prettier than anything you'll find in the hostels back in Luzern. And don't forget to hang in the beautiful common or conference rooms with art on the walls, the scene of frequent off-beat events like sculpture classes and a "Tibetan rites" program of breathing, exercise, meditation, and relaxation. Om.

Historical footnote: The town, tiny and pretty, was actually its own small republic for 500 years before someone put a stop to that administrative loophole. But it was nice while it lasted, we're sure.

How to get there:

By bus: From Brunnen Station, take bus to Rotschuo and walk ¼ mile to hostel.

By car: Call hostel for directions.

By train: From Brunnen Station, take bus to Rotschuo and walk ¼ mile to hostel.

HOSPENTAL HOSTEL

Gotthardstrasse, CH-6493 Hospental
Telephone Number: 041–887–1889

Fax Number: 041–887–0902
E-mail: hospental@youthhostel.ch
Rates: 20.40 SF (about $13.60 US) per HI member
Credit cards: No
Beds: 65
Private/family rooms: No
Kitchen available: Yes
Season: January 1–April 5; May 16–October 16; December 16–31
Office hours: 7:00 to 10:00 A.M.; 5:00 to 10:00 P.M.
Affiliation: Hostelling International
Extras: Bike storage, breakfast, meals ($)

Cheaper-than-usual meals are one of the bonuses of this remote hostel, which is primarily for groups but does allow individual hostellers in, too.

It's a quite plain building, with dorms that are too large to be fun when they're full—eight or more beds per room is the rule. They let you store bikes inside the building, though, include breakfast, and serve dinner for a charge.

This area on the northern boundaries of Ticino is remote, as we say, with quiet hikes and good skiing. No nightlife at all, though.

Best bet for a bite:
Dinner here

What hostellers say:
"Didn't see a soul."

Gestalt:
General Hospental

Hospitality:

Cleanliness:

Party index:

How to get there:

By bus: Call hostel for transit route.
By car: Call hostel for directions.
By train: From Hospental Station, walk ½ mile to hostel.

BUSSKIRCH HOSTEL

(Jona-Rapperswil Hostel)
Hessenhofweg 10, CH-8645 Jona
Telephone Number: 055–210–9927

Fax Number: 055–210–9928
E-mail: jona@youthhostel.ch
Rates: 29.60–50.00 SF (about $19.75–$33.00 US) per HI member; doubles 79.60 SF (about $53 US)
Credit cards: Yes
Beds: 74

Private/family rooms: Yes
Single rooms: Yes
Kitchen available: No
Season: January 3–November 1
Office hours: 7:00 to 10:00 A.M.; 5:00 to 10:00 P.M.
Affiliation: Hostelling International
Extras: Meeting room, bike rentals, bike storage, breakfast, meals ($)

This hostel occupies a three-story low-rise outside the town of Jona, a bit like a motel in the country. You don't come to hostels for the architecture, right? Of course not. You come for the scenery, and this one's got some. Rapperswil is a town on Lake Zürich, and a fairly quaint one at that.

There are mostly four-bedded dormitory rooms here, with good facilities for the traveling cyclist or hosteller; they rent bikes and let you store them here as well. You get an included breakfast, meal service, and a conference room, and the hostel is wheelchair-accessible. It's well run, and we'd rate it fine as a stopping place, with the bonus that the surrounding terrain—as well as the train ride to get to these parts—is very nice.

Rapperswil, known as the "town of roses," has everything you'd need for a quiet day of sightseeing—an old castle, winding streets, gardens, and a zoo.

Best bet for a bite:
Dinner at hostel

Insiders' tip:
Hit the road on a bike

What hostellers say:
"Up and at 'em!"

Gestalt:
Magic Busskirch

Hospitality:

Cleanliness:

Party index:

How to get there:

By bus: Take bus to Südquartier and walk ½ mile to hostel.
By car: Call hostel for directions.
By train: From Rapperswil Station, walk 1 mile to hostel.

SOLDANELLA HOSTEL

(Klosters Hostel)

Talstrasse 73, CH-7250 Klosters

Telephone Number: 081–422–1316

Fax Number: 081–422–5209
E-mail: klosters@youthhostel.ch
Rates: 26.50–31.50 SF (about $18–$21 US) per HI member; doubles 67–75 SF (about $45–$50 US)
Credit cards: MC, VISA, AMEX, DISC
Beds: 84
Private/family rooms: Yes
Kitchen available: No
Season: July 2–October 18; December 17–April 12

Office hours: 7:00 to 9:30 A.M.; 5:00 to 10:00 P.M.
Affiliation: Hostelling International
Extras: Bike storage, breakfast, meals ($), garden, pool table, jukebox, piano, game room, table tennis, spa, patio

A simple, homey chalet in a field with good views, this place succeeds by packing a medium-size hostel with giant-size amenities— try a piano and a jukebox! We liked that. For kids there's a game room, table tennis, pool table, and children's play area; for adults, a nice garden area, terrace, Jacuzzi-like spa, and loads of scenery. The kicker is that they host some pretty wild events and activities here, like Senegalese music and dance nights one year.

It's the kind of place where the wooden floorboards creak when you walk over them, a nice antidote to the usual Hostelling International sterility. For rooms, they've got four singles, a good supply (ten) of doubles—most of them with sinks—two triples, one five-bedded room, seven six-bedded dorms, and an eight-bedded room, spread out among two buildings. Nothing too large, which is nice. Bathrooms are on the hallways.

Breakfast is included, and they make good meals in the kitchen; they just ask that you reserve for dinner a day in advance, so you might need to mention that when you make your booking. It's very quiet here; you'll savor the silence, the stars, and the mountains at night. They sometimes fix campfires outside, too, adding to the friendliness and conviviality of the place. It's a bit of a hike from Klosters proper, meaning that if you want to hit the discos or pubs, you've gotta weave your way back to the edge of town. The even more chichi nightspots in Davos are farther out, a taxi ride away.

Best bet for a bite:
In the Bündnerhof

Insiders' tip:
Rufinis pub

What hostellers say:
"Loved the campfires."

Gestalt:
Klosters-phobic

Hospitality: 👍

Cleanliness: 👍

Party index:

KEY TO ICONS

🍁 Attractive natural setting	🛏️ Comfortable beds	👪 Especially well suited for families
🌍 Ecologically aware hostel	🏅 Among our very favorite hostels	🚲 Good for active travelers
✗ Superior kitchen facilities or cafe	**S** A particularly good value	🎨 Visual arts at hostel or nearby
Offbeat or eccentric place	Handicapped-accessible	🎵 Music at hostel or nearby
Superior bathroom facilities	Good for business travelers	Great hostel for skiers
♥ Romantic private rooms		Bar or pub at hostel or nearby

Summertime hikes abound in these parts. In winter hit the slopes at one of several internationally famous hills in the area, or head over to Davos to do the same. You can even go night skiing in Selfranga. And local instructors will teach you skiing, snowboarding, and cross-country skills if you don't come equipped with 'em.

If you want history, on the other hand, hit the Reformed Church in town, with some windows designed by none other than Giaccometti. Another building, the history museum, was constructed in 1565.

How to get there:

By bus: Call hostel for transit route.
By car: Call hostel for directions.
By train: From Klosters-Platz Station, walk around rotary and take right on Talstrasse, continuing to follow signs uphill ½ mile to hostel.

VILLA HORNLIGERG

(Kreuzlingen Hostel)

Promenadenstrasse 7, CH-8280 Kreuzlingen

Telephone Number: 071–688–2663

Fax Number: 071–688–4761
E-mail: kreuzlingen@youthhostel.ch
Rates: 23.50–36.75 SF (about $15–$25 US) per HI member; doubles 53 SF (about $35.30 US)
Credit cards: Yes
Beds: 97
Private/family rooms: Yes
Single rooms: Yes
Kitchen available: No
Season: March 1–November 30
Office hours: 8:00 to 9:00 A.M.; 5:00 to 9:00 P.M.
Affiliation: Hostelling International
Extras: Breakfast, meals ($), bike rentals, kayak rentals

This hostel's in Switzerland, but you are much more likely to use it if you are visiting Germany. The interesting German city of Konstanz (or Constance to language-challenged Anglos) is a heckuva interesting place, but its hostel isn't too great. And if you're older than twenty-six, you can't stay there anyway. Bingo! Instant short walking trip across the border to the Swiss city of Kreuzlingen, where you'll have to show a passport to the unsmiling Swiss guards, but they probably won't give you a hard time.

Once there you'll find this to be a pretty good hostel: a homey old three-story building in quiet surroundings right on the lake. The dorms are a little too big for our taste, with many of them containing eight or more beds (and they get a lot of school groups here, to boot), but we liked the emphasis on fresh air here—staff will rent you a bicycle, a kayak, or both.

If you're not on a bike or on the lake, you'll probably be spending most of your free time over in Konstanz. It's a cool town, fueled by scores of university students—that means more and later-night bars, discos, and clubs than you'll often find in a small European city. Good beaches on the lake, too.

Konstanz is also the starting point for numerous excursions around the lake, which is served by a tremendous network of ferries, trains, and bus lines; get all the details at the hostel. We recommend a bus over to Mainau in Germany, with its terrific gardens, or a ferry ride over to the spooky medieval town of Meersburg.

Best bet for a bite:
Rheingasse, in Konstanz

Insiders' tip:
Gardens in Mainau, Germany

What hostellers say:
"Perfect base for seeing Germany."

Gestalt:
Konstanz comment

Hospitality:

Cleanliness:

Party index:

How to get there:

By bus: Call hostel for transit route.
By car: Call hostel for directions.
By ferry: Take ferry to the Kreuzlingen-Hafen ferry dock and walk ¼ mile to hostel.
By train: From Kreuzlingen-Hafen station, walk ¼ mile to hostel. Or from Konstanz, walk 1 mile around lake path to park; turn right and walk away from water, turning to hostel entrance.

LA NICHÉE HOSTEL

(Leissigen Hostel)

Horbacher, CH-3706 Leissigen

Telephone Number: 033–847–1214

Fax Number: 033–847–1497
E-mail: leissigen@youthhostel.ch
Rates: 25.50–51.00 SF (about $17–$34 US) per HI member; doubles 71.40 SF (about $47.60 US)
Credit cards: Yes
Beds: 42
Private/family rooms: Yes
Single rooms: Yes
Kitchen available: No
Season: Late April to mid-October
Office hours: 7:00 to 10:00 A.M.; 5:00 to 10:00 P.M.
Affiliation: Hostelling International
Extras: Breakfast, meals ($)

A very handsome little three-story chalet beneath hills, this hostel's a good place—especially so if you get one of the cottages they have in

Best bet for a bite:
Soup's on here

Insiders' tip:
Listen to the quiet

What hostellers say:
"Loved the woods."

Gestalt:
Chalet okay!

Hospitality:

Cleanliness:

Party index:

the woods. Quiet is the watchword here, quiet and privacy: Dorms are mostly doubles or four-bedded rooms, a rare treat in a country full of huge antiseptic dorms. The lack of a bar adds to the blissful silence.

Ignore the higher-than-usual price for a bed, and consider how lucky you are to have a bed like this for the night. There's no kitchen, but the hostel provides meals for an extra charge.

How to get there:

By bus: Call hostel for transit route.
By car: Call hostel for directions.
By ferry: Take ferry to Leissigen and walk ½ mile to hostel from dock.
By train: From train station, follow signs and walk ½ mile to hostel.

LOCARNO

Locarno is a sleeper of a town; it sneaks up on you. You don't expect much of it, and then suddenly you show up and it surprises you with the views, the friendliness, the great weather. (This is the sunniest town in the land, don'cha know.)

Located on Lake Maggiore, most of which lies in Italy, this is the lowest-elevation and hottest (well, climatically speaking) town in Switzerland. The old center is a maze of cobblestones, squares, and narrow streets with lots of Italian and hand gestures being bandied about. The old center alone provides hours of enjoyment just walking around. The local Madonna church, way up on top of the hill—you can get there by funicular lift or walk it—is the most popular destination.

You can also take a boat all around the lake to various Italian and Swiss towns or places like the Brissago Islands' botanical gardens and their unusual subtropical flora. And one of Switzerland's best train rides, through the Centovalli ("one hundred valleys"), begins here in Locarno. Not bad, eh?

Best of all, the place has not one, not two, but four hostels of different kinds to satisfy even the most jaded traveler. None of 'em is bad, either, and all are actually within reasonable distance of the city center. Go ahead. Enjoy the good life for a few days and pretend you've got a deep-pocketed Swiss bank account.

OSTELLO GIACIGLIO

via Rusca 7, CH-6600 Locarno

Telephone Number: 091–751–3064

Fax Number: 091–743–5406
Rates: 30 SF (about $21 US) per person
Credit cards: Yes
Beds: 50
Private/family rooms: Sometimes
Kitchen available: Yes
Office hours: 8:00 to 11:00 A.M.; 5:00 to 11:00 P.M.
Affiliation: None
Extras: TV, sauna, tanning booth

Good dorms that aren't too big and a pleasant atmosphere are the hallmarks of this independent joint, one of four in the resort town of Locarno.

Dormitories contain four to eight beds, and if they're not too full they might let you share a smaller one with your sweetie; it's worth a shot. They charge you for the extra touches, but what extra touches these are—both a sauna and a tanning booth, the second one a little hard to figure, given that no place in Switzerland sees more annual UV than Locarno.

The huge film festival in early August means that you shouldn't think you'll snag a last-minute bed here. Luckily, they've got a good booking system in place and you can reserve far ahead if you know you'll be coming this way. A tip of the hat, too, for being centrally located near the Piazza Grande.

Best bet for a bite:
Near Piazza Grande

Insiders' tip:
Break out the sunscreen

What hostellers say:
"Good enough."

Gestalt:
Locarnoval

Hospitality:

Cleanliness:

Party index:

How to get there:

By bus: Call hostel for transit route.
By car: Call hostel for directions.
By train: Call hostel for transit route.

OSTELLO PALAGIOVANI

(Locarno Hostel)

Via Varenna 18, CH-6600 Locarno

Telephone Number: 091–756–1500

Fax Number: 091–756–1501
E-mail: locarno@youthhostel.ch

Rates: 31.60–38.00 SF (about $21–$25 US) per HI member; doubles 71.40 SF (about $47.60 US)
Credit cards: Yes
Beds: 188
Private/family rooms: Yes
Kitchen available: No
Office hours: 7:00 to 10:00 A.M.; 3:00 to 11:30 P.M. (summer); 8:00 to 10:00 A.M.; 4:00 to 11:30 P.M. (winter)
Affiliation: Hostelling International
Extras: Breakfast, meals ($), bike rentals, tourist information, TV, laundry, lockers, garden, table tennis

A three-story, functional place with nice lawns, this hostel has outstanding facilities despite its size. Staff, however, could be more hospitable.

Rooms are good for families, couples, or backpackers—fifty-four doubles and fourteen quads of various sizes, all kept clean. Some of the double rooms even come with small kitchens, which you'll rarely find at a hostel anywhere (the Hostelling International hostel in nearby Lugano also has this perk, interestingly). The grounds are pretty peaceful, yet you're right in the center of the city.

The extra touches here are tremendous, beginning with a television lounge and laundry and extending to a garden area, table tennis room, and included breakfast. They serve meals and rent bikes for an extra charge, too. Perfect, right?

However, we did hear a few troubling complaints of occasional unfriendliness at the front desk and an overemphasis on rules. We're sure that won't continue—especially now that this book is in your hot little hands.

Best bet for a bite:
Migros on Piazza Grande

Insiders' tip:
Occasional snowboarding classes

What hostellers say:
"OK place."

Gestalt:
Locarno sweat

Hospitality:

Cleanliness:

Party index:

How to get there:

By bus: Take #31 or #36 bus to Cinque Vie and walk 200 yards to hostel.
By car: Call hostel for directions.
By train: From Locarno Station, walk ¾ mile to hostel or take #31 or #36 bus to Cinque Vie; walk 200 yards to hostel.

PENSIONE CITTÀ VECCHIA

Via Toretta 13, CH-6600 Locarno

Telephone Number: 091–751–4554

Fax Number: 091–751–4554
E-mail: cittavecchia@datacomm.ch
Web site: www.cittavecchia.ch

Rates: 22–35 SF (about $15–$23 US) per person; doubles 64–76 SF (about $43–$51 US)
Credit cards: No
Beds: 22
Private/family rooms: No
Kitchen available: No
Season: March 1–September 30
Office hours: 8:00 A.M. to 9:00 P.M.
Affiliation: None
Extras: Breakfast ($), sheets ($)

$

This very, very popular backpacker-style hostel—probably because of its incredibly low prices in a resort town—guarantees that it will often be packed full. There are few rules, and though they charge extra for breakfast and sheets, you won't mind.

Bright is the watchword here: bright paint, bright ideas, bright decorations on the interior and a very central spot in the city. Just get used to the laid-back groove; it means you're sharing bathrooms with everyone (guys and gals together), for instance, and that cleanliness can occasionally slide. Unusually, they have a couple of single rooms here in addition to the dorms.

This is a decent place, one more in a town already chock-full of 'em.

Best bet for a bite:
Aperto, Coop, or Migros—all good

Insiders' tip:
Film fest in August

What hostellers say:
"Cool."

Gestalt:
Locarno hero

Hospitality:

Cleanliness:

Party index:

How to get there:

By bus: Call hostel for transit route.
By car: Call hostel for directions.
By train: Call hostel for transit route.

REGINETTA HOSTEL

Villa della Motta 8 CH-6600 Locarno
Telephone Number: 091–752-3553

Fax Number: 091–752-3553
E-mail: reginetta.hotel@bluewin.ch
Web site: www.reginetta.ch
Rates: 49 SF (about $27 US) per person; doubles 98 SF (about $65 US)
Credit cards: Yes
Beds: 38
Private/family rooms: Yes
Kitchen available: No

Season: March 1–September 30
Office hours: 8:00 A.M. to 9:00 P.M.
Affiliation: None
Extras: Breakfast ($)

Best bet for a bite:
Casa del Popolo self-serve

Insiders' tip:
You may snag a double

What hostellers say:
"We love it!"

Gestalt:
Locarno knowledge

Hospitality:

Cleanliness:

Party index:

Lots of renovation has brought this hostel into line with the other three good ones in Locarno. It's another dolled-up building with plenty of coats of fresh paint and new fixtures; you can get a dorm room or, if you're fortunate, a double all to yourself.

Breakfast costs extra, a little surprising given what you're paying already for the bed. But it's a nice, comfortable place, with friendly staff to help plan your kick-back time in the area. What can we say? Another winner.

How to get there:

By bus: Call hostel for transit route.
By car: Call hostel for directions.
By train: Call hostel for transit route.

LUGANO–SAVOSA HOSTEL

Via Cantonale 13, CH-6942 Savosa (Lugano)
Telephone Number: 091–966–2728

Fax Number: 091–968–2363
E-mail: lugano@youthhostel.ch
Rates: 31.60–54.00 SF (about $21–$36 US) per HI member; doubles 87.70 SF (about $58.50 US); apartments 100–170 SF (about $67–$113 US)
Credit cards: Yes
Beds: 110
Private/family rooms: Yes
Single rooms: Yes
Kitchen available: Yes
Season: Mid-March–late October
Office hours: 7:00 A.M. to 12:30 P.M.; 3:00 to 10:00 P.M.
Curfew: 10:00 P.M.
Affiliation: Hostelling International
Extras: Breakfast ($), meals, swimming pool, laundry

If you're looking for a party, hit Lugano's backpackers-style hostel (see below). But if you want a quiet rest and a base from which to hike, swim, and relax, this is as good as any hostel in Europe.

Maybe the best. It is definitely a hostel of two distinct personalities—one that caters to groups and families, which it does well with loft-style rooms containing kitchenette and shower and toilet facilities, and the other, which provides bunk beds for individual backpackers in a separate wing. Above all, it draws an interesting crowd.

Dorms are rather large, ten beds, but there is an outside common room. Rooms are outfitted with desks and chairs for writing those postcards. The bathrooms are kept sparkling clean. There are no lockers, though, a small sticking point with our snoops.

On the flipside, the family apartment rooms are a dream. You can lounge on a balcony overlooking the tropical-like paradise below while your honey is whipping up an Italo-Swiss meal in the tiny kitchenette complete with cutlery, cookware, sink, and stovetop. These rooms are real beauts and can sleep at least five people. They have huge picture windows and spiral staircases, too—and, obviously, they cost extra. If you don't know your neighbors, the proximity to the next room could be somewhat annoying, particularly if they have young children who like to scream a lot. Otherwise these rooms are ideal for families or couples traveling together who want to share the same floor. Management asks that you stay a minimum of seven nights in these rooms, so take note of that.

Best bet for a bite:
Innovazione Supermarket, a mile downhill

Insiders' tip:
Get yer Ovomaltine here

What hostellers say:
"Fabulous and peaceful."

Gestalt:
Tropical paradise

Hospitality:

Cleanliness:

Party index:

The grounds are positively peaceful and beautiful. You can tell they like to garden here, too: The unusual palmettos, conifers and even banana fronds scattered around the property are lovingly tended—and set against splashing fountains. A retirement home next door brings some interesting characters over once in a while for a chat, too. Out back, they maintain a small swimming pool in a peaceful enclosed yard of trees that's good for your dive-bombing seven-year-old kid. If you have one.

Other stuff of note? Well, the breakfast here is wonderful (not included with your room rate; about $5.00 US), with genuine Swiss hot chocolate, a variety of cereals, breads, cheese, and juice. Remember that it starts real early, though—at 7:00 A.M. sharp—and ends abruptly at 8:30 A.M. Management is incredibly helpful here: They'll even lend you a transformer so that your laptop, hair dryer, or whatever will work at the hostel. You can get a key with your room, too, so even though curfew is an early 10:00 P.M., you can get in later. This being Ticino, Italian is the primary language spoken here, with French, German, and English all being at least understood. Management is quadralingual!

The surrounding area is nice and tidy and good for a short stroll. Walking away from town from the hostel, you'll walk past an interesting antiques store and come to a smaller village with a commercial zone that boasts an Innovazione store that is similar to the Swiss-French version, La Placette. Basically it's a high-concept store where the idea is to provide a farmers' market atmosphere with the convenience and low prices of a supermarket. You're getting fresh produce, seafood, as well as grocery store stuff at reasonable prices. It's a relief from the monotonous Co-op/Migros/EPA trio you must use in every other Swiss town for cheap eats.

If you get bored—which you might if you stay too long, since Lugano doesn't score too high on the backpacker's excitement scale—you can check out the Alprose chocolate factory outside town in Caslano, where you can watch the chocolate-making process from a catwalk. Or hike the huge mountains nearby; staff can tell you how to do that. Lugano really is mostly a retirement town catering to rich Swiss who want the comfort and efficiency that the rest of the country provides, without the quirky weather.

OK, so it's not a party on wheels. But if you want a warm, sunny, green, and quiet hostel experience, you could do no better than to rest your bones *qui*.

How to get there:

By bus: From bus station at Piazza Manzoni, take #5 blue streetcar to Crocifisso stop, then walk back less than 50 yards, make a left, and go uphill 100 yards to hostel on left.

By car: Take motorway to Lugano-Nord exit, take left-hand lane at first set of traffic lights and follow signs to Savosa. Continue following signs to hostel.

By train: From Lugano Station, walk outside and turn left. Walk down ramp to street, go straight across, then turn right and cross street again. Now turn left and walk uphill 100 yards to bus stop. Catch #5 blue streetcar or yellow postbus marked COMASO to Crocifisso stop. Walk back less than 50 yards, make a left and go uphill 100 yards to hostel on left.

MONTARINA HOSTEL

Via Montarina 1, CH-6903 Lugano

Telephone Number: 091–966–7272

Fax Number: 091–966–0017
E-mail: info@montarina.ch
Web site: www.montarina.ch
Rates: 25 SF (about $17 US) per person; doubles 100–120 SF (about $66–$84 US)
Credit cards: Yes
Beds: 170
Private/family rooms: Yes
Kitchen available: Yes
Office hours: 8:00 A.M. to 10:00 P.M.

Affiliation: Swiss Backpackers
Extras: Pool, table tennis, massages ($), tours, laundry, breakfast ($), lockers, meals ($), sheets/towels ($)

Lugano does it again! This little city, perched way down in southern Switzerland near the gateway to Italian lake country, has not just one great hostel but two—and two of the best in the land.

This big pink hostel is part of a hotel that is itself a converted villa; the two houses were built early in the twentieth century (which, come to think of it, is no longer turn-of-this-century.) Its position could not possibly be more central: It's literally right behind the train station, and yet you don't really hear the trains because it sits on a little rise above the station. Views of the town and the lake are stupendous. Better still, the hostel grounds are a peaceful enclave from the urban noise surrounding it: Birds chirp, thick tropical foliage is everywhere (this town is south of the Alps, after all, so the weather is going to be much better here than in the big mountains), and a nicely groomed lawn provides places to lie out and picnic in the sun or shade.

Absolutely come for the swimming. The hotel-quality pool is one of the nicest we've ever seen in a hostel—no, make that *the* best. It's clean, pretty, and surrounded by well-to-do tanners. You'll feel like a movie star at hostel prices.

The regular dorms here are okay, too, although beds are packed a little closer together than we like. Some are of the mattress-on-wooden-shelf variety, good for your back maybe but not always the most comfortable sleep. But you probably won't mind, since everything here is brand spankin' new. Every dorm room comes with a sink and plenty of lockers for hosteller valuables, an added bonus.

In another wing usually earmarked for groups, things get a bit tighter: These high-ceilinged dorms are arranged in triple high-rises linked by big ladders. We're talking nine to fifteen bunks to a room, plus a shared bathroom and trough-style sink. You probably won't end up here, though, as there are plenty of other dorms, too.

The double rooms are amazing, basically hotel rooms; you can pay extra for rooms with bathrooms in another building, but the hostel's doubles are almost as good.

One more bonus that sets this one above most others. It's got a kitchen, and a well-stocked one at that; despite the fact that it's small, it really does the job. Plates, tongs, mitts, an oven, everything you need to whip up a gourmet feast—heck, even a dishwasher! (To find fresh local produce, take the cable car from the station downtown and emerge at a couple of greengrocers. They close at 6:30

Best bet for a bite:
Station grocery store

Insiders' tip:
Walk instead of taking cable car

What hostellers say:
"Cannonbaaaaall!!!"

Gestalt:
Think Pink

Hospitality:

Cleanliness:

Party index:

P.M. sharp.) Breakfast buffet costs, and so do the tours and massages you can book here.

In short, it's everything you could want in a hostel. Since this one's sometimes booked full with groups, though, you may not get the chance to stay here. Good thing there's another great hostel on the outskirts of Lugano.

How to get there:

By bus: From downtown bus station, take funicular cable car up to train station (0.80 SF/about 50 cents US; free with Swisspass). Exit station, turn right, and walk 100 yards to railroad crossing. Make a right, cross tracks (if train isn't coming), and walk uphill to left; follow signs to reception.

By car: From expressway, take Lugano-Nord exit and drive toward CENTRO (center). Follow signs to train station and continue 200 yards beyond; turn right and cross train tracks, then go 200 yards uphill to hostel parking at entrance on left.

By train: From Lugano Station, turn right and walk 100 yards to railroad crossing. Make a right, cross tracks (if train isn't coming), and walk uphill to left; follow signs to reception.

TOLAIS HOSTEL

(Pontresina Hostel)

Langlaufzentrum, CH-7504 Pontresina

Telephone Number: 081–842–7223

Fax Number: 081–842–7031
E-mail: pontresina@youthhostel.ch
Rates: 42.30 SF (about $28 US) per HI member; doubles 135.70 SF (about $90.50 US)
Credit cards: Yes
Beds: 130
Private/family rooms: Yes
Kitchen available: No
Season: June 18–October 23; December 10–April 10
Office hours: Vary; call hostel for hours
Curfew: 11:00 P.M.
Affiliation: Hostelling International
Extras: Breakfast, restaurant ($), terrace, bike rentals, bike storage, lockers, TV, VCR, library, ski rentals, ski lessons, waxing room, laundry ($)

Despite the bland and foreboding exterior, this place is nice, a good facility in spectacular mountain-pass countryside—and a place with especially terrific stuff for skiers.

The hostel has a lot of beds in rooms that are bland but efficient. We're talking three double rooms with sinks, seven quadruple rooms with sinks and—the bulk of the space—sixteen six-bedded dorm rooms; all bathrooms are on the hallways. Beds have quilts, a nice touch.

The cafeteria here features a big terrace for catching some sun, and the common-room facilities are modern and plentiful—a television lounge with VCR, a reading room, a children's playroom, and a playground. They also rent top mountain bikes in summer and cross-country skis in winter, give lessons at discount rates, and maintain a waxing room.

Best bet for a bite:
Engadiner torte at any bakery

Insiders' tip:
Toboggan runs abound

What hostellers say:
"What views!"

Gestalt:
Peak experience

Hospitality: 👍

Cleanliness: 👍

Party index:

The town itself is about a mile high, with good weather and not too much wind for an Alpine retreat. This is the Engadine, one of Switzerland's prettiest and most popular (among locals) vacation spots. Ski trails—both downhill and cross-country—are easy to find. Rumor even has it that you can actually hire a bobsled-style taxi to go from St. Moritz to Celerina! We've heard it's not cheap, but talk about a story to tell your friends . . . inquire at the hostel for current details of the service.

In summers you might spring for a scenic train or bus ride on the Rhätische Bahn through the stunning Bernina pass to Tirano, Italy. Aromatic trees cover the hills and make them good for summer hiking; walking to the Swiss National Park is popular, as is the huge peak called Piz Languard—almost a ten-thousand-footer, by gosh.

How to get there:

By bus: From Pontresina bus stop, walk less than 100 yards to hostel.

By car: Cross Punt Muragl and enter Pontresina, turn right towards train station and continue to hostel.

By train: From Pontresina Station, walk less than 100 yards to hostel.

KEY TO ICONS

🍁 Attractive natural setting

🌍 Ecologically aware hostel

✗ Superior kitchen facilities or cafe

🛸 Offbeat or eccentric place

🚿 Superior bathroom facilities

❤️ Romantic private rooms

🛏️ Comfortable beds

🏅 Among our very favorite hostels

S A particularly good value

♿ Handicapped-accessible

💼 Good for business travelers

👨‍👩‍👧 Especially well suited for families

🚴 Good for active travelers

🎨 Visual arts at hostel or nearby

🎵 Music at hostel or nearby

⛷️ Great hostel for skiers

🍺 Bar or pub at hostel or nearby

HORN HOSTEL

(Richterswil Hostel)

Hornstrasse 5, CH-8805 Richterswil

Telephone Number: 01–786–2188

Fax Number: 01–786–2193
E-mail: richterswil@youthhostel.ch
Rates: 29.60 SF (about $19.75 US) per HI member
Credit cards: Yes
Beds: 82
Private/family rooms: Yes
Kitchen available: No
Season: March 1–December 19
Office hours: 7:00 to 10:00 A.M.; 5:00 to 10:00 P.M.
Affiliation: Hostelling International
Extras: Breakfast, meals ($), meeting rooms, bike storage, foosball, terrace

A huge, modern complex that looks a bit like a spaceship, sitting right on Lake Zürich under big shade trees, this hostel is also a water-sports complex. Part of it occupies a former silk factory—interesting, huh? The best part is, it's just a short commuter-train ride from Zürich.

Best bet for a bite:
Meals and snacks available here

Insiders' tip:
Bring a towel or two

What hostellers say:
"Liked the lake."

Gestalt:
Lake effect

Hospitality:

Cleanliness:

Party index:

They do a great job for families here, with fourteen double rooms and twelve quadruples—the family rooms are even in a separate section, which both backpackers and the families will probably appreciate. There's one six-bedded dorm room, too. There's a game room, a play area for kids with a mock castle, and a foosball table; youngsters will love this stuff. Or they could just frolic in the large park grounds outside.

For the rest of us they serve cafeteria-style meals in the big modern dining room, as is usual—and the hostel restaurant also stays open between meals to supply snacks, light salads, and ice cream.

Richsterwil is a small town on Lake Zürich, unknown to many travelers but popular as a day trip by city-worn locals in Zürich. You can swim, row a boat, windsurf, or take a cruise nearby on the lake—there's a good beach with snacks, grills, and so forth.

Einsiedeln, nearby, is another good visit—its Benedictine monastery has long been a pilgrimage spot for travelers coming to see its black Madonna figure. Remember that you have to take the SOB (Südostbahn, not son-of-a-biscuit) railway from Burghalden Station to get there, about a half-hour ride.

Horn Hostel
Richterswil

(courtesy of HI-SI)

How to get there:

By bus: Call hostel for transit route.

By car: Take highway to Richterswil exit, follow road into town, and then make a left at Seestrasse; follow signs to hostel.

By ferry: Take ferry to Richterswil; from dock, walk 200 yards around lake to hostel.

By train: From Zürich Station, take #2 or #8 S-Bahn (suburban) train to Richterswil. From Richterswil Station, walk ¼ mile around lake to hostel.

ROMANSHORN HOSTEL

Gottfried Keller-Strasse 6, CH-8590 Romanshorn

Telephone Number: 071–463–1717

Fax Number: 071–461–1990
E-mail: romanshorn@youthhostel.ch
Rates: 21.40 SF (about $14.30 US) per HI member
Credit cards: No
Beds: 114
Private/family rooms: No
Kitchen available: No
Season: March 1–October 31
Office hours: 7:00 to 10:00 A.M.; 5:00 to 10:00 P.M.
Affiliation: Hostelling International

Extras: Breakfast, meals ($), bike storage, bike rentals

We can't imagine getting excited about this centrally located place, which packs you in dorms that typically average fifteen beds per room. Obviously it's a tour-group leader's dream—but it might be your nightmare.

Best bet for a bite:
Breakfast and dinner here

Insiders' tip:
Use eyeshade and earplugs

What hostellers say:
"Now I know what cattle feel like."

Gestalt:
Romanshorn o' plenty

Hospitality:

Cleanliness:

Party index:

They do rent bikes and let you store 'em, and they serve meals for a charge. The only reason you might come is that Romanshorn is on big Lake Konstanz, and you can take boats from this seaside town to others. We'd recommend staying in one of the others, if only because we don't like huge warehouse dorm rooms.

How to get there:

By bus: Call hostel for transit route.
By car: Call hostel for directions.
By ferry: Take ferry to Romanshorn; from dock, walk ½ mile to hostel.
By train: From Romanshorn Station, walk ¼ mile to hostel.

RORSCHACH–SEE HOSTEL

Churerstrasse 4, CH-9400 Rorschach

Telephone Number: 071–844–9712

Fax Number: 071–844–9713
E-mail: rorschach.see@youthhostel.ch
Rates: 32.65 SF (about $22 US) per HI member
Credit cards: No
Beds: 32
Private/family rooms: Yes
Kitchen available: No
Season: April 1–October 31
Office hours: 7:00 to 10:00 A.M.; 5:00 to 10:00 P.M.
Affiliation: Hostelling International
Extras: Breakfast, meals ($), bike rentals

This is a rather bland building at first glance, but you've got to like a hostel that almost literally touches a lake.

Basically a house in a green field, this new Swiss hostel augments the other one in town, which is open only to groups; we applaud the division of labor (and hostellers) here, having been awakened one too many times by the trampling feet of kiddies arriving back off their bus in the middle of the night. Anyhow, the place enjoys great position right next to the lake and a small beach, practically touching Lake Konstanz and the bike trail that encircles it. Yet you're in a green field at the edge of woods, too. Nice.

Best bet for a bite:
Strap on the feed bag at hostel

Insiders' tip:
Old Grange Museum

What hostellers say:
"Nice grounds."

Gestalt:
Rorschach test

Hospitality:

Cleanliness:

Party index:

It's a rather small joint, though, just thirty-two beds doled out as seven quad rooms and two coveted doubles. None have private bathroom facilities, unfortunately. They serve meals and, importantly, rent bikes—probably the best way to explore the lake at your leisure if you've got the time.

Rorschach as a town is no big deal at all, just a few churches and museums and the usual lake-resort restaurants. We'd likely opt instead for a boat trip over to the gardens of Mainau, Germany, or maybe a night boat to another lake town nearby. Just make sure you know when the last boat to Rorschach runs.

How to get there:

By bus: From the port, take postbus to Jugendherberge (hostel) stop and walk ¼ mile to hostel.

By ferry: Take ferry to Rorschach; from dock, walk ½ mile to hostel.

By car: Call hostel for directions.

By train: From Rorschach Station, walk ¼ mile to hostel.

ST. GALLEN HOSTEL

Jüchstrasse 25, CH-9000 St. Gallen

Telephone Number: 071–245–4777

Fax Number: 071–245–4983
E-mail: st.gallen@youthhostel.ch
Rates: 25.50 SF (about $17 US) per HI member; doubles 71.40 SF (about $47.60 US)
Credit cards: Yes
Beds: 104
Private/family rooms: Yes
Kitchen available: No
Season: March 6–December 12
Office hours: 7:00 to 10:00 A.M.; 5:00 to 10:30 P.M.
Affiliation: Hostelling International

Extras: Laundry, breakfast, meals ($), information desk, TV, library, lockers, garden, playground, table tennis, grill, patio, meeting rooms, jukebox, patio, disco

A boring concrete building with huge windows, sure, but this nice spot above lively little St. Gallen is one of the better hostels in this half of Switzerland. A good staff and some nice extras—disco, jukebox (cool)—complete the surprising picture here. You may not even need to leave the place at night to have a good time.

Best bet for a bite:
Bratwurst stands

Insiders' tip:
Local lace makes great souvenir

What hostellers say:
"Surprisingly fun."

Gestalt:
Gallen the family

Hospitality:

Cleanliness:

Party index:

The inside's decorated with modern murals, green things, bright paint—good touches. They've got six double rooms, two six-bedded dorms, and six eight-bedded dorms. Then there are the five special family rooms in their own separate wing, each with in-room sinks, showers, and private bathrooms. The terrace is popular, especially when hostel cooks decide to put on a barbecue; the garden with its children's play area is also well liked. Other interior touches include a small library, a television room, and a rec room with table tennis and what have you.

You can walk the mile down into town for nightlife and attractions (take a streetcar, bus, or private rail back up, though). St. Gallen's got plenty to see despite its small size, including a good cathedral, convents in the old town, and fun bars, discos, and restaurants galore. The single most stunning thing to see, if you're pressed for time, is the city's abbey library, the Stiftsbibliotek, wondrous if you're into old buildings or books or Umberto Eco novels.

One day trip could be a stroll across Europe's highest footbridge (yikes) to a working dairy. There's also a game park with ibex and wild boar in the area and an interesting trail up in the Appenzeller, where you actually walk barefoot from Gonten to Gontenbad; your shoes are waiting for you at the end. Wild! Finally, near the hostel there's a pond where you can swim.

Good hostel, good area of Switzerland. All good.

How to get there:

By bus: Take #1 bus to Singenberg stop and walk ⅓ mile to hostel. Or take streetcar to Schülerhaus stop and walk ⅓ mile to hostel.

By car: Call hostel for directions.

By train: From St. Gallen Station, take orange Trogenerbähn train to Schülerhaus stop and walk ¼ mile to hostel. Or walk 1 mile up to hostel.

STILLE HOSTEL

(St. Moritz Hostel)

Via Surpunt 60, 7500 St. Moritz-Bad (St. Moritz)

Telehone Number: 081–833–3969

Fax Number: 081–833–8046
E-mail: st.moritz@youthhostel.ch
Rates: 44.40 SF (about $27 US) per HI member; doubles 114 SF (about $76 US)
Credit cards: MC, VISA, AMEX
Beds: 190
Private/family rooms: Yes
Kitchen available: No
Office hours: 7:00 to 10:00 A.M.; 4:00 to 10:00 P.M. (summer); 7:30 to 10:00 A.M.; 4:00 to 10:00 P.M. (winter)
Curfew: Midnight
Affiliation: Hostelling International
Extras: Breakfast, meals, TV, VCR, meeting rooms, laundry, lockers, information desk, garden, bike rentals, bike storage, waxing room, foosball

A few miles outside superwealthy St. Moritz, this concrete block of a hostel is an okay choice even if is too big, bland, expensive, and far from town. It's expensive because they include the breakfast buffet and dinner in your room charge, whether you eat or not—so make sure you stock up, buddy boy. And be seated at the dinner table prior to 7:15 P.M.—otherwise you lose out. At least the food's good. As for the other problems—big, bland, far away—we can't offer much solace except to say that any hotel in this town would surely break your bank.

But back to basics. A blocky structure, this hostel looks like the progressive high schools and college campus everyone in the States starting building during the seventies. Not too impressive at first glance. Yet it sits on the edge of woods and not too far from the local lake, so you're going to start mellowing out immediately.

All rooms are double- or quadruple-bedded, so that's a plus: privacy. If you're really lucky, you might even get to reserve one of the two coveted double rooms with its own bathroom. The other fourteen doubles have just sinks, as do the remainder of the rooms—forty-two quads.

Best bet for a bite:
You're gonna have to eat here

Insiders' tip:
Cross-country trails right outside

What hostellers say:
"Got any wax?"

Gestalt:
Stille the one

Hospitality:

Cleanliness:

Party index:

Common facilities abound here; try five recreation rooms and two game rooms with everything from foosball to table tennis. They've also got a ski storage room, a waxing room, and a special playroom for kids.

As good as the place is for families (especially those with their own cards), it's really ace for hardbody hostellers who wanna hit the mountains. We're talking mountain bike rentals and easy access to tons of ski, bike, and hiking trails. The Swiss National Park, down in the Lower Engadine, is a wonderland for hikers; when the snow flies, you've got a hundred miles of local cross-country ski paths to check out, including some that pass right by the hostel door.

You might also hit a local village like Zuoz or Guarda, or check out the eleventh-century chapel in Celerina—good fresco work here. Locally the Engadine Museum teaches the history and culture of the region over the past 400 years.

How to get there:

By bus: From St. Moritz Station, take postbus to Hotel Sonne and walk ¼ mile to hostel.

By car: Call hostel for directions.

By train: From train station, walk 1¼ mile west around lake to hostel. Or from train station, take postbus to Hotel Sonne and walk ¼ mile to hostel.

SANTA MARIA IM MÜNSTERTAL **NR** HOSTEL

Chasa Plaz, 7536 Santa Maria im Münstertal GR

Telephone Number: 081–858–5052

Fax Number: 081–858–5496
E-mail: sta.maria@youthhostel.ch
Rates: 24.50 SF (about $16.30 US) per HI member
Credit cards: No
Beds: 62
Private/family rooms: No
Kitchen available: Sometimes
Season: May 22–October 23; December 18–April 10
Office hours: 7:00 to 10:00 A.M.; 5:00 to 10:00 P.M.
Affiliation: Hostelling International
Extras: Meals (sometimes), meeting room, bike storage

This interesting-looking, half-timbered building is the real Switzerland for sure; it's a beautiful structure in quiet territory.

Best bet for a bite:
Occasional dinners here; call hostel for schedule

Dorms are larger than you might like, though, as they're geared (sigh, once again) to the ever-present school groups who come for the rural terrain and local ski slopes. They sometimes serve meals here and will store your bike. Otherwise, you're on your own.

Note that the place closes in spring for six weeks and then again in fall for about two months.

How to get there:

By bus: From Zernez Station, take postbus to Santa Maria (takes one hour) and walk less than 200 yards to hostel.

By car: Call hostel for directions.

By train: From Zernez Station, take postbus to Santa Maria (takes one hour) and walk less than 200 yards to hostel.

Insiders' tip:
Try a more backpacker-friendly hostel

What hostellers say:
"I can't hear myself think!"

Gestalt:
Downhill mogul

Party index:

BELAIR HOSTEL
(Schaffhausen Hostel)

Randenstrasse 65, CH-8200 Schaffhausen

Telephone: 052–625–8800

Fax Number: 052–624–5954
E-mail: schaffhausen@youthhostel.ch
Rates: 23.50 SF (about $15.65 US) per HI member; doubles 60.20 SF (about $40 US)
Credit cards: MC, VISA
Beds: 86
Private/family rooms: Yes
Kitchen available: Yes ($)
Season: March 1–October 31
Office hours: 8:00 to 10:00 A.M.; 5:30 A.M. to 10:00 P.M.
Curfew: 10:30 P.M.
Affiliation: Hostelling International
Extras: Breakfast, meals ($), meeting room, bike storage

A cool three-story building with twin, vaguely onion-domed towers that used to be a villa and looks vaguely like an Orthodox church, this hostel—surely one of the prettiest hostels in this part of the world—is mighty attractive outside if a little simple inside. It's remote from town, too, which means plenty of beautiful grounds to romp around in; those are hundred-year-old trees in the park. Just remember that late-night access back from town is going to be difficult to arrange unless you get a key before you set out. But it's hard to complain when you're sleeping in rooms where people like author Herman Hesse once sat as guests.

The beds here come one to twelve beds per room, though most of 'em contain six or eight; the nice singles and doubles cost a little more. They charge you to use the kitchen, which we found ridiculous; must be an attempt to get you to buy the hostel meals, served in a dining room.

Schaffhausen is a so-so destination, not the most interesting place actually. But it's near everything else you might be on your way to or from—the Rhine, the waterfall, Zürich, and Germany. This is a major rail and ferry hub, so boats and trains head from here to Lake Konstanz and other German points. If you're really stuck in town, prowl the alleys like a cat. There are a number of old churches and decent museums (including a good natural history museum) to occupy your time, plus a local brewery.

Best bet for a bite:
Falken brewpub, of course

Insiders' tip:
Bring change for kitchen

What hostellers say:
"I've got to catch an early train."

Gestalt:
Hermans' hostellers

Hospitality:

Cleanliness:

Party index:

How to get there:

By bus: From Schaffhausen Station, take #3 or #6 bus to Wesli stop and walk 200 yards to hostel.

By ferry: Take ferry to Schaffhausen; from dock, walk 1 mile to hostel.

By car: Call hostel for directions.

By train: From Schaffhausen Station, walk ¾ mile to hostel. Or take #3 or #6 bus to Wesli stop and walk 200 yards to hostel.

SEELISBERG HOSTEL

Gadenhaus Stöck beim Rütli, CH-6377 Seelisberg

Telephone Number: 041–820–1784 or 041–820–1274

Fax Number: 041–820–1784 or 041–820–1274
E-mail: seelisberg@youthhostel.ch
Rates: 18.90 SF (about $12.60 US) per HI member
Credit cards: No
Beds: 25
Private/family rooms: Sometimes
Kitchen available: Yes
Season: April 1–October 31
Office hours: 7:00 to 10:00 A.M.; 5:00 to 10:00 P.M.
Affiliation: Hostelling International

This hostel occupies a low wooden house that feels like a home—or maybe a hut—it's so rustic, and the location, up a dirt path next to a big tree, enhances that feeling. This is one of the small hostels of Switzerland: only twenty-five beds here, so creature comforts are few and far between.

Most of the guests tend to be school-groups. If you do get out here, take advantage of the hostel kitchen and cook your own meal (but bring food). It's a hard place to reach without a car, though if you ride a ferry to Treib and then a gondola up to Seeligsberg, you'd be all set.

How to get there:

By bus: Call hostel for transit route.

By car: Call hostel for directions.

By ferry: From Brunnen Station, take ferry to Rütli and walk ½ mile to hostel. Or take ferry to Treib, then gondola to Seelisberg. From top of lift, walk ¾ mile to hostel.

By train: From Brunnen Station, take ferry to Rütli and walk ½ mile to hostel.

Best bet for a bite:
Stock up at a supermarket before you get here

What hostellers say:
"Where am I??"

Gestalt:
Tiny town

Party index:

STEIN AM RHEIN HOSTEL

Hemishoferstrasse 711

CH-8260 Stein am Rhein

Telephone Number: 052–741–1255

Fax Number: 052–741–5140

E-mail: stein@youthhostel.ch

Rates: 23.50 SF (about $15.65 US) per HI member; doubles 59 SF (about $39.30 US)

Credit cards: None

Beds: 121

Private/family rooms: Yes

Kitchen available: Yes

Season: March 1–October 31

Curfew: 10:30 P.M.

Office hours: 8:00 to 9:30 A.M.; 5:30 to 10:00 P.M.

Affiliation: Hostelling International

Extras: Breakfast, meals ($), meeting room

This hostel's quite a ways from downtown Stein am Rhein, but it's so well run that you might not mind—more relaxed than many "official" Swiss hostels, that's for sure, though the curfew is early.

Beds mostly come in biggish dorm rooms, eight hostellers per room. There are also some decent double rooms, an included breakfast, and dinners for extra. You probably won't use the meeting room, but they've got one here just in case.

Best bet for a bite:
Co-op to the rescue

What hostellers say:
"Good old town."

Gestalt:
Rhein-stone cowboy

Hospitality:

Cleanliness:

Party index:

Stein is okay, pretty if a bit too quaint and touristed. But you gotta admit that those bright half-timbered buildings look darned good. The old Kloster church is suitably formidable. It's worth noting that you can start boat trips down the Rhine from here; heading downriver to Lake Constance is mighty fine riding, and it's covered by railpasses.

How to get there:

By bus: From Stein am Rhein Station, take bus to Strandbad stop.

By car: Call hostel for directions.

By train: From Stein am Rhein Station, walk 1¼ miles to hostel. Or take bus to Strandbad and walk ¼ mile to hostel.

VALBELLA-LENZERHEIDE HOSTEL

Voa Sartons 41, CH-7077 Valbella

Telephone Number: 081–384–1208

Fax Number: 081–384–4558
E-mail: valbella@youthhostel.ch
Rates: 24.50 SF (about $16.30 US) per HI member; doubles 67 SF (about $44.70 US)
Credit cards: Yes
Beds: 115
Private/family rooms: Yes
Kitchen available: Sometimes
Season: Mid-December–April 23; end June–end October
Office hours: 7:00 to 10:00 A.M.; 5:00 to 10:00 P.M.
Affiliation: Hostelling International
Extras: Breakfast, meals ($)

Best bet for a bite:
Reserve ahead for
dinner here

Insiders' tip:
Parla Italiano un poco,
if you can

What hostellers say:
"Grazie mille!"

Gestalt:
Schusser's Valhalla

Hospitality:

Yet another little chalet-style hostel tucked up in hills near the Italian border, this place has got more beds than you'd think possible—more than a hundred. Yet it's really pretty simple, with meal service and included breakfast being the only true perks.

Dorms contain four to eight beds each, and they sometimes open a kitchen to the hostellers, depending both on time of year and day and, possibly, their whim. The local skiing and hiking are good, but then, again, where in Switzerland isn't it?

How to get there:

By bus: From Chur Station, take bus to Valbella (takes thirty minutes) and walk 1 mile to hostel.

By car: Call hostel for directions.

By train: From Chur Station, take bus to Valbella (takes thirty minutes) and walk 1 mile to hostel.

Cleanliness:

Party index:

ZUG HOSTEL

Allmendstrasse 8, beim Sportstadion Herti, CH-6300 Zug

Telephone Number: 041–711–5354

Fax Number: 041–710–5121
E-mail: zug@youthhostel.ch
Rates: 28.60 SF (about $19 US) per HI member;
doubles 88 SF (about $58.70 US)
Credit cards: No
Beds: 92
Private/family rooms: Yes
Kitchen available: Yes
Season: Mid-March–January 3
Office hours: 7:00 to 10:00 A.M.; 5:00 to 10:00 P.M.
Affiliation: Hostelling International
Extras: Breakfast, meals ($), meeting rooms, bike storage, laundry, information desk, garden, grill, game room

A two-story building with so little character that it actually looks like it's still on some architect's drawing of a perfect village, this place nevertheless is okay inside. The city of Zug donated the building, wedged between a lake and sports fields, to its townspeople in 1987, and—this is true—what had been little more than a shack was redeveloped into a modern hostel with all the amenities you'd expect. And a few more.

For starters it's a very good hostel for families, especially because it has cooking facilities—pretty rare in Switzerland—and other useful stuff like a laundry, bicycle shed, garden, barbecue, included breakfast, and tourist information. The art on the walls lends a happy touch, too. It does tend to get some school groups, however, who come here en masse to use the sports fields.

Best bet for a bite:
Migros in town

Insiders' tip:
Open-air cinema on lake

What hostellers say:
"We're gonna Zug, zug, zug-a, zug."

Gestalt:
European vacation

Hospitality:

Cleanliness:

Party index:

Zug Hostel
Zug

(courtesy of HI-SI)

Too bad its unimpressive dorms look a bit like prison cells. Most of these rooms are small here, intimate in a good way. There are four double rooms with showers (all bathrooms are communal here), eight quad rooms and six six-bedded dorms. Two more dorms contain eight beds apiece, and these have showers, too. Almost everything—including most rooms—are handicapped-accessible, too.

The old center of town has a distinctive thirteenth-century tower, ancient town hall, old churches, and snaky streets. Come the right weekend in June (the third) and you'll participate in a famous lake festival. Also in the area, check out the Höllgrotten in Baar—the largest set of stalactite-filled caves in Switzerland, where (this is a little bizarre) classical concerts are held now and then. Or just stroll up Zugerberg Mountain.

How to get there:

By bus: From Zug Station, take #6 or #11 bus to Stadion stop and walk less than 200 yards to hostel. Or walk ½ mile to hostel.

By car: Call hostel for directions.

By train: From Zug Station, take #6 or #11 bus to Stadion stop and walk less than 200 yards to hostel. Or walk ½ mile to hostel.

ZÜRICH

Zürich gets a bad rap from some, but our feeling was that young travelers who want to experience a hip city should come here. Along with Geneva—a *very* different place, by the way—this town's got the most vibrant nightlife in all Switzerland, one part Berlin/Zoo Station/fly shades and one part Teutonic cool.

The two hostels here, as usual, are total opposites in character: One's strict, hygienic, pastoral, and staid, while the other's central, hopping, noisy, young, and fun. Take your pick.

Zürich's public transit is decent, not great—a network of buses and trams fans out from the train station into the commercial, tourist, and residential areas.

One option, if you think you're going to be hopping around the city doing a lot of sight-seeing, is the "9 o'clock Travelcard" (in German, *9-Uhr-Tagespass*). It gets you free public transit within city limits on weekdays from 9:00 in the morning until the time when everything stops running (around 1:00 A.M. for most lines) and all day long on weekends. The cost is 20 SF (about $14 US), so it's not cheap, and you'd have to ride a whole lot to make it worth your while. Still, it's something to think about.

There's obviously lots to do around town, including several theater companies, a variety of cruises on Lake Zürich, and huge and impressive department stores right on Bahnhofstrasse outside the train station. If you like movies, the city has an interesting promotion each Monday: big reductions on tickets. The theaters are packed! So get in line early.

The Swiss National Museum, directly behind the train station (and pretty close to the independent hostel), showcases Swiss history—old stoves, weapons, artifacts, and lots of other stuff that traces the story of this fascinating mountain-rimmed land. The Kunsthaus museum downtown exhibits modern art; the Fraumunster church's Chagall stained-glass work is also worth a look. The "Züri-Tip" newspaper supplement clues you in on cultural happenings each Friday.

Mid-August is a good time to come—the city hosts its biggest party, the annual Lake Parade. Begun in 1991 the parade now throws a half-million crazed Germans, locals, traveling Americans, and other visitors into one heaving stewpot. It's a lot of fun as the normally reserved Swiss let it loose for a day.

ZÜRICH HOSTELS at a glance

	RATING	PRICE	IN A WORD	PAGE
City Backpacker	👎	29 SF	central	p.200
HI-Zürich	👍👎	31.60–65.00 SF	staid	p.201

THE CITY BACKPACKER

Hotel Biber
Niederdorfstrasse 5, CH-8001 Zürich
Telephone Number: 01–251–9015

Fax Number: 01–251–9024
E-mail: backpacker@access.ch
Rates: 29 SF (about $20 US) per person; doubles 65–88 SF (about $46–$62 US)
Credit cards: Yes
Beds: 64
Private/family rooms: Yes
Kitchen available: Yes
Office hours: 8:00 to 11:00 A.M.; 5:00 to 10:00 P.M.
Affiliation: Swiss Backpackers
Extras: Laundry, lockers, travel store, Internet access

🎵

This is probably the better bet of Zürich's two hostels, mostly because it's quite central to Zürich's considerable action—but also because it is looser and more laid back than its HI counterpart, while being kept decently clean and fun at the same time.

Its location is smack in the Niederdorf, the city's really fun old town—think dance clubs, cafes, souvenir shops, and poseurs, all crammed into every available square inch of the winding lanes, avenues, and very old town houses that make up the area.

Don't be discouraged when you arrive and are faced with a steep climb up winding stairs to reception. There's no elevator, but the hostel is worth it. Don't duck into the restaurant kitchen on the first couple of floors; the cooks might come at you with cutlery. (Just kidding.)

There are four or five doubles here, plus fifty other beds, most of those in six-bedded rooms; there are also some quads. Rooms are nice and airy, with lockers and a little furniture—well done, we say. Each floor comes with relatively clean bathrooms, and—this is the real reason for coming here—its own little kitchen featuring fridges, rangetops, a nice little table, plus a window onto Zürich. Breaking up the kitchen space this way, by floor, avoids the dinnertime crush that often plagues a bigger hostel.

As we said, there are few rules here: No lockout, no curfew; you come and go as desired. They've got a laundry downstairs and now have added an Internet station for e-mail-happy hostellers. The little front desk shop sells Swiss army knives and other souvenirs at reasonable (not rip-off) prices. One more bonus: The manager is one of the cofounders of Switzerland's independent association, Swiss Backpackers, so he can brief you (well, in addition to this book) on other backpacker-style digs around the country.

This place is incredibly convenient to Zürich's main train station—it's a five- to ten-minute walk away—and that means you can day-trip just about anywhere in Switzerland: Geneva, the Alps, even Italy are only a three- to four-hour ride. But more likely you'll be hanging out in the place that calls itself "little big city" and does indeed pack a lot of nightlife and fun into the old core.

You can stay right in this neighborhood and get the best of the bars, discos, and other nightlife. Or walk around the area, checking out the city's numerous clock towers.

Best bet for a bite:
All along
Niederdorfstrasse

What hostellers say:
"Couldn't be more central—
this rocks!"

Gestalt:
Zürich man, poor man

Hospitality:

Cleanliness:

Party index:

How to get there:

By bus: Call hostel for transit route.

By car: Call hostel for directions.

By train: From Zürich Station, walk out front entrance and turn immediately left. Walk to river and cross little bridge, then turn right on Limmatquai. Go ½ block, turn left up alley, then turn right onto Niederdorfstrasse. Hostel is on right, above Spaghetti Factory restaurant. Climb stairs up and up to reception.

ZÜRICH HOSTEL

Mutschellenstrasse 114, CH-8038 Zürich

Telephone Number: 01–482–3544

Fax Number: 01–480–1727
E-mail: zuerich@youthhostel.ch
Rates: 31.60–65.00 SF per HI member (about $21–$22 US); doubles 92 SF (about $61.30 US)
Credit cards: MC, VISA, AMEX
Beds: 310
Private/family rooms: Yes
Kitchen available: Sometimes

Office hours: Twenty-four hours
Affiliation: Hostelling International
Extras: Breakfast, meals ($), information desk, laundry, meeting rooms, TV, lockers, garden, table tennis, bike storage, pool table, jukebox, fireplace, snack bar

This hostel—in an institutional set of bunkerlike, five-story buildings that could probably withstand a bomb blast—delivers the goods in some ways. It's not convenient to town at all; it's not fun or spic-and-span, but it has enough services for families or backpackers who have cars to survive the night.

Yeah, you heard right. You've got to get wayyyy out of town to get to this place. The entrance area features the usual hanging-out lounge, in this case a *huge* one with a TV that even has an English-language channel. That room's adjacent to the dining area, where they serve the daily, included, breakfast buffet starting at the ungodly hour of 6:00 A.M. They did serve a good breakfast, we'll give 'em that.

Snacks are served throughout the day, and dinner can be purchased at night in the hostel restaurant; the kitchen claims to be renowned for its Asian buffet, but we wouldn't traipse all the way out here just to eat; our feeling is that the hostel food and drink is frankly overpriced, especially since you're so far from town that you'll be forced to eat their dinners.

Inside, all dorms contain no more than six beds, which is a nice switch from the usual sardine job. In addition to the forty-six six-bedded rooms, there's one double room and eight rooms with four beds each for families, couples, or buddies traveling together. Each

Best bet for a bite:
Not around here

What hostellers say:
"Overpriced and disappointing."

Gestalt:
Far and away

Hospitality:

Cleanliness:

Party index:

KEY TO ICONS

 Attractive natural setting

 Ecologically aware hostel

 Superior kitchen facilities or cafe

 Offbeat or eccentric place

 Superior bathroom facilities

 Romantic private rooms

 Comfortable beds

 Among our very favorite hostels

 A particularly good value

 Handicapped-accessible

 Good for business travelers

 Especially well suited for families

 Good for active travelers

 Visual arts at hostel or nearby

 Music at hostel or nearby

 Great hostel for skiers

Bar or pub at hostel or nearby

dorm comes with lockers and one desk. Though staff is as Swissly efficient and impersonal as ever, we were surprised to find the place not all that clean.

Showers, toilets, and hair dryers are available on each floor and sometimes in rooms, too. Other amenities include a courtyard, giant chess board outside, bike shed, and lots more services—almost like a rustic hotel, really, except with much less charm or attention.

You can tell they're really geared to groups at this place when you stumble across the huge, 200-seat auditorium; the rec room—yeah, that's a big-screen TV in there, along with foosball, a pool table, and a jukebox—or one of the two seminar rooms. Don't even think about cleaning your bike in there or taking a nap or eating a picnic. They *won't* like it.

The hostel's far from town but close to Lake Zürich, which is one possible trip. But you didn't come here to see that, did you? Yes? Well, then this hostel is perfect for you. The only other interesting option around here is the Rote Fabrik cultural centre, a showplace for avant-garde art, music, dance, and the like. It's practically next door, lending some much-needed culture to this too-remote place.

How to get there:

By bus: From Zürich Station, take #7 streetcar to Morgental stop and walk ¼ mile north to hostel. Or take #66 bus to hostel.

By car: Call hostel for directions.

By subway: Take #8 S-Bahn (suburban train) to Wollishofen stop, then walk 3 blocks to Musthecllenstrasse; turn right and continue 2 more blocks to hostel, following signs.

By train: From Zürich Station, take #7 streetcar to Morgental stop and walk ¼ mile north to hostel. Or take #8 S-Bahn (suburban train) to Wollishofen stop, then walk 3 blocks to Musthecllenstrasse; turn right and continue 2 more blocks to hostel, following signs.

LIECHTENSTEIN

The tiniest of lands, Liechtenstein nevertheless possesses one slim hostel—an interesting notch to add to your hostelling belt if you can swing it, and mighty scenic. Getting here isn't too hard, either; you just stay on the train from Feldkirch, Austria.

SCHAAN BEI VADUZ HOSTEL

Untere Rüttigasse 6, L-9494 Schaan

Telephone Number: 075–232–5022 (same as dialing Switzerland)

Fax Number: 075–232–5856 (same as dialing Switzerland)
E-mail: schaan@youthhostel.ch
Rates: 28.15 SF (about $18.75 US) per HI member;
private rooms 74.20–113.20 SF (about $49.50–$75.00 US)
Credit cards: None
Beds: 96
Private/family rooms: Yes
Kitchen available: No
Season: January 4–November 31
Office hours: 7:00 to 10:00 A.M.; 5:00 to 10:00 P.M.
Lockout: 9:30 A.M. to 5:00 P.M.
Curfew: 10:00 P.M.
Affiliation: Hostelling International
Extras: Breakfast, meals ($), lockers, laundry, meeting room

In a nice enough spot a little ways outside the only city of "size" in little Liechtenstein, Vaduz is itself not worth a trip here. But if you're coming (and most do) to add the unique, interesting stamps from the post office to your collection, this hostel makes a good night's stop.

The hostel's quite a ways from the station, however: It's out in the countryside, quite close to a farm. There aren't many buses running in these parts, either, so you might have trouble making it to the door.

At least the staff is superhelpful once you're here, and the sleeping is very quiet. Dorms are six-bedded, with lockers and your own key. There's no furniture in the dorm rooms, a surprise. Breakfast was coffee, bread with jam,

Best bet for a bite:
Load up at breakfast

What hostellers say:
"Steep country."

Gestalt:
Schaan shine

Hospitality:

Cleanliness:

Party index:

salami, and cheese—a typical breakfast in Germanic Euro-parts. There's no bar, thank goodness, no kitchen, but there *is* a laundry; the bathrooms are as efficient as they would be in any other Hostelling International–affiliated joint.

As we said, a nice stop if you can swing it.

How to get there:

By bus: From Feldkirch, Austria, take Bundesbus to Schaan; change buses and continue to Vaduz. Call hostel for directions from Vaduz.

By car: Call hostel for directions.

By train: From Buchs Station, walk ½ mile to hostel. Take #5 bus to Schaan/Mühleholz and walk ¼ mile to hostel.

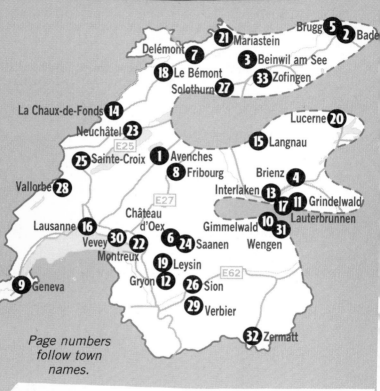

WESTERN SWITZERLAND

Brugg **5** **2** Baden
21 Mariastein
Delémont **7**
3 Beinwil am See
18 Le Bémont **33** Zofingen
Solothurn **27**
La Chaux-de-Fonds **14**
Lucerne **20**
Neuchâtel **23**
E25
15 Langnau
25 Sainte-Croix **1** Avenches
8 Fribourg Brienz **4**
Vallorbe **28** Interlaken **13**
17 **11** Grindelwald
E27 Lauterbrunnen
Château
Lausanne **16** d'Oex **10**
Gimmelwald **31**
30 **22** Vevey **6** **24** Saanen Wengen
Montreux
19 Leysin
9 Geneva Gryon **12** **26** Sion
E62
29 Verbier
32 Zermatt

*Page numbers
follow town
names.*

WESTERN SWITZERLAND

Western Switzerland covers a lot of ground. From lakeside grape-growers and dairy farmers who speak French to the biggest, most spectacular mountains in Europe in a solidly Germanic corner of the country, we're talking about a major must-see part of the world on your European itinerary. Trying to cram all the scenery into one trip is pointless, but we'll happily make a few suggestions.

The area surrounding Lake Geneva (or Lac Leman) is beautiful and often overlooked in the rush to get to grander heights. We'd definitely work a couple days in the Geneva-Lausanne-Montreux corridor into a trip. Some of the country's best hostels are here in French Switzerland, so that's another reason to come.

Then we'd go on to the Berner Oberland, a raised area of mountains with the best views in the land, hands-down. Stock up in the valley town of Interlaken and get your bearings, but don't spend too much time there unless the weather's yucky; in towns like Lauterbrunnen, Gimmelwald, and Wengen—and, to a lesser extent, Grindelwald—you'll find the bucolic Alpine paradise you've only ever seen before in postcards: cows, glaciers, huge hanging waterfalls, great-smelling air, loads of wildflowers (if you come in spring or summer). The hostels in that rarified air rise to the occasion, too, with personality and a down-home charm that's absent from most of the cities of Switzerland.

As a bonus our favorite train ride in Switzerland—the Panoramic Express—connects these two regions. Once in the Bernese Oberland, you can take the famous Jungfraubahn and a bunch of funiculars, gondolas, and smaller-gauge trains up and around the cliffs, valleys, and mountains. One very expensive train even takes you to the summit of the Jungfrau.

No, there's no hostel up top. But never fear. Head back to one of our faves for the night instead, safe in the knowledge that you've taken the best Switzerland could throw at you.

AVENCHES HOSTEL

Rue de Lavoir 5, CH-1580 Avenches

Telephone Number: 026–675–2666

Fax Number: 026–675–2717
E-mail: avenches@youthhostel.ch
Rates: 25 SF (about $17 US) per HI member;
doubles 65.30 SF (about $43.50 US)
Credit cards: No

> **Beds:** 76
> **Private/family rooms:** Yes
> **Kitchen available:** No
> **Season:** February 27–October 31
> **Office hours:** 7:00 to 9:30 A.M.; 5:00 to 11:30 P.M.
> **Affiliation:** Hostelling International
> **Extras:** Breakfast, meals ($), television, table tennis

$

This three-plus–story building on nice lawn fills the bill nicely for those wanting a quieter side of Switzerland, without huge peaks or high, high prices. Think cows, regular folks, and Roman ruins—that's right—and you're starting to get the picture.

The ruins just outside town are really the only concrete reason to come to this town, but we felt it made a nice day-off destination when cities and trains and tourists become a bit too much. The well-run hostel's got dorms of four to ten beds (some of the quads become family rooms as necessary) and—like everything else in town—isn't far from the ruins.

There's no kitchen, but they do serve free breakfast and dinner for a charge; the television lounge is the main draw at night. The owners are pleasant and attentive and will point you around town. That's a real bonus, especially considering how affordable this place already is. Nice to know that free local guides come with the package!

This little French-style community was once a mighty Roman outpost called Helvetica. A museum and bits of wall tell the story today, and the ruins make a great stroll late in the day when you can smell the grass. Avenches's old center is delightful, too.

If you're into opera (which we're not yet, but no matter), an annual festival brings performances here. Hostellers like to grab bikes and take some leisurely rides around the surrounding cheese-cows-and-meadows country, which isn't so challenging that you'll be doubled over gasping for air.

How to get there:

By bus: Take bus to Restaurant Croix Blanc and walk ¼ mile to hostel.

By car: Call hostel for directions.

By train: From station, walk ¾ mile to hostel.

BADEN HOSTEL

Kanalstrasse 7, CH-5400 Baden
Telephone Number: 056–221–6736
Fax Number: 056–221–7660
E-mail: baden@youthhostel.ch

Rates: 25.30 SF (about $17 US) per HI number; doubles 77.10 SF (about $51.40 US)
Credit cards: Yes
Beds: 83
Private/family rooms: Yes
Kitchen available: Yes
Season: March 16–December 23
Office hours: 7:00 to 10:00 A.M.; 5:00 to 10:00 P.M.
Affiliation: Hostelling International
Extras: Laundry, breakfast, meals ($), table tennis, game room, fireplace

Once a stable, Baden's hostel has been retooled to suit groups of sports-minded kids from Germany and Switzerland. It's got a few perks, though, that might lead you to consider it as a backup choice if you really want to get here—like a big room with an open fireplace, for instance.

There's one double room, one quad room, two six-bedded dorms, five eight-bedded dorms, and three ten-bedded dorms, plus that big twenty-five–bedded room with its own fire. They serve breakfast and dinner in the dining room and will make a vegetarian meal if you ask for one. Out back, there's an open-air chess set. The hostel touts its location near a bunch of sports complexes and fields, but what we liked was its position on the banks of the Limmat River.

Baden's not a bad place to get stuck for a night; it's a cute spa town with an attractive old core and a Governor's Castle standing next to a wooden covered bridge. The town's nineteen thermal springs have been known since Roman times, and they contain the highest mineral content of any water in Switzerland—a million liters' worth gushing forth each day. All this mineral-laden water has obviously made Baden a popular spot to soak (Baden means "baths," after all), and famous folks like Goethe, Hesse, and Thomas Mann have indeed soaked here through the ages. There's also a vibrant drama scene in town, with at least four different theater companies and venues, plus loads of art galleries and frequent summertime concerts by orchestral or other musical groups.

With even more time to spend, we'd skip the local casino and hit the small but decent museums—like Villa Langmatt, a wealthy family's home-turned-museum of Impressionist art, or the fun Child and Toy Museum—instead. Even better, strap on your walking shoes and follow a system of local ridges and pathways to a wide range of

Best bet for a bite:
Restaurant Manora

Insiders' tip:
Toy museum

What hostellers say:
"I'm goin' walkin'!"

Gestalt:
Bath time

Hospitality:

Cleanliness:

Party index:

monasteries, castles, and panoramic viewpoints. We would most likely opt for the walk from Schartenfels castle past vineyards to Wettingen; there we'd check out the Klosterkirche (monastery church) and a sporting center with lots of entertainment and games.

How to get there:

By bus: Take #1, #3, or #4 bus to Kantonsschule (Canton school) stop and walk ¼ mile to hostel.

By car: Call hostel for directions.

By train: From Baden Station, walk ¾ mile to hostel. Or take #1, #3, or #4 bus to the Kantonsschule (Canton school) stop, then walk ¼ mile to hostel.

BEINWIL AM SEE HOSTEL

Seestrasse 71, CH-5712 Beinwil am See

Telephone Number: 062–771–1883

Fax Number: 064–771–6123
E-mail: beinwil@youthhostel.ch
Rates: 15.30 SF (about $10.20 US) per HI member; doubles 53 SF (about $35.30 US)
Credit cards: No
Beds: 98
Private/family rooms: Yes
Kitchen available: Yes
Season: February 13–December 12
Office hours: 8:00 to 10:00 A.M.; 4:00 to 10:00 P.M.
Affiliation: Hostelling International
Extras: Meeting room, breakfast, meals ($), laundry

Forgive us if we get a little lump in our throat reviewing this one—it's got a lot of history, and though a recent addition to the building sacrificed charm in favor of comfort and space, it's still got good atmosphere.

Best bet for a bite:
Co-op

Insiders' tip:
Say hello to the pigs

Gestalt:
See-side

Hospitality:

Cleanliness:

Party index:

Opened back in 1931 this was the Ur-Swiss hostel; it was originally filled with straw mattresses and a single woodstove. Back then it cost 90 Swiss centimes (about 60 cents US) for a night's rest—and that included the cost of wood for heating. Then, in 1977 a god-awful-looking but comfortable concrete annex was tacked onto this beautiful, three-story gabled and shuttered farmhouse, now extremely popular with groups. Dorms are mostly six-to-eight-bedded affairs.

Beinwil am See Hostel

Beinwil am See

(courtesy of HI-SI)

There's a soccer field on the property, and the place is set back from a lake, behind an actual hotel constructed much more recently (which ruined the view). There are two resident pigs, too. A splendid little dining room with patio views, where they serve both free breakfast and meals for a charge, adds to the fun. A good place, if a bit out of the way.

How to get there:

By bus: Call hostel for transit route.
By car: Call hostel for directions.
By ferry: Take ferry to Beinwil am See dock, then walk 50 yards from dock to hostel.
By train: From train station, walk ¾ mile to hostel.

BRIENZ HOSTEL

Strandweg 10, am See, CH-3855 Brienz
Telephone Number: 033–951–1152

Fax Number: 033–951–2260
E-mail: brienz@youthhostel.ch
Rates: 23.75 SF (about $15.85 US) per HI member; doubles 57.75 SF (about $38.50 US)
Credit cards: AMEX, MC, VISA
Beds: 86

Private/family rooms: Yes
Kitchen available: Yes
Season: April 15–October 17
Office hours: 7:30 to 10:00 A.M.; 5:00 to 10:00 P.M.
Affiliation: Hostelling International
Extras: Bike rentals, hiking boot rentals, breakfast, meals ($)

A simple two-story structure by Brienzersee lake with grounds and hills, this place has got its priorities straight—they rent mountain bikes and hiking boots to those who wanna get close to the land, so that should tell you something good.

Best bet for a bite:
Co-op close by

Insiders' tip:
Check out local woodcarvings

Gestalt:
Mountain tops

Hospitality:

Cleanliness:

Party index:

Dorms are mostly eight-bedded, offering plain comforts. Breakfast is included, meals are served, and the smaller rooms are especially nice. The area is notable for local woodcarvings, as well as a good Swiss folk museum in the great outdoors called Ballenberg. Other folks enjoy taking the old train up the Brienzer Rothorn to get a wider view on things.

How to get there:

By bus: Call hostel for transit route.
By car: Call hostel for directions.
By ferry: Take ferry to Brienz dock and walk ¾ mile along lake to hostel.
By train: From Brienz Ost Station, walk ¾ mile along lake to hostel.

BRUGG HOSTEL

Schlössli Altenburg
Im Hof 11, CH-5200 Brugg
Telephone Number: 056–441–1020

Fax Number: 056–442–3820
E-mail: brugg@youthhostel.ch
Rates: 16.30 SF (about $10.90 US) per HI member; doubles 47 SF (about $31.30 US)
Credit cards: AMEX, MC, VISA
Beds: 52
Private/family rooms: No
Kitchen available: Yes
Season: March 1–October 31
Office hours: 7:30 to 10:00 A.M.; 5:00 to 10:00 P.M.
Affiliation: Hostelling International
Extras: Bike rentals, breakfast, meals ($)

A little stone-towered "castle"—well, sorta, but actually a pretty sixteenth-century chalet—this one comes with pleasant scenery that might cancel out the cattlelike effect of sleeping in bigger dorm rooms.

There are two parts, a main building and an annex, both equally comfortable beneath nice trees. They rent bikes, serve breakfast and meals, and enforce the usual rules of German Switzerland. The dorms all have eight to twelve beds, though, a minus in our view. Still, it's a decent stop for the night.

How to get there:

By bus: Call hostel for transit route.

By car: Call hostel for directions.

By train: From Brugg Station, walk 1 mile to hostel. Turn onto Sröhlibastrasse from main street, turn right, pass by hospital, come to a cross road, and see YOUTH HOSTEL sign, follow street and turn left; cross under tracks and see castle from railroad bridge. Continue to follow signs to hostel, or take taxi for 10 to 15 Swiss francs.

Best bet for a bite:
Migros close to train station

Insiders' tip:
Take a nap 'neath the trees

What hostellers say:
"Don't lock me in the dungeon!!"

Gestalt:
No-hassle castle

Hospitality:

Cleanliness:

Party index:

CHÂTEAU D'OEX HOSTEL

Les Riaux, CH-1837 Château d'Oex

Telephone Number: 026–924–6404

Fax Number: 026–924–5843
E-mail: chateau.d.oex@youthhostel.ch
Rates: 26.50 SF (about $17.70 US) per HI member; doubles 79.60 SF (about $53 US)
Credit cards: AMEX, MC, VISA
Beds: 50
Private/family rooms: No
Kitchen available: Yes
Season: December 23–October 24
Office hours: 7:30 to 10:00 A.M.; 5:00 to 10:00 P.M.
Affiliation: Hostelling International
Extras: Bike storage, breakfast, meals ($)

A two-story, flat-topped institutional type of chalet beneath towering hills, this one's hard to get to but possibly worth it. You can take a panoramic train to get here—it requires a reservation and thus costs extra, but the views are great en route if it's not a rainy day.

Dorms are four-to-eight-bedded. They serve breakfast and meals here, as usual in this part of the country, and the chief attractions are biking the

Best bet for a bite:
Co-op supermarket

Gestalt:
Oex marks the spot

Hospitality:

Cleanliness:

Party index:

back roads or skiing the hills in winter. Another hospitable, well-run place in the middle of nowhere.

How to get there:

By bus: From Château d'Oex bus stop, walk ½ mile to hostel.

By car: Call hostel for directions.

By train: Call hostel for transit route.

DELÉMONT HOSTEL

Route de Bâle 185, CH-2800 Delémont

Telephone Number: 032–422–2054

Fax Number: 032–422–8830
E-mail: delemont@youthhostel.ch
Rates: 24.50–49.00 SF (about $16.30–$32.65 US) per HI member; doubles 69.40 SF (about $46.25 US)
Credit cards: AMEX, MC, VISA
Beds: 80
Private/family rooms: Yes
Single rooms: Yes
Kitchen available: Yes
Season: March 6–November 1
Office hours: 7:30 to 10:00 A.M.; 5:00 to 9:00 P.M.
Affiliation: Hostelling International
Extras: Meeting room, bike storage, breakfast, meals ($), laundry

This place, just two simple buildings in evergreen woods, is maybe a cut above the usual rural Swiss hostel. Of course that means it will probably be hosting a huge gaggle of kids when you get here, but it's worth a stop if you're kicking around this corner of the country.

Best bet for a bite:
Migros or Co-op supermarkets in town

What hostellers say:
"Nice management."

Gestalt:
Full Delémonty

Hospitality:

Cleanliness:

Party index:

Dorms contain two to ten beds apiece, and they're nicer than they have to be—not hotel-nice, but what did you expect? They do meals, breakfast for free, let you stash your bike in the hostel if you've brought one, and maintain a conference room, too. Also, they've got a kitchen—something the vast majority of "official" Swiss hostels lack utterly.

Friendly and good.

How to get there:

By bus: Take bus to Morépont and walk ¼ mile to hostel.

By car: Follow the Route de Bâle; hostel is on the left.

By train: From Delémont Station; walk fifteen minutes to hostel.

FRIBOURG HOSTEL

2 rue de l'Hôpital, CH-1700 Fribourg
Telephone Number: 026–323–1916

Fax Number: 026–323–1940
E-mail: fribourg@youthhostel.ch
Rates: 25.50–46.00 SF (about $17.00–$30.60 US) per HI member; doubles 78.50 SF (about $52.30 US)
Credit cards: No
Beds: 90
Private/family rooms: Yes
Single rooms: Yes
Kitchen available: Yes
Season: February 26–November 1
Office hours: 7:30 to 9:30 A.M.; 6:00 to 10:00 P.M.
Curfew: 10:00 P.M.
Affiliation: Hostelling International
Extras: Bike storage, breakfast, meals ($), laundry, lockers

Hard to get excited about a place that looks a bit like a bomb shelter (and apparently was one at one time), but Fribourg tries. The white three-story structure is undeniably hospital-like from the outside, set at least in grounds with nice topiary work around. And you've gotta hand this to the place: It is certainly well placed near the city's university, train station, and amazing old town—one of Europe's best, say some.

Groups descend en masse in summertime, so book ahead! Dorms are six-bedded, mostly, nothing special at all. The laundry's a big boon, though, as are lockers, meals, breakfast and a place to store bicycles.

As we've already said, the old town is a spectacular little walk. Founded back in 1157 on a cliff above the Sarine River, its most impressive feature is St. Nicholas Cathedral's tower. Tiled roofs, pieces of old city walls, bridges spanning the river—all combine to give that medieval flavor you've been seeking ever since you got to Europe. Climb the cathedral (inside, of course), check out the monasteries, and make time for the tremendous art museum.

Best bet for a bite:
La Placette

Insiders' tip:
Check out art museum

Gestalt:
French Fribourg

Hospitality:

Cleanliness:

Party index:

How to get there:

By bus: Call hostel for transit route.
By car: Call hostel for directions.
By train: From Fribourg Station, turn left and cross avenue de Tivoli; continue to de Criblet, turn left, and walk ¼ mile to hostel.

GENEVA

Set beside a pretty lake, with a decent climate and views of the Alps on a very clear day, Geneva's got some serious advantages when you're considering a travel itinerary. It's very close to France if you're going to or coming from that way. And this city lets its hair down in a way that no other place in Austria or Switzerland, except maybe Vienna, quite does.

That alone makes it worth a stop. And despite its position way over at one edge of the country, superb transportation connections mean that you can be in Paris, Zürich, or Italy within a little more than half a day.

Getting around is very easy, thanks to a comprehensive network of buses and, especially, streetcars (also called trams) that wind through the alleys, boulevards, hills, and streets. As a bonus, a SwissRail pass will get you free rides on all of 'em. Clear maps of all routes are posted at each stand, and you're never far from one.

Eating and going out to clubs at night are two of the joys of being here. Some tourists want to catch boats and cruise around the lake; that's fine, particularly on a sunny day, but we found the mélange of cultures that have gathered here—most of them speaking French—so interesting that we never got far away. Clubs and bars are numerous, ranging from Anglo to African to Euro-pop in feel. Restaurants, well, there are so many that we can't begin to describe the options. Just know that most are good; the French insistence on quality eats has shaped the town's culinary habits.

An expensive city to eat and play in, sure, but so's all of Switzerland—and this is probably the best food town in the country. So enjoy yourself.

GENEVA HOSTELS at a glance

	RATING	PRICE	IN A WORD	PAGE
Nouvelle Auberge de Jeunesse	👍👍	24.50 SF	classy	p.219
City Hostel Geneva	👍	24–50 SF	central	p.217
Forget Me Not Hostel	👍👎	45 SF	shabby	p.218

CITY HOSTEL GENEVA

2 rue Ferrier, CH-1202 Geneva

Telephone Number: 022–901–1500

Fax Number: 022–901–1560
E-mail: info@cityhostel.ch
Rates: 24–50 SF (about $18–$35 US) per person;
doubles 75–82 SF (about $50–$55 US)
Credit cards: No
Beds: 98
Private/family rooms: Yes
Kitchen available: Yes
Season: Open year-round
Office hours: 8:00 A.M. to noon; 3:00 to 10:00 P.M.
Affiliation: Swiss Backpackers
Extras: Internet access, parking ($), currency exchange, lockers,
TV, book exchange

This newest entry in the Geneva hostelling sweepstakes is already getting decent reviews for friendly management, a very central location, and affordable pricing. They're still working out some growing pains, though, so be patient if your reservation gets lost or something similar happens.

The place is open twenty-four hours, with no curfew or lockout, yet it doesn't party all night like many independent big-city hostels do. Dormitories here come in various sizes, but none is too, too big; they range from a cheaper three-or-four-bedded room to shared doubles, private doubles (more expensive ones have private bathrooms and television sets in them), and even some single rooms. No matter what you pay, there are always sinks in the rooms and lockers in the halls. On the other hand, these are not the most spacious rooms we've ever seen. Try to get out. A lot.

There's no included breakfast or laundry at the hostel, but there is a laundromat around the corner—and tons of eating options almost right outside your door in an interesting ethnic neighborhood. Some are described on the hostel's comprehensive bulletin board guide to local eats. We also liked the fact that the place claims to invest a small percentage of its profits in a local nonprofit that brings disadvantaged youth to the city. The non-smoking policy (inside) was even better. Other extras include a currency exchange at the front desk, parking in a private lot, and four

Best bet for a bite:
Any produce market (ask the staff)

What hostellers say:
"Good new place."

Gestalt:
Swiss please

Hospitality:

Cleanliness:

Party index:

Internet terminals for e-mailing the latest on Switzerland back home.

How to get there:

By bus: Contact hostel for transit details.

By car: Contact hostel for directions.

By train: From Cornavin Station, exit and make an immediate left onto big rue de Lausanne. Walk ¼ mile to rue Prieure, turn left, and continue to rue Ferrier on right.

FORGET ME NOT HOSTEL

8 rue Vignier, CH-1205 Geneva

Telephone Number: 022–320–9355

Fax Number: 022–781–4645
Rates: 45 SF (about $30 US) per person; doubles 90 SF (about $60 US)
Credit cards: No
Beds: 88
Private/family rooms: Yes
Kitchen available: Yes
Office hours: 9:00 A.M. to 8:00 P.M.
Affiliation: None
Extras: Laundry, lockers

It's always a bad sign when a hostel has weekly rates . . . but this one has *monthly* rates. As soon as you hear that, you know who's going to show up here—the local unemployed, scraggly students, and the occasional bewildered backpacker who blundered in here late one night on the recommendation of some student guidebook. And so they do.

OK, back to basics. This place in the hip Plainpalais student district of Geneva, across the bridge and a ways from the train station, has only singles, doubles, and cramped quads. Each room does have a bit of furniture—usually a desk to write at. It's basically a student-dorm tower.

Sure there are great views from the terraces and rooftops—but the kitchens on each floor were scummy and furniture and carpets were worn. Though the pictures in this hostel's slick brochure look really nice, the words "beat up" apply in spades to the real thing—these floors and beds have seen much better days.

Good stuff? The single rooms are the best ones, although they're also the priciest; they do your laundry for a

Best bet for a bite:
Numerous in Pleinpalais

Insiders' tip:
Flea markets in the square

What hostellers say:
"Not quite what I expected."

Gestalt:
Forget it

Hospitality:

Cleanliness:

Party index:

fee; and there are common study rooms on each floor in addition to the tiny kitchen we mentioned earlier. The breakfast room is nice, too.

One undeniable plus, though, is the youthful and happenin' neighborhood the place is set in. Pleinpalais and the adjacent Carouge area are the city's university hangout, with loads of cheap eateries, cheap and expensive shops, nightlife, and such. Mornings are even fun, too, with a wild outdoor market right below the hostel and a produce market in the same square twice a week.

But buyer beware. The brochure claiming that it's five minutes from Central Station is a cruel joke; it takes quite a bit longer. And once you're here, you might not like what you find.

How to get there:

By bus: From train station, take #12 or #13 tram to Rondeau de Plainpalais stop; turn down rue Vignier. Hostel is at end, on right. Or take #4 or #44 bus to Plainpalais stop and walk 100 yards to hostel.

By car: Call hostel for directions.

By train: From train station, take #12 or #13 tram to Rondeau de Plainpalais stop; turn down rue Vignier. Hostel is at end, on right. Or take #4 or #44 bus to Plainpalais stop and walk 100 yards to hostel.

NOUVELLE AUBERGE DE JEUNESSE

(New Geneva Hostel)

30 rue Rothschild, CH-1202 Geneva

Telephone Number: 022–732–6260

Fax Number: 022–738–3987
E-mail: booking@yh-geneva.ch
Rates: 24.50 SF (about $17 US) per HI member; doubles 76.50 SF (about $51 US)
Credit cards: MC, VISA
Beds: 350
Private/family rooms: Yes
Kitchen available: Yes
Office hours: 6:30 to 10:00 A.M.; 2:00 P.M. to 1:00 A.M (June–September); 6:30 to 10:00 A.M.; 4:00 P.M. to midnight (October–May)
Lockout: 10:00 A.M. to 4:00 P.M.
Affiliation: Hostelling International
Extras: Breakfast, meals ($), TV, laundry, Internet access

A classier place you'd be hard pressed to find. Add in this hostel's decent location and its modern facilities, and you've got a real winner—one that actually cares about travelers' needs.

The entrance area is typical of French-style hostelling—it's cavernous and dedicated to a variety of activities. One part's been sectioned off to form a "bistro" (read: cafeteria); another, the laundry room; there's a television somewhere in there and, finally, the hosteller kitchen. Though you have to figure out the weird system for using these things—it costs a "token," which you buy from the hostel desk, to cook for forty-five minutes and three tokens to do laundry—it all actually works quite well once you deduce that you're supposed to put tokens and not money into the machines. Lots of people had trouble with this operation, not surprising since instructions were variously printed in German, French, Italian, or English.

It's a six-stage building, which actually means eight floors in American terms: a ground floor, six floors above that, and a basement. The rooms are upstairs, and the doubles here are real stunners—two single bunks, a bathroom, a closet, and a concrete balcony overlooking the lake and mountains. Whoever designed these was really thinking.

Dorm rooms aren't bad, either, divided mostly into six-bedded rooms with bathrooms and sinks. The laundry is unusually good, containing multiple washers and dryers, and the kitchen has a long table and enough burners to accommodate up to four or five folks at once. The reception staff get very busy but somehow usually manage to keep any cynicism in check and get the job done quite efficiently.

The hostel neighborhood is ethnically diverse, meaning that you can nibble kebabs, cruise the Internet, and buy great French bread—all within half a block. You can also walk a block and sun by huge Lake Leman, one of the prettiest we've seen; that's big Mont Blanc looming way off in the distance, while vineyards and France cover the opposite shore. On the way, stroll past the UN's European headquarters, just a stone's throw away in Wilson Palace. (The guy with the Uzi and the earpiece guarding the entrance won't joke around with you. Don't even try.)

For eats you've got a wealth of choice. Back toward the station, in just ten minutes we found a superific Swiss grocery store, a daily produce market, an Italian grocer, and a hole-in-the-wall veggie joint. (Since this is basically France, people were smoking inside while they ate the health food!) Penetrating farther into the old city, we located lots of cafes where people sipped coffee or mineral water and ate pastries, a popular pasttime around here.

How to get there:

By bus: Take #1 bus to Wilson Place, then walk less than 50 yards to hostel.

Best bet for a bite:
Public Market, rue de Coutance

Insiders' tip:
Free bikes available on waterfront

What hostellers say:
"C'est beau!"

Gestalt:
Geneva pool

Safety: 👍

Hospitality: 👍

Cleanliness: 👍

Party index:

By car: Call hostel for directions.

By train: From front of Geneva Station, turn left and walk down rue de Lausanne less than ½ mile. Turn right at hostel sign down AMAT Street, then left at next sign to hostel on corner of rue Rothschild.

MOUNTAIN HOSTEL

CH-3826 Gimmelwald

Telephone Number: 033–855–1704

Rates: 17 SF per person (about $11.50 US)
Credit cards: No
Beds: 50
Private/family rooms: No
Kitchen available: Yes
Office hours: 8:30 to 11:00 A.M.; 5:30 to 10:30 P.M.
Lockout: 9:30 to 11:00 A.M.
Affiliation: None
Extras: Food store, travel store, patio, Internet access, showers ($)

It certainly takes quite a bit of effort to get here; either brave a gondola ride or funicular train or attempt the steep walking trails on your own steam. You'll find a pleasant, though somewhat rustic, hostel with loads of Europe Through the Back Door–worshipping American college students and guitar noodlers.

The hostel is pretty much a DIY (do-it-yourself) affair. If you show up looking for a bed while reception is closed, you'll have to put your name on a list; otherwise you may lose out. Backpackers have no real storage area other than the indoor common space that also doubles as a dining room, but it works out. Dorms contain six to fifteen beds apiece, and are just simple wooden beds— homey with stunning views, but not real spacious.

Toilets and showers are coed, and the friendly owners have made sure there's never a TP shortage; about fifteen rolls of recycled TP were lined up when we popped in, eliminating the need to ask your neighbor if he/she can spare a square. However, the showers here cost you— and can run out of hot water quickly at times.

Unlike many of the HI hostels, there is a kitchen for use here, and you can fill your sack with the surprisingly well-stocked Co-op store in

Best bet for a bite:
Mürren Co-op

Insiders' tip:
Late spring is nice

What hostellers say:
"Ain't no mountain high enough . . ."

Gestalt:
Rocky mountain high

Hospitality:

Cleanliness:

Safety:

Party index:

Mürren before you begin the thirty-minute descent to Gimmelwald. However, we recommend also stopping at one of the first buildings you'll encounter in town, which has, among other things, a farm store featuring locally made products like yogurt, cheese, cream cheese, and sausage. People tend to cook meals together here, just as it should be. The back deck is the most popular place, with the best view we've ever seen at a hostel.

One drawback: The place seems to draw almost 100 percent Americans, and they hang around on the deck a lot doing nothing. You feel like slapping some of these guys around and saying, "Hey! There's a mountain over there!" But no. It's another beer, another nap, dude.

Oh, well. You're still sure to find a hiking buddy here, and there are loads of trails in the area, ranging from easy to difficult. You may tire of lame American college-isms and the constant presence of Back Door pilgrims. But you'll never find a better view from a hostel porch.

How to get there:

By bus: Call hostel for transit route.

By car: Drive to Stechelberg and park at lift station; take lift to Mürren, then walk down to Gimmelwald (thirty minutes).

By train: Call hostel for transit route.

SCHLAF IM STROH

(Sleep in Straw Hostel)

Chilchstatt, CH-3826 Gimmelwald

Telephone Number: 033–855–5488

Fax Number: 033–855–5492
E-mail: evallmen@bluewin.ch
Rates: 20 SF (about $13.30 US) per person
Credit cards: No
Beds: 15–20; varies
Private/family rooms: No
Kitchen available: No
Season: June 20–October 10; contact hostel for current season
Office hours: Be reasonable
Affiliation: None
Extras: Straw, breakfast

This place is unique, run by a sweet, hardworking local family that makes yogurt and other products up top of a high ridge with just incredible views. It's just down the street from a much more popular hostel in Gimmelwald, but this one's an equally good bet—*if* you don't mind sleeping in straw.

That's right. You get real familiar with a cow's life here, sleeping on the floor of a barn that becomes a hostel when the cows go home. OK, actually they're taken over to Mürren to graze on the sweet summertime grass. But you get the picture. It's supersimple, no-frills, and absolutely fun. Remember that you bring the sleeping bags, pads, whatever you need to be comfortable.

Bathrooms are in the handsome family home, and the views are the ultimate. A little musty, perhaps, but authentically rural and Alpine, and quite hygienic. The proprietors couldn't be sweeter, either. Signing e-mails with "sunny greetings from the Swiss Alps," they ask only that you contact them ahead of showing up so that they can find you room in the straw.

Best bet for a bite:
Esther's yogurt

Insiders' tip:
Hike down to the valley

What hostellers say:
"So rustic! Loved it!"

Gestalt:
Moo juice

Hospitality:

Cleanliness:

Party index:

How to get there:

By bus: Call hostel for transit route.

By car: Drive to Stechelberg, park at lift station and take lift (7.40 SF/about $5.00 US) to Mürren, then walk down to Gimmelwald (thirty minutes).

By train: Call hostel for transit route.

GRINDELWALD HOSTEL

Weid 12, Terrassenweg, CH-3818 Grindelwald

Telephone Number: 033–853–1009

Fax Number: 033–853–5029
E-mail: grindelwald@youthhostel.ch
Rates: 26.30–34.80 SF (about $17.50–$23.00 US) per HI member; doubles 100 SF (about $66.70 US)
Credit cards: Yes
Beds: 123
Private/family rooms: Yes
Kitchen available: No
Season: Mid-December–mid-April; May 23–end October
Office hours: 6:30 to 9:30 A.M.; 3:00 to 11:00 P.M. Monday through Saturday; 6:30 to 9:30 A.M.; 5:00 to 11:00 P.M. Sunday
Affiliation: Hostelling International
Extras: Breakfast, meals ($), garden, playground, TV, library, laundry, lockers, table tennis, Internet access

Word to the wise: First, do *not* bring much luggage to this place unless you like back-breaking walks or splurging for public transportation. The hostel's perched on the edge of a green hillside facing the awesome face of the Eiger Mountain, but to get there from the train station you've gotta climb almost straight up—and then you're likely to get lost because the signage is just plain terrible.

Once here, though, the fantastic views and amiable sheep lurking about (and a pig, we hear, very soon) just might entice you to stay awhile.

Recently installed solar panels on the roof, plus lots of windows, mean the sun is used to the max here—when it's shining, that is. The rustic main building has mostly four-bedded rooms and is the most sociable, with dining and common spaces seeing lots of foot traffic; balconies here are also at a premium and have outstanding views. The common area features a fireplace, game room, hostel guitar, foosball, and table tennis. There's a laundry (though the balky dryer doesn't always work) down in the basement, plus good storage lockers also downstairs for stashing your stuff.

Best bet for a bite:
Hearty meals at hostel

Insiders' tip:
Drying room free

What hostellers say:
"Baa."

Gestalt:
Hill of a hike

Hospitality:

Cleanliness:

Party index:

The annex building is more boring, without the Eiger views, but up-close contact with the sheep made a nice side benefit and the clanking of their bells lulled us to sleep in a jiffy. (A slide connects the two buildings, by the way; you'll have to see what we mean.) That building's all quads, except for two doubles with private bathrooms. You get into all the hostel rooms using a weird paper-key system we've never seen before.

The rooms themselves are okay, and recent renovations have made them even better. Some quad rooms even have amazing—and we mean amazing—views of the face of the Eiger. If it's a clear day, you'll get a view you'd gladly pay a million dollars for. You need only spring for a handful of francs instead. The upstairs dorms of the main building do get a bit cramped because of low ceilings and a large number of beds, but groups traveling together didn't seem to mind a bit.

The staff will sell you a few essentials like chocolate, beer, wine, and expensive bottles of the local water that they bottle and put fizz into—not as good as true bottled waters, in our opinion, but a cute (if heavy) glass souvenir of your trip. Staff are erratic, sometimes ultrahelpful and sometimes irksome.

The place doesn't have a kitchen but does offer an extremely rib-sticking dinner each night. The breakfast, which is free with your bed, is the real star here—a buffet of all-you-can-eat yogurt, good cereal, great bread (get us that recipe!), cheese, and other healthful stuff for a change. Mountain flowers grace the tables, too. They admonish you not to fill your pockets up for lunchtime but otherwise leave you alone during the day's first meal. It's a good way to start a hard day of Oberland sight-see-ing and/or hiking.

As we said before, spend the extra 3.00 SF (about $2.00 US) for the bus ride on the orange or purple lines to the hostel (it's at the stop called "Gaggi"). You'll thank us later when you still have the energy left to do some hiking.

Only drawback? Lots and lots of American guests. Like, you know what we mean??

Grindelwald itself is freely accessible to cars and as a result looks awfully overdeveloped. You're not gonna hang around here if you can help it; although when rain socks in the valley, there's little else to do. If the weather's good, though, there are a million and one places to hike, bike, sightsee, and more in the area.

How to get there:

By bus: From Grindelwald Station, take #4 bus toward Terrassenweg to Gaggi Säge stop and walk downhill about 50 yards to hostel on left. Or walk ¾ mile to hostel.

By train: From Interlaken-Ost Station, take train to Grindelwald Station. Then take #4 bus (bus station across the street and to the left of station) toward Terrassenweg to Gaggi Säge stop and walk about 50 yards downhill to hostel on left.

MOUNTAIN HOSTEL

Grund, CH-3818 Grindelwald

Telephone Number: 033–853–3900

Fax Number: 033–853–4730
E-mail: mhostel@grindelwald.ch
Rates: 32 SF (about $21 US) per person; doubles 84 SF (about $56 US)
Credit cards: Yes
Beds: 120
Private/family rooms: Yes
Kitchen available: Sort of ($)
Office hours: Twenty-four hours
Affiliation: Swiss Backpackers
Extras: Table tennis, pool table, Internet access, TV, breakfast, lockers, laundry, meals ($), bike rentals

This extremely blue hostel with cool murals painted on its back has an odd name, considering that it's actually down in a valley and not on top of a mountain. On the other hand, it's snuggled right up to the foot of the huge Eiger Mountain, giving it one of the most amaz-ing views of any hostel in Europe. Hmmm. Guess the name does make sense after all.

A clean and efficient place, it could use a little help in the hospitality department. But there's no denying it's comfortably furnished, starting with a huge open lounge outfitted with table tennis, foosball, a television, a pool table, and some cool snaky couches to lounge around (or even snooze) on. There's one Internet terminal for getting your e-mail, too, and you can do laundry for a charge.

Rooms come in doubles and three-, four-, and six-bedded rooms, nothing special but they're fine, each with lockers inside; the triples were kinda squeezed-in tight, we noticed. Hallways are extremely wide and extremely blue (just like the outside).

Best bet for a bite:
Grund train station
restaurant

What hostellers say:
"Look at that freakin'
mountain!"

Gestalt:
Déjà view

Hospitality:

Cleanliness:

Party index:

The kitchen out back is a little odd, requiring 50-centime coins to get cooking. And it's outside—we mean literally outside—which could be daunting if it's cold. Since it basically consists of two hot plates, a tiny fridge, an ancient wood-fired grill, and some picnic tables under an awning, it's really suitable only for pasta or cookouts anyway. At least the kitchen is located next to a pretty rushing river, with the requisite Swiss cows grazing peacefully away as though posed for snapshots.

To get here from Grindelwald Station, be prepared for a twenty-minute downhill hike with your stuff. One alternative—especially for the trip up, when you're in a hurry—is to buy a ticket on the Jungfraubahn railroad and go from Grund Station just up the street to the main station. The ride takes a couple minutes, and the 3.00 Swiss franc (about $2.00 US) fare is a rip-off in our view, but it'll save you a half-hour of huffing and puffing.

Look for the blue building with the buses in front. That's right. Buses. They get lots and lots of groups here, so there's always one parked out front. But this is one of the hipper hostels in Switzerland, and for that alone—some personality—it deserves a close look.

How to get there:

By bus: From Grindelwald Station, take blue-line city bus (3.80 SF/about $2.50 US) to Grund Station stop and walk back uphill toward town about 100 yards to hostel on left.

By car: From Interlaken, drive up to Grindelwald and turn right off main road at sign for Grund Station. Hostel is on right, just before station.

By train: From Grindelwald Station, walk into town and follow signs downhill 1 mile to Grund Station; hostel is on right, just before station. Or take train (3.80 SF/about $2.50 US) one stop to Grund Station and walk back uphill toward town about 100 yards to hostel on left.

SWISS ALPS RETREAT HOSTEL

Chalet Martin

CH-1882 Gryon

Telephone Number: 024–498–3321

Fax Number: 024–498–3531
E-mail: chaletmartin@yahoo.com
Rates: 25–28 SF (about $17–$19 US) per person
Credit cards: No
Beds: Number varies
Private/family rooms: Yes
Kitchen available: Yes
Office hours: 9:00 A.M. to 9:00 P.M.
Affiliation: None
Extras: Fireplace, grill, rental discounts, Internet access, TV, VCR, movie rentals

You can't miss the flyers for this place; we ran into them all over Europe, and we mean *every*where—from Munich to London and back. The real thing is good, but we still gotta wonder how they cover so much ground with those flyers . . . we're expecting to see 'em the next time we hit Antarctica.

Owners Robyn and Bertrand Kohli have done a fun job with the place, outfitting it with a barbecue, fireplace, Internet terminal, and television lounge; they rent movies for use with the VCR, offer discounts on ski rentals, and have a very liberal checkout policy.

Gryon's a pretty little town of terraced streets way up in the hills, nice for kicking back. It takes some doing to get here, but it's worth it.

Best bet for a bite:
Throw something on the grill

Insiders' tip:
Flyers make good scrap paper

What hostellers say:
"Okay, we're here already!"

Gestalt:
Frequent flyers

Hospitality:

Cleanliness:

Party index:

How to get there:

By bus: Call hostel for transit route.
By car: Call hostel for transit route.
By train: From Lausanne, take SBB train toward Brig to Bex; at Bex, change to cog rail train and continue to Gryon. From Gryon Station, walk up main road and follow BACKPACKER signs to hostel.

INTERLAKEN

Yes, Interlaken has sold its soul to tourism. But if you poke around enough, you can actually find neat wooden houses with lots of trees and vines, an antidote to the rampant package-tour crowd that storms the downtown on a daily basis.

Being a town in a valley beneath major-sized peaks, it has become something of a supply depot and way station to travelers heading up to or coming down off the stupendous heights. Package tourists like it here because it's completely flat and unchallenging. You'll like the fact that it has actual nightlife and restaurants, unlike the poorer options as you ascend. But if you're hoping to get away from it all, this is *not* the place to spend the night.

Our advice? Get ahold of a schedule and map for the Bernese Oberland Regional Pass, which gives discounts on all the local lifts and small trains and cable cars, then head up to the big scenery.

If you are staying the night down in Interlaken, the half-dozen hostels here range from the notorious (Balmer's) to the should-be-famous (Backpackers Villa) to the downright strange (Heidi's). A couple other choices, each of them with a distinctive personality, fill out the bill. Almost all are adequate, and all are a short walk from Interlaken's two train stations. Hooray to that, for once, we say.

INTERLAKEN HOSTELS at a glance

	RATING	PRICE	IN A WORD	PAGE
Backpackers Sonnehof	👍👍	29–34 SF	outstanding	p.229
HI-Bönigen	👍	25.50 SF	sedate	p.232
Happy Inn Lodge	👍👎	20–39 SF	beery	p.233
Balmer's	👍👎	19–28 SF	mayhem	p.230
Heidi's	👍👎	20–60 SF	musty	p.234

BACKPACKERS VILLA SONNEHOF

Alpenstrasse 16, CH-3800 Interlaken

Telephone Number: 033–826–7171

Fax Number: 033–826–7172
E-mail: backpackers@villa.ch
Rates: 29–34 SF (about $19–$23 US) per person;
doubles 82–92 SF (about $55–$61)
Credit cards: MC, VISA, AMEX
Beds: 70
Private/family rooms: Yes
Kitchen available: Yes
Office hours: 7:45 to 11:00 A.M.; 4:00 to 9:00 P.M.
Affiliation: Swiss Backpackers
Extras: Lockers, Internet access, breakfast, store, table tennis, laundry, tours, garden, foosball, shuttle, swing set, TV, tennis, grill, patio, bike rentals ($)

With cheesy mottos like "the only villa *you* can afford" and "the cheapest way to get Swiss quality," this new place might seem at first glance like just another cash-cow warehouse—one of many in trendy Interlaken. Take another look, though, folks, because in our view this one's the best hostel in town. Easily.

A former rest home for elderly folks and now run by a Methodist church group (but don't let that scare ya), it's set on a beautiful little pocket of green property. You've got views of the fabulous Jungfrau, and you're right across the street from a pretty park. It's right between the town's two train stations, too.

The place is beautifully decked out and kept very clean. Up neat granite steps, the dorms are good, not too big, with two to six beds apiece; some of the six-bedded rooms are a little tight, but otherwise everything's good. These dorms feature extra high bunks, reading lights, nightstands, and killer views. They also contain an interesting type of locally built flip-up pine locker that can fit an entire frame backpack, a real plus.

The four private rooms with quilts, double beds (not two twins shoved together), and sinks are just stellar. There's a stone patio for grilling and a backyard with a swing set; a decent TV lounge that gets CNN; a game room with pool table, foosball, and table tennis; and an Internet access area with a growing number of terminals. The most unique feature, however, is an upstairs "meditation room" where you can bliss out, read, nap, or think. The Christian message is available in

Best bet for a bite:
Supermarket near station

Insiders' tip:
Use that kitchen

What hostellers say:
"Fantastic and quiet."

Gestalt:
Park place

Hospitality:

Cleanliness:

Party index:

leaflets, but it's not pushed on you at all—honest. There are few rules.

Other perks at this great place include a van shuttle around town, free showers, a tennis court, and a small but good common area that opens onto the outside. The front desk runs a small store selling Toblerone, hardtack, pasta meals, and suntan lotion. (They'll also book you with any adventure tour in town if you want.) The breakfast room has a tape and CD player for tunification. Towels, sheets, and lockers are free. And there's a laundry, plus an outstanding kitchen with two big stovetops, three sinks, and a breakfast of bread and milk included for free.

In a town stuffed full with hostels, most of them only barely acceptable, this place stands head and shoulders above the pack. Make it your first call before you get to town.

How to get there:

By bus: Call hostel for transit route.

By car: Call hostel for directions.

By train: With back to Interlaken Ost (east) Station, turn right and walk up main road ½ mile into town. Turn left at front corner of park and walk 2 blocks to hostel on left.

BALMER'S HERBERGE

23–25 Hauptstrasse, CH-3800 Matten (Interlaken)

Telephone Number: 033–822–1961

Fax Number: 033–823–3261
E-mail: balmers@tcnet.ch
Rates: 19–28 SF (about $13–$20 US) per person; doubles 56–70 SF (about $39–$49 US)
Credit cards: MC, VISA, AMEX
Beds: 400
Private/family rooms: Yes
Kitchen available: Yes ($)
Office hours: 6:30 A.M. to 11:00 P.M. (summer); 6:30 to 9:00 A.M.; 4:30 to 11:00 P.M. (winter)
Affiliation: None
Extras: Bar, restaurant ($), rip-off store, outings, tours, shuttle, TV, laundry, lockers, breakfast, Internet access, table tennis, currency exchange, bike rentals, shuttle, movies, library, ski passes, jukebox, library, hammocks, showers ($)

See it here, see it now, see it all: the sad state of American youth on parade for the amused Swiss locals. Yeah, it's Balmer's, the place you've heard about everywhere—and if you're the beer-swigging, gotta-get-laid kind of hosteller, then you're ripping this book to shreds right now. If you're a normal human being, however, sit back down in your seat and read on. We'll give you the skinny—good, bad, and very ugly.

Balmer's is a one-of-a-kind concept, an American enclave nestled in one of Europe's most beautiful places.

But you don't come here to see the scenery, unless it's during one of the (Balmer's-sponsored) rafting, hiking, gliding, or other adventure tours. (About those adventure tours, in view of the tragedy that involved eighteen deaths during a canyoning expedition, you really better think twice about trusting your survival to complete strangers.) Instead you'll want to buy a souvenir—the Balmer's store will sell it to you, at a jacked-up price. And get bombed: Beer is cheaper here than anywhere else in Switzerland, probably, and it's consumed in huge quantity by college kids flashing mommy and daddy's credit cards. We noted more than a few young hostellers wandering around dazed and drunk, ordering more beer . . . and this was only 2:00 in the afternoon. Geeeez.

Anyway, let's try to find the good in this. The beds weren't completely terrible, and some hostellers we talked to actually liked 'em; comforters and blankets come free, surprisingly. Other beds resembled cots, though, painful on the back. The dorm rooms contain anywhere from two to twenty of these good-or-bad beds, none with their own bathrooms of course, and then there's the notorious tent (in a different location in town)—in a field, kinda like camping uncomfortably close to about a hundred other smelly people you may or may not like. There is a bathroom, at least.

Best bet for a bite:
Co-op supermarket nearby

Insiders' tip:
Use protection

What hostellers say:
"Dude, where's the bar?"

Gestalt:
Pit party

Hospitality: 👎

Cleanliness: 👎

Party index:

The common facilities are nothing short of awe-inspiring: movies, beer, TV, beer, Internet access, beer, library, bike rentals, beer. The list goes on in similar fashion. Supposedly they sell no beer after 10:00 P.M. (hmmm . . .), and supposedly everyone is shooed inside at midnight to appease the neighbors.

What else? Showers cost, like everything else you can do here, and they don't take reservations—you've just gotta show up. There's open-air luggage storage (a huge backpack graveyard, really), which raises questions about security since nobody's really watching. Almost 100 percent of the clients are from the United States or Japan, it seemed to us, so you won't learn much about European culture here.

You might wake up next to someone you don't know, however.

How to get there:

By car: Call hostel for directions.

By train: From Interlaken West Station, turn left and walk along main street to traffic circle; turn right and follow signs to hostel. From Interlaken Ost Station, walk straight out of the station to the traffic light; continue through to traffic circle and follow signs to hostel.

BÖNIGEN BEI INTERLAKEN HOSTEL

Aareweg 21, am See, CH-3806 Bönigen (Interlaken)

Telephone Number: 033–822–4353

Fax Number: 033–823–2058
E-mail: boenigen@youthhostel.ch
Rates: 25.50 SF (about $17 US) per HI member;
doubles 78.40 SF (about $52 US)
Credit cards: Yes
Beds: 150
Private/family rooms: Yes
Kitchen available: Yes
Season: January 23–November 13; December 18–January 9
Office hours: 7:00 to 10:00 A.M.; 2:00 to 11:30 P.M. (summer);
7:30 to 9:30 A.M.; 4:00 to 11:00 P.M. (winter)
Affiliation: Hostelling International
Extras: Bike rentals, bike storage, breakfast, meals ($), TV, lockers, laundry, library, tourist information, garden, playground, table tennis, volleyball, badminton, snack shop

Not exactly in Interlaken but not far away at all—like a half-hour walk at most, on the shores of a lake, this is a decent pick for people who want to get away from the madding Japanese crowds or the boozing Americans. Backpackers might also enjoy the quiet, though they will probably hate the rules and the oversize dorms. At least it's clean . . .

Best bet for a bite:
Stock up at Migros near Ost

Insiders' tip:
Try two-wheelin' the Aare bike path

What hostellers say:
"I've been Bönigen!"

Gestalt:
Land o' lakes

Hospitality:

Cleanliness:

Party index:

The hostel occupies two buildings in a field beneath majestic mountains and just beside that lake we mentioned. Dorms are divided into four quads, four six-bedded dorms, and a few larger ones as well. As in *huge*—seventeen to twenty-five beds apiece! You could get lost in there, and don't count on a quiet sleep.

They try to make up for this fault with lots of amenities: bikes and skis for rent (it's directly on the Aare bike path that runs to Koblenz, Germany), lockers, meals, a breakfast, a game room, and, of course, the lovely views. They even have a children's playroom on premises.

Bönigen itself is small and quiet, but the wood carvings on the local houses are actually quite nice. Inquire at the tourism office or the hostel for details about when to take tours of these houses, which are open to visitors only in the summertime. Also hit the beach on Brienzersee lake just a couple hundred yards away.

How to get there:

By bus: From Interlaken, take #1 or #3 bus toward Bönigen to Lütschinenbrücke stop and walk ¼ mile toward lake to hostel.

By car: Call hostel for directions.

By train: From Interlaken Ost Station, walk 1 mile along Lake of Brienz (Brienzersee) to hostel. Or take #1 or #3 bus toward Bönigen to Lütschinenbrücke stop and walk ¼ mile toward lake to hostel. From Interlaken West Station, take #1 bus or walk ½ mile to hostel.

HAPPY INN LODGE

Rosenstrasse 17, CH-3800 Interlaken
Telephone Number: 033–822–3225

Fax Number: 033–822–3268
E-mail: happyinn@tcnet.ch
Web site: www.happy-inn.com
Rates: 20–39 SF (about $13–$26 US) per person; doubles 60–78 SF (about $40–$52 US)
Credit cards: No
Beds: 48
Private/family rooms: Yes
Single rooms: Yes
Kitchen available: No
Office hours: 6:00 A.M. to midnight
Affiliation: Swiss Backpackers
Extras: Breakfast ($), bar, meals ($), lockers, tours ($)

Attached to an interestingly decorated blues bar called Brasserie 17, this hostel is so-so but could get better over time, who knows? They made sure to keep you some personal space by not packing too many beds into each room and making the place kinda homey, so there's hope. The downside is that the place could be in better shape; it's getting worn out.

The hostel sits above a semigrungy bar where you do the check-in formalities. It's not a wild place, but you will certainly hear the noisy goings-on later at night. (They have live music every Thursday here, except in summer for some strange reason.) Anyway, you can get five local beers on tap at the bar, which is nice to know.

Dorms contain four to six metal bunk beds each, all coming with sinks and lockers, and all adequate. The views are decent, as are the bath-

Best bet for a bite:
All over town

Insiders' tip:
Bring some earplugs

What hostellers say:
"Du-u-u-u-de!"

Gestalt:
Happy daze

Hospitality:

Cleanliness:

Party index:

rooms. In fact the homey doubles are especially nice for a so-so place like this. Breakfast costs here, and they also serve meals in the bar; needless to say, you gotta pay for 'em.

The place is sandwiched between two Internet places, a definite bonus; there's no kitchen, but you've got restaurants around, and the lack of a laundy is also compensated by the proximity to a public one. There are no bikes for rent, but you can rent them right next door.

It's marginal, by our standards, but certainly acceptable if you don't mind smoke and noise—and beer.

How to get there:

By bus: Call hostel for directions.

By car: Call hostel for directions.

By train: From Interlaken West Station, make a left, then turn right onto town's main street and walk into town. At main crossroads, shortly turn right onto Rosenstrasse and continue to hostel on left.

HEIDI'S HOSTEL

Bernastrasse 37, CH-3800 Interlaken

Telephone number: 033–882–9030

Rates: 20–60 SF (about $16–$40 US) per person; doubles 60–80 SF (about $40–$53 US)
Credit cards: No
Beds: 35
Private/family rooms: Yes
Kitchen available: Sometimes
Office hours: Vary; call hostel for hours
Affiliation: None
Extras: Bike rentals, TV

Located just off a strip of gas stations and car dealerships on the edge of Interlaken, this is definitely one of the oddest hostels in normally staid Switzerland: a place where dogs feel at home and you can't book a dorm bed without paying for a complete double or quad room.

Best bet for a bite:
Back in town

What hostellers say:
"Here, doggie, doggie."

Gestalt:
Dog daze

So come with a friend and expect strangeness, or else head elsewhere in town.

The double and quad rooms—some with showers and balconies—are scattered about a small, old, fading hotel that's seen better days.

The, um, quirky proprietors are harmless, but they're not quite the usual bunch. The real Switzerland, this definitely is.

They don't serve breakfast, but they do bikes for 25 Swiss francs (about $17 US) per day; they'll sell you tour tickets and maybe invite you into their own living room, which has a TV with CNN and a Swiss sports channel. There is a laundry across the street, the owners claim; you might need it if the resident Afghan climbs onto you (unlikely, but possible). The kitchen was on the mend when we showed up—torn out is more like it, actually—but staff said they'd boil water if we needed tea. Thanks.

Hospitality:

Cleanliness:

Party index:

The owners, as we said, are harmless and in fact pretty hospitable, happy to invite you over for a pastry and a sit by the tube. But if you're looking to socialize or save money in a big dorm, this is *not* the place, as there are no dorms and no common space.

Not our first pick, as you can probably tell.

How to get there:

By bus: Call hostel for transit route.
By car: Call hostel for directions.
By train: Call hostel for transit route.

LA CHAUX-DE-FONDS HOSTEL

Rue du Doubs 34, CH-2300 La Chaux-de-Fonds
Telephone Number: 032–968–4315

Fax Number: 032–968–2518
E-mail: chaux.de.fonds@youthhostel.ch
Rates: 24.50 SF (about $16 US) per person; private rooms 63–122 SF (about $42–$81 US)
Credit cards: MC, VISA, AMEX, DISC
Beds: 80
Private/family rooms: Yes
Kitchen available: Yes
Season: January 1–November 5
Office hours: 7:30 to 9:30 A.M.; 5:00 to 10:30 P.M. (summer); 7:30 to 9:30 A.M.; 5:00 to 10:00 P.M. (winter)
Curfew: 10:00 P.M.
Affiliation: Hostelling International
Extras: Meeting room, bike storage, breakfast, meals ($), recreation room, garden, TV

Tucked in one of La Chaux's checkerboard grids of streets—unusual for Switzerland—it's a five-story place behind gates and fairly institutional. Through the front doors, you come to a foyer and then the dining room where free breakfast and meals (for a charge) are served. There's a game room and a garden beyond those.

Room setups consist of four quad rooms, half with sinks, plus six more dorms of six to eight beds each. All have lots of sunny windows, and the ground floor is wheelchair accessible.

Best bet for a bite:
Cheese farm in Les
Ponts-de-Martel

What hostellers say:
"Not bad."

Gestalt:
La Chaux must go on

Hospitality:

Cleanliness:

Party index:

Some notable folks who've lived in this watch-making capital have included the architect Le Corbusier and auto magnate Louis Chevrolet. Not bad company. For fun, hit the town's free zoo—a short walk from the hostel—or get to the peat bog reserve called Le Bois-des-Lattes.

Half an hour or so away by train from Neuchâtel, in the town of La Chaux-de-Fonds, the Time Museum (that's our rough translation) dispenses a fascinating and comprehensive history of calendars, watches, and clocks. What else did you expect from the Swiss?

How to get there:

By car: From Neuchâtel, drive through Vue-des-Alpe tunnel and continue to La Chaux-de-Fonds.

By train: From La-Chaux-de-Fonds Station, walk ½ mile to hostel. Or take #4 bus toward Hôpital (hospital) to Bois du Petit-Château or Stavay-Mollondin stops and walk ¼ mile to hostel.

By bus: From La-Chaux-de-Fonds Station, take #4 bus toward Hôpital (hospital) to Bois du Petit-Château or Stavay-Mollondin stops and walk ¼ mile to hostel.

LANGNAU HOSTEL

Mooseggstrasse 32, CH-3550 Langnau

Telephone Number: 034-402-4526

E-mail: langnau@youthhostel.ch
Rates: 14.30 SF (about $9.50 US) per HI member
Credit cards: No
Beds: 50
Private/family rooms: No
Kitchen available: Yes
Season: January 1–February 12; February 22–September 24; October 18–December 31
Office hours: 7:00 to 9:00 A.M.; 5:00 to 8:00 P.M.
Affiliation: Hostelling International

S

This place is supercheap, located in an atmospheric Swiss chalet, and very well run. What more do you want? Turn the most obvious weakness here—the simplicity—to your advantage and enjoy a hostel that, for once, doesn't so much resemble a prison as it does a country inn.

Dorms in the gabled, three-story farmhouse contain four to ten beds each and are your standard-issue deal. No, actually, they're much better than standard-issue. There are absolutely no extras here. Wait. There *is* one perk: the kitchen, a rarity anywhere in Switzerland. So cook away.

Langnau's not exactly right on your usual itinerary, but it is smack between two other places that might be: Lucerne and Bern.

How to get there:

By bus: Call hostel for transit route.
By car: Call hostel for directions.
By train: From Langnau Station, walk ½ mile to hostel.

Best bet for a bite:
Emmental

Insiders' tip:
Stock up at grocery store

What hostellers say:
"So rural."

Gestalt:
Lang-uid

Hospitality:

Cleanliness:

Party index:

JEUNOTEL

(Lausanne Hostel)

Chemin du Bois-de-Vaux 36, CH-1007 Lausanne

Telephone Number: 021–626–0222

Fax Number: 021–626–0226
E-mail: lausanne@youthhostel.ch
Rates: 25.50 SF (about $17 US) per HI member;
doubles 88–104 SF (about $59–$70 US)
Credit cards: MC, VISA, AMEX, DISC
Beds: 240
Private/family rooms: Yes
Kitchen available: No
Office hours: Twenty-four hours
Affiliation: Hostelling International
Extras: Breakfast, meals ($), laundry, bike rentals, bar, lockers, store

We've never seen a hostel before that looked so darn much like a Motel 6. Hey, they don't call it the Jeunotel for nothin', and when you get here you'll see why: This is a two-story concrete complex that appears to have been designed to deflect bomb blasts.

Surprisingly, however, some people report liking the insides, despite this place's institutional feel and its way-too-distant location from downtown Lausanne. This requires either a car, some skillful bike-riding, or a familiarity with the city's late-night transit system (which isn't that great).

You enter through a big heavy front door that looks like a garage door. There's some art along the walls of the huge, hospital-like complex, and that might distract you from its overall drabness long enough for the front desk to check you in and give you the lowdown on all the rules. They'll also sell you lighters, Toblerone—you know, essential stuff—as well as Olympic souvenir tack. They rent bikes (15–19 Swiss francs/about $11–$13 US per day), too—just keep in mind that they'll dock your credit card a solid 400 Swiss francs (about $280 US) as a deposit until you bring it back in one piece.

You'll notice plenty of people smoking in the common area, which is hangarlike and filled with the strains of echoey, piped-in (and bad) Europop. Hightail it to your room, which will be as charmless as a hotel no matter how many beds it contains. Clean, comfortable—yeah, fine. Boring. And the superhighway running right behind the hostel doesn't do anything to dispel that feeling.

Rooms are mostly doubles, triples, or four-bedded, all with private bathrooms—a big plus. They also have furnished studio apartments for around 1,000 Swiss francs per week, though we'd be hard pressed to imagine someone liking this place *that* much. There's a laundry, a so-so breakfast in another big soulless room, a giant chessboard with big pieces, and tons of groups staying with you. Yippee.

At a bar with an incredibly buxom waitress, we checked out the array of coffees, liquor, and beer but didn't order anything. There's a lively little hotel-bar just up the street (almost the only place with food, drink, and life within walking distance of this remote outpost), and that's where we found some Caribbean musicians and dancers working themselves into a steamy lather. Much more interesting than the antiseptic hostel, which is one of the most boring we have ever seen anywhere.

Back in town, though, you could find plenty to do for a day. This is a sleepy town, but as sunset approaches the beautiful people filter downhill to Ouchy, the lakeside port area of the city. There they walk or cruise their cars slowly down the strip, as bar after lakeside bar fills with life. The Lausanne Marathon passes by here once a year, and the cross-lake swimming race is a social event for locals. Use the city's funicular "metro" lift to get to the rest of town, where you'll find a few steep streets of shops, restaurants, and other stuff—fairly humdrum but full of some interesting characters, at least, a combination of wealth, beauty, and artsiness.

This is also the town where the International Olympic Committee is based, of course, so the really good Olympic Museum is a must-see.

How to get there:

By bus: Take #2 bus to Bois-de-Vaux and walk 2 blocks to hostel, following signs.

By car: Call hostel for directions.

By train: From Lausanne Station, take Metro subway to Ouchy stop. Then take #2 bus to Bois-de-Vaux and walk 2 blocks to hostel, following signs.

LA CROISÉE HOSTEL

Avenue Marc Dufour 15, CH-1007 Lausanne

Telephone Number: 021–321–0909

Fax Number: 021–321–0908
Rates: 30–40 SF (about $21–$27 US) per person;
doubles 130 SF (about $90 US)
Credit cards: No
Beds: 81
Private/family rooms: Yes
Kitchen available: No
Office hours: 7:30 A.M. to noon; 3:30 to 6:30 P.M.; 7:00 to 8:00 P.M.
Affiliation: None
Extras: TV, garden, cafeteria ($), playroom, meals ($), laundry

This former church is really more a hotel than a hostel, but it's the second of two hostels in fun Lausanne—definitely the more central and atmospheric of the two, but the prevalence of people living here (not staying, living) set off warning buzzers.

The main draw here? Great doubles with TVs. But dorms are just as good. They've got a garden, a cafeteria serving meals, a lounge, and a playroom for kiddies, among other good points. It's a good pick for families, actually for anyone, because it is right in the old town. (The other hostel's so far from the action that it requires work to get there.) Don't forget the views of the lake and mountains, either, which are terrific.

All may seem perfect here, but the hostel allows long-termers—ya know, people who live at the hostel while they look for a job or avoid life (although it seems incomprehensible to us how one could live in Switzerland without some kind of regular cash flow).

Best bet for a bite:
Train station grocery

Insiders' tip:
Informative map of train station at station

What hostellers say:
"Yup. I'm stayin' another month!"

Gestalt:
Cross my heart

Hospitality: {NR}

Cleanliness: {NR}

Party index:

How to get there:

By bus: Call hostel for transit route.

By car: Call hostel for directions.

By train: Leave central station, turn left at avenue Louis Ruchonnet, and go up hill; follow to Clinique Cecil; at traffic light turn left to avenue Marc Dufour 15.

MATRATZENLAGER STOCKI HOSTEL

CH-3822 Stocki (Lauterbrunnen)

Telephone Number: 033–855–1754

Rates: 13 SF (about $9.00 US) per person
Credit cards: No
Beds: 32
Private/family room: Yes
Kitchen available: Yes
Season: January 1–October 31; December 15–31
Office hours: 10:00 A.M. to 6:00 P.M.
Affiliation: None
Extras: Clotheslines, views

Exceedingly simple but with drop-dead views, this homey place sits beneath big ridges and waterfalls. It's in a small village just across the river from larger (but still small) Lauterbrunnen, a major jumping-off point for excursions higher in the Jungfrau region. You've also got amazing views of huge Staubbach Falls, which appear suspended in midair and can be reached from downtown within about fifteen minutes by postbus.

The hostel name means "mattress-house," and that's just what it is: a place where the beds are packed in, clean and adequate but just very close together—as many as three or four to a row, stacked two high. (Come with a group and you'll love it; get rolled on top of by a stranger and you might not . . . .) There are a total of twenty-two beds on this ground floor.

Enter the nice reception area with antique wooden chairs and you might think you've gone to heaven. However, this isn't the hostel—it's the owner's house. The upper floor was once a carpenter's loft, and that's where the beds are now. The seven-bedded dorm

Best bet for a bite:
Co-op supermarket in Lauterbrunnen

Insiders' tip:
Mürren funicular ho-hum; try walking up mountain

What hostellers say:
"Tight fit, but what views . . ."

Gestalt:
Lumbar yard

Hospitality:

Cleanliness:

Party index:

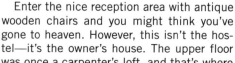

upstairs is one big open room, a combination common area and sleeping area; it's sorta like someone's summer camp slumber party, with the jumble of a fridge, scattered tables and chairs, a space-heater, and people sleeping on the floor. There's also one separated double up here with its own table and heater, perfect for a family.

The big draw here, besides the great location, is the kitchen—mighty popular with hostellers when we dropped by, especially those folks cooking up piles of ramen noodles, as it has two stoves, cutting boards, and all the other assorted culinary tools you require to whip up a simple feast.

Take careful note that winter is higher season here, so you'll see lots of ski groups booking it up full; you also need to stay for a minimum of two nights in winter. Realistically, if you come then you probably will not be able to find a bed anywhere around here. Sad but true. Also, there's one sticking point: just two bathrooms and one shower for the entire hostel. So you may stand in line awhile come morning. You can't rent towels, either.

But we digress. While there are very few frills here, that double room is nice and private—probably the cheapest double room in Alpine Switzerland besides a tent—and you're sure to meet people. Friendly management (it's been a hostel for thirty years, always run by the same family) has kept this place a safe, low-priced option for decades.

Lately, word on the street has it that the aging owner may close down within a few years. That's a shame, because this offers a budget bed and a chance to get to know other travelers well—sometimes too well—in a spectacular setting.

How to get there:

By bus: Call hostel for transit route.

By car: Call hostel for directions from Lauterbrunnen.

By train: From Interlaken, take Jungfraubahn train up to Lauterbrunnen. Descend into underground section of station, turn right and emerge in back of station. Turn right again, then go left, following signs to Stocki and Matrazenlager. Cross river on small bridge, continue to village, and stay straight; hostel is on right.

VALLEY HOSTEL

CH-3822 Lauterbrunnen

Telephone Number: 033–855–2008

Fax Number: 033–855–2008
Rates: 20 SF (about $14 US) per person; doubles 50 SF (about $35 US)
Credit cards: No
Beds: 53

Private/family rooms: Yes
Kitchen available: Yes
Office hours: 8:00 A.M. to 10:00 P.M.
Affiliation: Swiss Backpackers
Extras: Laundry, breakfast ($), dinner ($), store

This fairly new place consistently gets rave reviews and full bookings, thanks to terrific hospitality and a super location right on little Lauterbrunnen's main street.

They've even had a marriage at this place, for gosh sakes—two Australians who fell in love with the area (and apparently the hostel too) sight unseen and came here to do the deed. The wedding was a small affair, the reception a mixture of hill-country locals and Aussies . . . all imbibing some good cheer.

Best bet for a bite:
Co-op across street

Insiders' tip:
Walk to Gimmelwald is pretty

What hostellers say:
"I do!"

Gestalt:
Falls in love

Hospitality:

Cleanliness:

Party index:

Owners Alfred and Martha Abegglen keep a happy spirit alive in the place, and hostellers congregate at dinnertime to share wine, pasta, and salad—fixed in the good little kitchen they have here—and trade tales of death-defying hikes above the clouds. Martha and Alfred also offer a fondue dinner, and if you'd like to try that Swiss specialty, it's cheaper here than in any restaurant or hotel. Homemade, too.

Rooms are basic and certainly fine, with duvets and miniscule pillows, too. Push-button showers and most of the bathrooms are all the way down in the basement, a bit of a hassle if you're sleeping on the top floor, but there's also a really good laundry down there that you'll like a lot. They sell wine, beer, chocolate, and excursion train tickets at the front desk.

Lauterbrunnen itself is a one-street town—but it's a street we'd say has maybe the best views of any main street in the world! Good grief; from the hostel garden and some rooms, you can gaze up at the mighty plume of the biggest waterfall in Europe, Staubbach Falls. That alone keeps folks coming back here, plus quick and easy connections up the cliffs to great skiing, walking, and looking. We'd personally recommend a jaunt up to Gimmelwald, though most folks opt to spring the bucks and take the cable car instead, which is obviously much quicker and vertiginously scenic.

How to get there:

By bus: Call hostel for transit route.

By car: From Interlaken, drive up to Lauterbrunnen. Hostel is on main street; turn left across from Co-op store and drive down into driveway.

Le Bémont Hostel
Le Bémont

(courtesy of HI-SI)

By train: From Interlaken Ost (east) Station, get into "Lauterbrunnen" half of the Jungfraubahn train and take it up to Lauterbrunnen. From Lauterbrunnen Station, walk up exit stairs to main street and turn left. Walk 100 yards to hostel on left.

LE BÉMONT HOSTEL
CH-2877 Le Bémont

Telephone Number: 032–951–1707

Fax Number: 032–951–2413
E-mail: bemont@youthhostel.ch
Rates: 24.50 SF (about $16.30 US) per HI member
Credit cards: Yes
Beds: 96
Private/family rooms: Yes
Kitchen available: Yes
Season: February 2–November 30
Office hours: Vary; call
Affiliation: Hostelling International
Extras: Bike rentals, breakfast, meals ($), laundry

In a corner of French Switzerland, this two-story building with a lawn and trees—a typical style of farmhouse in this region, by the way—is a rustic retreat with the basics and not a lot of cushy extras. In fact, we're not even sure the freakin' telephone works (see below).

Best bet for a bite:
Supermarket in town

Insiders' tip:
Parlez a little français

What hostellers say:
"To Bémont or not to Bémont . . ."

Gestalt:
Bé watch

Hospitality: 👎

Cleanliness: 👎

Party index: 🎉

Anyway, rooms are mostly large—four-bedded or bigger. They do breakfast for free, meals for a charge, and also rent mountain bikes if you want to go exploring the countryside. Not the most exciting place, but our hostellers seemed to enjoy it as a peaceful getaway.

Management rarely, if ever, answers the telephone here; instead, the fax seems to be on most of the time. If you need to make a quick reservation, either call the Swiss Hostel Association or send a fax asking when you can reach the management. We gave up.

How to get there:

By bus: From Tavannes or Glovelier Station, take bus to Bémont stop and walk less than 100 yards to hostel.

By car: Call hostel for directions.

By train: From Tavannes or Glovelier Station, take bus to Bémont stop and walk less than 100 yards to hostel.

HIKING SHEEP GUEST HOUSE HOSTEL

Villa La Joux, CH-1854 Leysin

Telephone Number: 024–494–3535

Fax Number: 024–494–3535
E-mail: hikingsheep@leysin.net
Rates: 26–30 SF (about $18–$21 US) per person; doubles 60–70 SF (about $42–$49 US)
Credit cards: Yes
Beds: 35
Private/family rooms: Yes
Kitchen available: Yes
Office hours: 8:00 A.M. to noon; 5:00 to 10:00 P.M.
Affiliation: Swiss Backpackers
Extras: Lockers, laundry, breakfast ($), fireplace, Internet access, grill, garden, TV, VCR, tours, meditation room, game room, library, hammocks

This hostel, located in the so-called "pre-Alps" that stand between the shores of Lake Geneva and the actual Alps, is one of the country's best located—and just plain one of the best—a laid-back, natural groove of a hostel in a great area. It's not often in our travels that we located a nature-lover's and backpacker's paradise, with great views and quiet, so sit up and pay attention.

The first thing you notice as you work your way up through the series of cog trains and such required to get here is that you're going, well, *up*. Up in the woods and fields and hills, high above cities and pollution. Nice. These pre-Alps may be just precursors to the real thing, but this hostel is just as splendid as those sharp-pointed mountains.

Owner Gérard Cheseaux, a former backpacker himself, has redecorated the nineteenth-century building—a former sanitorium where the unhealthy got well with the fresh air and views—in Art Deco fashion, then added plenty of personal touches that elevate this place far above the usual warehouse-style hostel.

He's got three nice private rooms and four dormitories, none with private bathrooms (oh, well); each floor has a balcony with views out over the valley, the Trient Glacier, or Mont Blanc. In a cozy dining room with a log fire, they serve two kinds of breakfast—a simple light one and a fuller, cooked one—for 8.00 to 10.00 Swiss francs (about $6.00–$7.00 US) plus dinners on request. Gérard also organizes impromptu Swiss cooking classes.

Best bet for a bite:
Prafandaz

What hostellers say:
"Simply the best."

Gestalt:
Good night's sheep

Hospitality:

Cleanliness:

Party index:

Prices are higher here in winter, but don't worry about that. Just come in spring, when the wildflowers that cover these hills are most spectacular. Until the cows eat 'em up, at least.

How to get there:

By bus: Call hostel for transit route.
By car: Call hostel for directions.
By train: Take SBB train to Aigle, then change to cog railway to Leysin and stay on train to last stop (Grand Hotel). Follow signs 100 yards to hostel.

KEY TO ICONS

- Attractive natural setting
- Ecologically aware hostel
- Superior kitchen facilities or cafe
- Offbeat or eccentric place
- Superior bathroom facilities
- Romantic private rooms

- Comfortable beds
- Among our very favorite hostels
- A particularly good value
- Handicapped-accessible
- Good for business travelers

- Especially well suited for families
- Good for active travelers
- Visual arts at hostel or nearby
- Music at hostel or nearby
- Great hostel for skiers
- Bar or pub at hostel or nearby

LUCERNE (LUZERN)

Freedom's just another word for nothin' left to Luzern.

OK, but seriously. Lucerne is okay if you like old, Germanic-style towns. Frankly speaking, we'd probably pass it up in favor of the lakes and big mountains within a few hours' train ride. Besides, once you get there you'll find the streets thick with tourists of every stripe elbowing one another out of the way to get a snapshot of the Kappelbrücke (Chapel Bridge)—basically a covered bridge with paintings on the inside and flowers on the outside. It's quaint, though this isn't the original deal; that one burnt down in 1993 and was rebuilt in a perfect copy. Wooden homes in the old town are also painted on their facades, making for interesting browsing if you've got time to spare. And there's a second bridge that crosses the river running through the city, painted with a strikingly different set of motifs.

Lake Lucerne is beautiful here, and some opt to go for a steamer cruise on the lake, a plodding way to enjoy a few cool hours beneath towering peaks.

For food there are fortunately a number of good places in town. Expense is always a concern in Switzerland, so do as we did—dine at the department store and grocery store restaurants. Take our word for it, they're a heck of a lot better than Kmart's! Also take note of the produce market that hits town twice a week (Tuesday and Saturday), bringing fresh food to the masses—and possibly you—in your times of direst need.

As for the hostels, there are three here, very different in character but all quite good. One, the official joint, is a bit out from the center of town but more than compensates with the best views and quietest surroundings. The backpacker-style digs are closer to the train station and nightlife—and obviously more relaxed in terms of rules.

LUCERNE HOSTELS at a glance

	RATING	PRICE	IN A WORD	PAGE
Backpackers Lucerne Hostel	👍	22 SF	cheap	p.247
Tourist Hotel Hostel	👍	30 SF	central	p.249
Luzern am Rotsee	👍	31.10 SF	noisy	p.247

BACKPACKERS LUCERNE HOSTEL

Alpenquai 42, CH-6005 Lucerne

Telephone Number: 041–360–0420

Fax Number: 041–360–0442

Rates: 22 SF (about $15 US) per person; doubles 56 SF (about $37 US)

Credit cards: Yes

Beds: 78

Private/family rooms: Yes

Kitchen available: Yes

Affiliation: Swiss Backpackers

Extras: Lockers, laundry, bike rentals

Everyone's been giving good marks to this recently renovated back-packer-style hostel, situated on famous Lake Lucerne and less than a twenty-minute walk from the city's lakeside train station.

For one thing, it's all quads and doubles—no huge, huge rooms to get lost in at night with lots of stinky feet in 'em. And every room has a balcony, they claim. How about that! Plus they've got a kitchen and they rent bikes for just 7.00 Swiss francs (about $5.00 US) a day, insanely low for Switzerland.

They tout the fact that they're next to the beach and call themselves "the friendly hostel" in Lucerne. We've seen nothing so far to indicate that isn't accurate. A good pick.

Best bet for a bite:
Co-op downtown

What hostellers say:
"Cool dudes."

Gestalt:
Lucerne change

Hospitality:

Cleanliness:

Party index:

How to get there:

By bus: Call hostel for transit route.

By car: Call hostel for directions.

By train: From train station, exit to front and make an immediate right; walk to lake, then walk along lake ¾ mile to hostel.

LUZERN AM ROTSEE HOSTEL

Sedelstrasse 12, CH-6004 Lucerne

Telephone Number: 041–420–8800

Fax Number: 041–420–5616

E-mail: luzern@youthhostel.ch

Rates: 31.10 SF (about $20.75 US) per HI member; doubles 76.50 SF (about $51 US)

Credit cards: MC, VISA, AMEX, DISC
Beds: 194
Private/family rooms: Yes
Kitchen available: No
Office hours: 7:00 to 10:00 A.M.; 2:00 P.M. to midnight (summer); 7:00 to 9:30 A.M.; 4:00 P.M. to midnight (winter)
Lockout: 10:00 A.M. to 2:00 P.M.
Curfew: 12:30 A.M.
Affiliation: Hostelling International
Extras: Breakfast, meals ($), bike storage, meeting room, library, laundry, TV, lockers, information desk, garden, table tennis, snack shop, pool, dartboard

This two-story hostel, way up on the northwestern edge of Lucerne, is not central at all but it is very close to a beautiful little lake and some community gardens. It's also blessed with good vistas from the rooms and a staff that do a good job elevating the hostel from its basic nature as a functional and not-real-exciting place.

You enter through an archway. Inside, the modern facilities are well geared to groups and families—think echoey concrete-block dorms and hallways, the usual hostel fare. There's kind of a garden, table tennis and TV room (which seemed like it got channels in about twenty different languages), lockers, and a snack shop at the front desk—lots of stuff to make your trip painless. Even the trip from the center of town is easy, a single hop onto a convenient bus at the train station; ten or fifteen minutes later, you're deposited at a stop signed JUGENDHERBERGE (German for youth hostel, of course) in the burbs.

Best bet for a bite:
EPA store cafe in town

What hostellers say:
"Taxi?"

Gestalt:
Lucerne up

Safety: 👍

Hospitality: 👍

Cleanliness: 👍

Party index:

The room arrangements consist of eight doubles—two of them are sorta hotel style, with twin bunks, a bit of furniture, and private bathrooms and lockers—four triples, eighteen quads, nine six-bedded dorms, and two huge twenty-bedded dorms for school groups and maybe unlucky you if you come in late at night during high season without a booking.

Nothing here is fancy, as you would have to expect of a place that houses almost 200 people at once. However, we've gotta hand it to HI this time: The beds here were plain but very comfortable and came with nice pillows, fluffy duvet comforters, and towels. Other amenities include good meals in the dining room until 8:00 each night and a library of books that were all in German—except for one inexplicable copy of Leonard Maltin's movie guide, so we (unsurprisingly) ended up reading that.

They give you day use of the large ground-floor lounge, though you'll probably opt instead for a hike in the surrounding hills—yeah, those green things with goats sticking out of them—or a look at the nice wooden guild houses in town and a stroll around the lake. You can book various tours of the area through the front desk.

Hostel staff also recommend visits to the Lion Monument, the city glacier garden, or the parkside Richard Wagner Museum. Personally, though, we found the Swiss Transport Museum even more interesting—and if you've ridden trains through impossible passes, tunnels, and loops, you might, too. In addition to the usual craft shops downtown, a once-a-month open market gets you in touch with the artists who actually make this stuff. And a twice-weekly (Tuesday and Saturday) produce market supplies the vittles for picnics on the lake.

A word of warning is in order here: Definitely book ahead in summer, when travelers and the dreaded school groups pack the place.

How to get there:

By bus: Take #18 bus to Jugendherberge stop and walk less than 200 yards to hostel.

By car: From expressway, take Emmen Süd exit; continue toward Rotsee/Spittal and follow signs to hostel.

By train: From Lucerne Station, take #18 bus to Jugendherberge stop and walk less than 200 yards to hostel.

TOURIST HOTEL HOSTEL

St. Karliquai 12, CH-6004 Lucerne
Telephone Number: 041–410–2474

Fax Number: 041–410–8414
E-mail: info@touristhotel.ch
Rates: 30–85 SF (about $20–$57 US) per person; doubles 98 SF (about $65 US)
Credit cards: MC, VISA, AMEX
Beds: 100
Private/family rooms: Yes
Office hours: 7:00 A.M. to 10:30 P.M.
Affiliation: None
Extras: Currency exchange, breakfast, laundry, lockers, bike rentals, Internet access, TV, bar

Only a few minutes from Lucerne Station and the lake, this place is getting popular among the backpacker set—not the least because it's really friendly and decently clean in addition to being quite central.

Room prices vary wildly according to room size, presence or lack of a private shower, and time of year; if you're sleeping in bigger dorms, it's just 30 to 32 Swiss francs (about $20 US). Things climb from there; a triple or quad goes for 35 to 57 Swiss francs (about $25 to $40 US), and your very own single room can cost as much as 51 to 85 Swiss francs (about $36 to $57 US). All prices include the good breakfast buffet of coffee, tea, milk, chocolate, orange juice, bread, butter, marmalade, yogurt, corn flakes, muesli, and cheese.

Best bet for a bite:
Anywhere along Karliquai

What hostellers say:
"So friendly!"

Gestalt:
Hangin' Lucerne

Safety: 👍

Hospitality: 👍

Cleanliness: 👍

And talk about services. They've got Internet access for a very reasonable 10 Swiss francs per hour (about $7.00 US) and rent bikes for exploring the area for 15 Swiss francs (about $10 US) per day, 10 Swiss francs (about $7.00 US) per half-day. There's also a well-used laundry and a currency exchange at the front desk.

The helpful owner offered plenty of suggestions about what kind of stuff to do in the area, such as a day-long excursion that involved getting to the top of a local mountain by cable car and back . . . it was a full day, that's for sure. Afterward we walked around the old town counting wooden bridges, happy with our visit and our hostel choice.

How to get there:

By bus: Call hostel for transit route.
By car: Call hostel for directions.
By train: Call hostel for transit route.

MARIASTEIN–ROTBERG HOSTEL 👍

Jugendburg, CH-4115 Mariastein
Telephone Number: 061–731–1049

Fax Number: 061–731–2724
E-mail: mariastein@youthhostel.ch
Rates: 21.30–24.00 SF (about $14–$16 US) per HI member; doubles 53 SF (about $35.30 US)
Credit cards: Yes
Beds: 86
Private/family rooms: No
Kitchen available: Yes
Season: March 1–December 11
Office hours: 8:00 to 10:00 A.M.; 5:00 to 9:00 P.M.
Affiliation: Hostelling International
Extras: Breakfast, meals ($)

This one's strange. At first glace, it's stupendous—inside a castle, with lots of beds and the unusual perk of a kitchen, too. On closer examination, though, there are drawbacks to this beautiful building—dorms are big, and groups love 'em.

The half-timbered building on green grounds has its own tower and fountain; that's how authentic it is. Inside, it's just as nice, and they serve an included breakfast and meals for a charge. The dorms are a little cavernous, though, none containing fewer than ten beds.

This place is just outside Basel and almost in France, a very pretty area, actually.

How to get there:

By bus: From Basel Station, take #10 street-car to Flüh stop. Board postbus to Rotberg and walk ½ mile to hostel.

By car: Call hostel for directions.

By train: From Basel Station, take #10 streetcar to Flüh stop. Board postbus to Rotberg and walk ½ mile to hostel.

Best bet for a bite:
Co-op supermarket near train station

Insiders' tip:
Best to rent a car in Germany and explore

What hostellers say:
"Yep, it's a castle."

Gestalt:
Ave Mariastein

Hospitality: 👎

Cleanliness: 👎

Party index:

HAUT LAC HOSTEL

(Montreux Hostel)

8 Passage de l'Auberge, CH-1820 Territet (Montreux)

Telephone Number: 021–963–4934

Fax Number: 021–963–2729
E-mail: montreux@youthhostel.ch
Rates: 29.60 SF (about $18 US) per HI member; doubles 77.50–94.00 SF (about $51.70–$63.00 US)
Credit cards: MC, VISA, AMEX, DISC
Beds: 112
Private/family rooms: Yes
Kitchen available: No
Season: February 1–November 30
Office hours: 7:00 to 10:00 A.M.; 4:00 to 11:00 P.M. (summer); 7:30 to 9:30 A.M.; 5:00 to 10:00 P.M. (winter)
Lockout: 10:00 A.M. to 4:00 P.M.
Curfew: Midnight
Affiliation: Hostelling International
Extras: Breakfast, meals ($), TV, meeting room, laundry, lockers, information desk, garden, table tennis, bike storage

Amazingly clean, cleverly designed, Montreux's hostel proves once again that the French Swiss know how to do a hostel right in their pastoral corner of the country.

Start outside, walking beneath the arched railway bridge to the building: The shutters are touched up with purple paint; bright flowers grace the window boxes; an attractive walkway welcomes you to reception. There you spot more clever mural work.

The dining room continues the local theme, with portraits of jazz greats all around. The dorms (six quads, nine six-bedded rooms, and three larger ones) are comfy and modern, for once, and the five doubles are especially good. Decent staff and management keep things relatively cheery and absolutely spic-and-span.

In fact, we'd award this five stars and call it one of the best in Switzerland—or Europe— but for one little nagging detail.

The lockout.

Yes, folks, you're kicked out from 10:00 A.M. to 4:00 P.M., and that ain't fun—especially since Montreux is more a chic and sleepy town than a happenin' one. The hostel is next to a nice green park with benches, and you may spend lots of time there hangin' out (or else sunning at the beach just downhill) just waiting for the lockout to end. And waiting.

This is not the most interesting stop as a town; a much-photographed castle stands about a mile away by foot (skip the torture chambers but check out the vistas), so that's one stop, and there's a covered farmers' market on Friday downtown. Otherwise we're stumped. You could walk around Lake Geneva on the promenade, catch a train into the nearby mountains for skiing or walking, or get the inside scoop on where to taste some local wines at the source—the area is full of little wineries— all preferable to sticking around town all day long.

Best bet for a bite:
Fish restaurant below Territet Station

Insiders' tip:
"Bus Accelere" 1 goes directly to Vevey

Gestalt:
Smoke on the water

Hospitality: 👎

Cleanliness: 👎

Party index:

KEY TO ICONS

🍁 Attractive natural setting

🌐 Ecologically aware hostel

✗ Superior kitchen facilities or cafe

Offbeat or eccentric place

🚿 Superior bathroom facilities

♥ Romantic private rooms

🛏 Comfortable beds

🏅 Among our very favorite hostels

S A particularly good value

Handicapped-accessible

💼 Good for business travelers

👫 Especially well suited for families

🚴 Good for active travelers

🎨 Visual arts at hostel or nearby

🎵 Music at hostel or nearby

Great hostel for skiers

🍺 Bar or pub at hostel or nearby

Remember that the famous annual jazz fest in early July fills all these beds up way ahead of time, so reserve superearly if you're thinking about coming for this event.

How to get there:

By bus: Take #1 bus to Territet and walk less than 200 yards to hostel.

By car: Call hostel for directions.

By ferry: Take ferry to Port de Territet. From dock, walk 200 yards east to hostel.

By train: From Montreux Station, walk 1 mile along lakeshore, going beneath railroad underpass, to hostel. From Montreux-Territet Station, walk less than 200 yards to hostel.

AUBERGE OASIS

(Oasis Hostel)

35 rue du Suchiez, CH-2000 Neuchâtel

Telephone Number: 032–731–3190

Fax Number: 032–730–3709
Rates: 23–28 SF (about $16–$20 US) per person; doubles 56 SF (about $39 US)
Beds: 38
Private/family rooms: Yes
Kitchen available: Yes
Office hours: 8:00 to 10:00 A.M.; 5:00 to 9:00 P.M.
Affiliation: Swiss Backpackers
Extras: Breakfast, lockers, camping, fax, dartboard, table tennis, grill, lockers

A small hostel with lake views, this homey building has dorms plus twin rooms in a fun, laid-back setting. Let's put it this way—it's so mellow it has tepees for camping in at night. (Just remember to BYOB: Bring Your Own sleeping Bag.)

Breakfast is included in the price here—fruit juice, snacks, and the like—and they serve vegetarian-only dinners for a charge as well. Free tea is served to you as you check in, another plus, and for a groovy place it's loaded with helpful extras like a fax, grilling capability, a dartboard, table tennis, and more. What else? Well, it's free on your birthday—if you happen to be in this French Swiss town on that blessed day. No lockouts or curfews to worry about, either. They'll even phone ahead and book your next night's bunk if they're able.

Neuchâtel, of course, is the chief town on the big lake of the same name—not our favorite lake in Switzerland but a restful one nevertheless. There are hiking trails close to the hostel, cheese

Best bet for a bite:
Co-op near hostel

Insiders' tip:
Use that grill!

What hostellers say:
"Groovy."

Gestalt:
Oasis in the desert

Hospitality:

Cleanliness:

Party index:

everywhere in the area, and the usual lakeside diversions to take care of your idle time.

How to get there:

By bus: From Neuchâtel Station, take #6 bus to place Pury. Change to #1 bus and continue toward Cormondreche to Vauseyon stop. Walk uphill toward Centre Sportive le Chanet to hostel.

By car: From Neuchâtel, drive toward Pontarlier or Peseux to Vauseyon bus station; after third stoplight, follow sign toward Centre Sportive le Chanet. Turn uphill on rue du Suchiez to hostel.

By train: From Neuchâtel Station, take #6 bus to place Pury. Change to #1 bus and continue toward Cormondreche to Vauseyon stop. Walk uphill toward Centre Sportive le Chanet to hostel.

CHALET RÜBLIHORN HOSTEL

(Saanen-Gstaad Hostel)

Chalet Rüblihorn, CH-3792 Saanen

Telephone Number: 033–744–1343

Fax Number: 033–744–5542
E-mail: saanen@youthhostel.ch
Rates: 28.15 SF (about $19 US) per HI member;
doubles 77.50 SF (about $51.70 US)
Credit cards: Yes
Beds: 76
Private/family rooms: Yes
Kitchen available: No
Season: December 11– October 31
Office hours: 7:00 to 10:00 A.M.; 4:00 to 10:00 P.M.
Curfew: 11:00 P.M.
Affiliation: Hostelling International
Extras: Breakfast, meals ($), bike rentals, volleyball, table tennis

Yes, it's a chalet, with stupendous views out the front windows of row after row of incredible peaks and valleys. What more do you want? This is one of Switzerland's best-located and best-run hostels, if a bit remote—tremendous for traveling couples and families.

The hostel's just outside and above the little town of Saanen, with great views (especially from the balcony rooms). There are three doubles, one triple, eight quad rooms, three six-bedded rooms, and an eight-bedded dorm. There's lots of common space, too, including several lounges, a kids' playroom, and a schoolroom (summer-only) for groups. There's a pool table, volleyball net, and foosball table, and they rent (and repair!) bikes. Meals are served, too—and they're darned good.

Did we mention the staff? This place is really friendly; it feels like a home, not an "official" hostel.

The town is okay, a good antidote to toney Gstaad. How plain-spoken is this area? The local mascot's a *goat!* There's some great train riding in the area, plus outdoor adventure stuff and a springtime film festival. Tennis nuts can catch the Swiss Tennis Open locally in July, while the Country Night celebration hits town in September. But many simply stroll Saanen's old downtown, checking out lots of historic buildings and ogling the fifteenth-century Mauritius church. Want still more culture? Inquire at the hostel about local folkarts like pottery, weaving, and—yes—Alpine horn making.

Best bet for a bite:
Dinner here with all the fixin's (i.e., salad bar)

Insiders' tip:
Panoramic Express well worth it

What hostellers say:
"They were *so* friendly."

Gestalt:
Saanen your shoulders

Hospitality:

Cleanliness:

Party index:

How to get there:

By bus: From Saanen bus stop, walk ½ mile to hospital and continue just past hospital to hostel on left.

By car: Drive to Saanen Station and park; walk ½ mile to hospital, then continue just past hospital to hostel on left.

By train: From Montreux, or Bern, take train to Saanen. Walk ½ mile to hospital, then continue just past hospital to hostel on left.

SAINTE-CROIX HOSTEL

16 rue Centrale, CH-1450 Sainte-Croix

Telephone Number: 024–454–1810

Fax Number: 024–454–4522
E-mail: ste.croix@youthhostel.ch
Rates: 27.55 SF (about $18.35 US) per HI member; doubles 73.50 SF (about $47.60 US)
Credit cards: No
Beds: 58
Private/family rooms: Yes
Kitchen available: Yes
Season: April 1–October 30
Office hours: 8:00 to 10:00 A.M.; 5:00 to 9:00 P.M.
Affiliation: Hostelling International
Extras: Breakfast, meals ($), bike storage, meeting rooms

A beautifully decorated villa on a hillside, right near pretty Lake Geneva, this one qualifies as a try-to-see on the basis of its looks alone—even if it takes a bit of work to get there. Facilities are good, staff are okay, and you'll be getting away from city bustle.

First off, it's right in the dead center of town, a switch from the usual Swiss hostelling modus operandi. The dorms are four-to-eight-bedded, and staff serve breakfast for free and meals for a charge. They'll store your bike, too.

The town's tiny, nestled among mountains and lakes and seemingly inches from France—yet another cute place to get off the beaten track and check out.

Best bet for a bite:
Migros right next door

What hostellers say:
"Good but quiet."

Gestalt:
Cross talk

Hospitality:

Cleanliness:

Party index:

How to get there:

By bus: Call hostel for transit route.
By car: Call hostel for directions.
By train: From Sainte-Croix Station, walk ¼ mile to hostel.

SION HOSTEL

2 rue de l'Industrie, CH-1950 Sion

Telephone Number: 027–323–7470

Fax Number: 027–323–7438
E-mail: sion@youthhostel.ch
Rates: 27.55 SF (about $18.35 US) per HI member; doubles 69.40 SF (about $46.25 US)
Credit cards: Yes
Beds: 80
Private/family rooms: No
Kitchen available: Yes ($)
Season: December 24–January 4; January 23–October 25
Office hours: 7:30 to 9:30 A.M.; 5:00 to 10:00 P.M.; 5:00 to 9:00 P.M. (December–April)
Lockout: 9:30 A.M. to 5:00 P.M.
Curfew: 11:00 P.M.
Affiliation: Hostelling International
Extras: Breakfast, meals ($), lockers, laundry

In an unusual, stern-looking building, this hostel nevertheless gets top marks from our snoops. It's very near Sion's train station, staffed by extremely friendly types, and is a quiet sleep—thanks to the lack of a bar, probably. The train that rumbles past can be noisy, however—one possible drawback.

Dorms are mostly four-bedded, wheel-chair-accessible, and possess good views and balconies; the interior decoration is artsy. They serve meals here, breakfast is included with your bunk, and lockers are available.

Sion almost hosted the Olympics twice, so there's obviously some great skiing in the neighborhood. The town's a bit of a disappointment, though, good really only as a base to explore the surrounding mountains maybe.

How to get there:

By bus: Call hostel for transit route.
By car: Call hostel for directions.
By train: From Sion Station, walk 200 yards down rue de la Blancherie beneath tracks to hostel.

Best bet for a bite:
La Placette
Insiders' tip:
Wine-tasting tours
What hostellers say:
"Friendly people."
Gestalt:
Sion of the times
Hospitality:
Cleanliness:
Party index:

AM LAND HOSTEL

(Solothurn Hostel)

Landhausquai 23, CH-4500 Solothurn

Telephone Number: 032–623–1706

Fax Number: 032–623–1639
E-mail: solothurn@youthhostel.ch
Rates: 27 SF (about $18 US) per HI member
Credit cards: MC, VISA, AMEX
Beds: 92
Private/family rooms: Yes
Kitchen available: Yes
Season: January 18–November 21
Office hours: 7:30 to 10:00 A.M.; 4:00 to 9:30 P.M.
Affiliation: Hostelling International
Extras: Breakfast, meals ($), TV, VCR, library, meeting room, laundry, lockers, information desk, piano, bike storage, game room, pool table, terrace, courtyard

Note: You'll be charged a surtax of 2.00 SF (about $1.50 US) if you're age seventeen and over and 1.50 SF (about $1.00 US) if you're younger.

In a beautiful old former customs house right in Solothurn's old center and by the Aare River, this is one of the better obscure hostels we turned up in Switzerland. Worth a trip for sure, and convenient to the riverside bike trail if you happen to be coming by that means of transportation.

There are four triple rooms with private bathrooms, a real find, plus two five-bedded rooms with sinks, four six-bedded rooms, and five more big dorms. The architecture of the smaller dorms is quite distinctive and homey, and the list of extras that comes with 'em is so long we almost can't fit it on the page, including a kitchen, a game room, free breakfast, and lockers.

Take some time to poke around Solothurn, a surprising destination you probably never heard of; the old town—which is traffic-free during all afternoons and all day Saturday—is a nice walk. Speaking of free, there's a huge museum of medieval stuff (armor, mail, weapons, you know) nearby, and it's free, too! As in no admission charge. Just like a half-dozen other museums that pepper the little town—a natural history museum, an art museum, a cathedral. Gratis. Believe it.

The farmers' market in town is a source of fresh foods, and—should the sky happen to clear up—you can head up to the Weissenstein's 3,800-foot peak and its set of limestone caves.

Best bet for a bite:
Restaurant Manora

Insiders' tip:
August is jazz month

What hostellers say:
"Fantastic architecture."

Gestalt:
Goin' Solothurn

Hospitality:

Cleanliness:

Party index:

How to get there:

By bus: Take #1, #2, or #4 bus to post office and walk 200 yards to hostel.

By car: Call hostel for directions; no parking at hostel.

By ferry: Take ferry to Solothurn; from dock, walk ½ mile east to hostel.

By train: From Solothurn Station, cross river using Kreuzacker bridge, then turn left onto Landhausquai and continue to hostel on right.

L'AUBERGE POUR TOUS

(The Hostel for Everyone)

11 rue du Simplon, CH-1337 Vallorbe

Telephone Number: 021–843–1349

E-mail: auberge.pour.tous@smile.ch
Rates: 21–26 SF (about $14–$15 US) per person; doubles 52 SF (about $35 US)
Credit cards: No
Beds: 75
Private/family rooms: Yes
Kitchen available: No
Office hours: 7:30 A.M. to 10:00 P.M.

Affiliation: Swiss Backpackers
Extras: Laundry, breakfast, meals ($), garden, grill, bike rentals, pool table, patio

This independent hostel does decently well by us, with a laid-back management and a combo of dorm rooms and private rooms.

It's a three-story home with all sorts of rooms—doubles, quads, and sixes for families and then ten-bedded dorms. There's one large shared bathroom on each floor. They also have one apartment with two rooms, a kitchen, and a bathroom.

Dinner is available for a charge, there are two gardens with table tennis and other games, a pool table, and bikes for rent. They just love kids here, too, furnishing a special "children's corner" where little ones can play or watch movies.

About half an hour's train ride from Lausanne, the town's on the Jura Road from Basel to Geneva—hostellers come by foot or by bike on their trip through the beautiful Jura. The area has grottoes with the requisite stalactites, stalagmites and such, plus lots of lakes and mountain-biking trails. Remember that winter, not summer, is high season here, and book ahead accordingly.

Best bet for a bite:
Supermarkets close by

Insiders' tip:
Meals on site

What hostellers say:
"My kids loved it!"

Gestalt:
Tous by Tous

Hospitality:

Cleanliness:

Party index:

How to get there:

By bus: Call hostel for transit route.
By car: Call hostel for directions.
By train: Call hostel for transit route.

THE BUNKER HOSTEL

Verbier Sports Center, CH-1936 Verbier
Telephone Number: 027–771–6602

Fax Number: 027–771–6603
E-mail: info@thebunker.ch
Rates: 21–35 SF (about $14–$24 US) per person
Credit cards: Yes
Beds: 144
Private/family rooms: Sometimes
Kitchen available: No
Season: January 1–April 30; June 15–December 31
Office hours: Contact hostel for current hours
Affiliation: Swiss Backpackers

Extras: Internet access, bar, restaurant, TV lounge, sports facilities, lockers, luggage storage, ski pass discounts

Just a half mile from Verbier's downtown and free shuttle buses to the town's terrific ski slopes, this is one of the weirder hostels we've come across. It's a bomb shelter. Yes, a bomb shelter. As in Cold War, hunker-down-and-head-beneath-ground.

No, there are no windows.

It's all part of the Verbier Sports Center, and that means what a European sports facility usually means: lots of pools, whirlpools, rinks, and the like, with pumped-up athletes working out while you down beers at the bar, shake it on the dance floor, catch some German CNN on the tube, or eat. They also put together package deals and can snag you discounts for the slopes. Sounds pretty good on the surface.

Best bet for a bite:
On-site dining

What hostellers say:
"Dude!"

Gestalt:
Bomb squad

Hospitality:

Cleanliness:

Party index:

However, it's an absolute Monster Mash of a place: There are only four "rooms" in the entire hostel, and three of 'em contain more than forty (yes, forty!) beds apiece . . . in other words, you'd better really like a barrackslike feel and the aroma of sweaty socks. We won't even get into the awful triple-decker bunks that make you feel like a sardine—or someone on all-night sleeper train to Hell. The place is wildly popular with snowboarders, who come to hit the local slopes for the long boarding season, but if you're a family or a couple or a reasonably clean person you might want to move along to somewhere else.

At least the place is safe in case of nuclear attack. We think.

Note: The hostel was said to be on the brink of adding new, summer-only double rooms that would be *much* more comfy than those other ones. If they pan out, this place will definitely rise to the level of a really good deal.

How to get there:

By bus: Contact hostel for transit route.
By car: Contact hostel for directions.
By train: Contact hostel for transit route.

RIVIERA LODGE

Place du Marché, CH-1800 Vevey
Telephone Number: 021–923–8040

Fax Number: 021–923–8041
E-mail: rivieralodge@bluewin.ch

Rates: 22 SF (about $15 US) per person; doubles 70 SF (about $49 US)
Credit cards: Yes
Beds: 60
Private/family rooms: Yes
Kitchen available: Yes
Office hours: 8:00 A.M. to noon; 5:00 to 8:00 P.M.
Affiliation: None
Extras: Laundry, lockers, TV, VCR, bar, breakfast ($), Internet access

Here's a surprise: You can sleep inexpensively in Switzerland and have fun, too. This is a super and laid-back place just yards from Lake Geneva. The early-July, two-week Montreux Jazz Festival is the main draw around here, and you're close enough to warrant staying in this great hostel if you can't stay in Montreux. Maybe even if you can, because the lack of rules compares favorably against the Montreux hostel's all-day lockout.

On a big square among lotsa cafes and restaurants, this place has one of the best common rooms we've seen in Europe. Think parquet floors, a salon with a good TV and VCR, tapestry-like drawings on the walls, tasteful couches and chairs, games, and books. It's like the arty crash pad you'd design if you had a little dough.

Each floor has a large common room with crazy mod furniture, like egg-shaped chairs. Dorms are eight-bedded, clean and homey. (As former apartments, they oughta be.) There are four doubles with dressers and mirrors for more money, but they're really worth it. The shared bathrooms have three sinks and stalls apiece, all incredibly clean when we popped in.

They serve breakfast for 7.00 Swiss francs (about $5.00 US) in the cool dining area, or you can fix your own meals in the very good hostel kitchen—a very modern area with a crescent-shaped bar and two (count 'em) rangetops. There's a great little laundry, too. They recycle, which is nice, and a woodstove in the reception area warms the place in winter. Top it all off with a very nice view of the lake and the local church from the hostel terrace and you've got a fun place to hang—with a fun crowd, usually. They're flexible about checkout and wake-up, too.

Vevey isn't a really quaint village, but it's okay as a burb. Lausanne is just thirteen minutes away by train, Montreux even closer, and local boats—the dock is just 50 yards away—goes to Montreux, Lausanne, and France. This steeply terraced stretch of the lakeshore

Best bet for a bite:
Migros restaurant up the street

What hostellers say:
"Near perfect."

Gestalt:
Jazzed

Hospitality:

Cleanliness:

Party index:

is quite scenic, with castles and wine villages very close by bike or foot. The square in front of the hostel offers wine tasting, music, and other stuff on Saturday plus a quieter market on Tuesday.

Guests sometimes include performing artists, which is cool, but lots of groups book in here, too. Reserve early if you possibly can.

How to get there:

By bus: From Montreux Station, leave station and walk down two sets of stairs to lower bus stop. On other side of street from lake, catch #1 bus to Vevey stop; get off and walk toward lake 50 yards into place du Marché square. Hostel is on right of square, in town house.

By car: Call hostel for directions.

By train: From Vevey Station, cross street and walk through place de la Gare; continue down avenue Ceresole to place du Marché square. Hostel is on right-hand side of square, in town house just before lake and docks.

EDDY'S HOSTEL

Eden Hotel, CH-3823 Wengen

Telephone Number: 033–55–1634

Fax Number: 033–855–3950
Rates: 30 SF (about $20 US) per person
Credit cards: Yes
Beds: 20
Private/family rooms: None
Kitchen available: No
Office hours: 7:00 A.M. to 10:00 P.M.
Affiliation: None
Extras: Breakfast ($), meals ($)

We can't say we liked this place, which is an add-on to a nicer hotel/restaurant next door, very much. The hostel consists of just one room; that's right, one room. We're talking twenty beds in the space, with triple bunks squashed together so that they're more like one wide bed than three tiny ones. Unfortunately, if Eddy's is booked full (it was completely empty when we came, but it was also summer), that means three heads pushed awfully close together.

There's just one toilet and one shower at the back in what looked like a closet. So mornings could get tricky, too, in this extremely basic hostel.

No denying that the area is spectacular, though, and if you get the place all to yourself you might actually not care one bit about the bunkroom's condition. We actually kinda liked Wengen—there are tons of good short hikes in the area, it's car-free and not too tacky, and nothing is more than walking distance from the train station or anything else.

For food, you're spoiled. You can buy a breakfast buffet (15 Swiss francs/about $10.50 US) at the Hotel Eden and eat dinners there, too, including a good and incredibly cheap (7.50 Swiss francs/about $5.00 US) all-you-can-gulp salad bar. More expensive but also more traditional and filling meals can also be had at the hotel. What's more, hotel owner Kerstin Bucher cooks the meals herself. There's a laundry in town, but in an emergency they'll do it at the hotel for a charge.

What to do? Bucher herself is the single best source in town, maybe, on where to walk. She'll tell you everything you need to know as you wander up toward the imposing Eiger, where foolish rock-climbers go to perish. In winter you can cross-country ski right up to the hostel door. Just be careful up there in wintertime—an unfortunate series of recent avalanches killed two persons in the winter of '98–'99 after heavy snowfalls. So look sharp.

Other travelers will want to take a gondola up to the very top of these mountains, so note that the lift runs only certain times of the year. The Jungfraubahn train system runs year-round, but it's very expensive if you're going all the way to the top of the Jungfrau and still expensive to get you just as far as Kleine Scheidegg. We found it more fun just to wander through the local cow pastures.

Best bet for bite:
Eden Hotel's restaurant

What hostellers say:
"Hello?"

Gestalt:
Fast Eddy's

Hospitality:

Cleanliness:

Party index:

Oh, and that name? It's Bucher's son, who runs a hotel over in much more-touristed Grindelwald now.

How to get there:

By train: From Interlaken Ost Station, take Jungfraubahn train up to Lauterbrunnen; change trains to Wengneralpbahn and continue to Wengen. From station, turn right and walk along path beside tracks. Continue to underpass, turn right and walk under tracks; hostel is on other side, on left. To check in, turn right and enter Eden Hotel through dining room.

HOT CHILI PEPPERS HOSTEL

P.O. Box 72, CH-3823 Wengen
Telephone Number: 033–855–5020
Fax Number: 033–855–5020
E-mail: chilis@wengen.com
Rates: 29 SF (about $20 US) per person; doubles 88 SF (about $60 US)
Credit cards: Yes

Beds: 30
Private/family rooms: Yes
Kitchen available: Yes
Office hours: 7:00 A.M. to 11:00 P.M.
Affiliation: None
Extras: Cafe, bar, dance club, lockers, breakfast ($), terraces

For a hostel above a bar—usually an unsavory kind of place—this one is great, scoring points with our hostellers for friendliness, coolness, hipness, and comfy beds, too. Owners Mirco and Zelia Plozza (one Canadian, one Swiss) are doing a great job so far of developing the bunkrooms above their Tex-Mex–themed bar—that's where the name comes from—and you'll need to book ahead in winter, as the word is out that pricey Wengen now has a great and affordable hostel option.

The bar pumps Brit-pop while serving beer and snacks (no full meals). Dorms are basic seven-bedded affairs, mostly with sinks and lockers inside them, and the communal bathrooms and showers are really tops. There's a small kitchen—rangetop, sink, and small tables—upstairs that you can use from 6:30 in the morning until 10:00 at night, nothing great but certainly adequate to fix small meals. The hostel has a couple terraces with good views of the mountains, popular as a hanging-out (just don't go hanging-too-far-out) spot.

We especially liked the eight huge, hotel-quality doubles here, which come without their own private bathrooms but *with* tables and couches. And one single with desk and sink, too. Really, really nice. This is a hostel? Oh, yeah, the rooms have fun new Southwestern-style curtains on the windows, in keeping with the motif of the bar, and you get in using keys with chili peppers on them. Cool.

Best bet for a bite:
Any hotel

Insiders' tip:
Shows last late

What hostellers say:
"Whooooe!"

Gestalt:
Hot stuff

Hospitality:

Cleanliness:

Party index:

The only problem we could see was the stage downstairs, where music often goes late into the night. Pretty much everyone stays up when the music is on, 'cause you gotta. Like it or not. If that doesn't bother you, though, this place will be just fine.

Not much goes on in sleepy Wengen, except the comings and goings of tourists, but an annual World Cup skiing event is a big draw for a very steep and fast downhill race. Book ahead if that's coming up. You can also ski right to the Jungfrau, Monch, and Eiger Mountains from Wengen. If you dare.

How to get there:

By bus: Call hostel for transit route.
By car: No cars allowed in Wengen; call hostel for transit route.

By train: From Wengen Station, cross street and turn left onto main road. Walk 100 yards down street. Hostel is on left, inside bar.

ZERMATT

Zermatt rocks. Literally. This place is the ultimate view-finder's dream destination—and if you ski you may never want to leave.

Electric cars and horse-drawn carriages are the only types of locomotion legal in this wonderland, so you'll feel like you're on another planet as you walk the quiet, snow-covered streets with the Matterhorn hanging above you.

Getting here isn't as hard as it sounds, though it takes a bit of cash, of course. International and long-distance Swiss trains stop at Brig, where you change to the narrow-gauge Zermatt railway; a scenic hour and a half later, you're here. By car, you drive to either Täsch (catch a shuttle train that runs three times an hour and then a taxi) or Visp.

Skiing, gawking, and sight-seeing are the main activities here. But you could also check out an interesting little Alpine Museum, the Radio Matterhorn broadcasting museum, or if you're into adrenaline, head for the (gulp) highest cable-car in Europe.

MATTERHORN HOSTEL

Schluhmattstrasse, Postfach 153, CH-3920 Zermatt

Telephone Number: 027–968–1919

Fax Number: 027–968–1915
E-mail: info@matterhornhostel.com
Rates: 24–29 SF (about $17–$20 US) per person; doubles 68–78 SF (about $48–$55 US)
Credit cards: MC, VISA, AMEX
Beds: 59
Private/family rooms: Yes
Kitchen available: Yes
Office hours: 7:30 to 11:00 A.M.; 4:00 to 10:00 P.M.
Affiliation: None
Extras: Laundry, Internet access, bar, TV, game room, garden, breakfast ($), restaurant ($), lockers

This place—the first one in Zermatt, they told us—fired up in 1997 to give budget travelers a viable option in a town notorious for sucking your wallet like a Hoover. It looks good to us, with a bar, a tele-

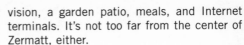

Best bet for a bite:
Big meals here

Insiders' tip:
Parking in Visp is free

What hostellers say:
"Laid-back and lotsa
fun."

Gestalt:
Matthorn o' plenty

Hospitality: 👍

Cleanliness: 👍

Party index:

vision, a garden patio, meals, and Internet terminals. It's not too far from the center of Zermatt, either.

Dorms come in lots of sizes: two doubles, one each of the quad and five-bedded rooms, five six-bedded rooms, and two eight-bedded dorms. There's an emphasis on a backpacker-style ethic here, which means no silly rules to hamper your good times. They do a five-night special in fall for 99 Swiss francs (about $69 US), which could take the sting out of prices a bit—though these are already the lowest in town.

Good show so far, guys. Let's see if they can keep it up.

How to get there:

By bus: Call hostel for transit route.

By car: Drive to Täsch and park, then take train 3 miles to Zermatt Station; walk ½ mile to hostel.

By train: From Zermatt Station, walk ½ mile to hostel.

ZERMATT HOSTEL

Winkelmatten, CH-3920 Zermatt

Telephone Number: 027–967–2320

Fax Number: 027–967–5306
E-mail: zermatt@youthhostel.ch
Rates: 47 SF (about $31.30 US) per HI member;
doubles 114 SF (about $76 US)
Credit cards: Yes
Beds: 140
Private/family rooms: Yes
Kitchen available: No
Season: January 1–May 7; June 18–November 1; December 17–31
Office hours: 6:30 to 9:30 A.M.; 4:00 to 11:00 P.M. (summer); 7:30 to 9:30 A.M.; 4:00 to 11:00 P.M. (winter)
Curfew: 11:30 P.M.
Affiliation: Hostelling International
Extras: Breakfast, meals, library, meeting rooms, laundry, lockers, information desk, garden, table tennis, patio, travel store, Internet access, bike rentals

A big four-story warehouse perched by the edge of a hill, this hostel is wildly popular for its view of huge mountains—dominated by the Matterhorn, probably the most distinctive-looking peak in the world. There's something about that crag of rock, jutting up impossibly fiercely into the sky right in front of you in perfect proportions, that just boggles the mind. And this hostel's got that vista in spades.

As a hostel it's not bad, either. This is a total S&G hostel. As in ski-and-gawk. Seriously, though, the famous Matterhorn looks right into your room! It might be the one double room, one of two quads, the six-bedded room, or one of the dozen others of varying sizes from eight to sixteen beds each—you'll probably get stuck in those, unfortunately. You must buy dinner with your bed, but at least that saves you the trouble of actually cooking it; and the food's pretty good. Eat in one of three dining rooms.

Best bet for a bite:
At the hostel

What hostellers say:
" "
(speechless at views)

Gestalt:
Zermatter of trust

Hospitality:

Cleanliness:

Party index:

Additional facilities include a laundry, lockers for stashing your stuff, a garden, and a game room.

The crowd is rather subdued, though, so you might not strike up lots of conversations. Stay at one of the two in-town backpackers for maximum social interaction.

No, this place isn't central or hopping, but who cares? Look up there . . . there's a *mountain!*

How to get there:

By bus: From Zermatt Station, take bus to Winkelmatten and get off at Luchre stop close to hostel.

By car: Drive to Visp train station, park for free; take train to Zermatt and walk ¾ mile to hostel.

By train: From Zermatt Station, take bus to Winkelmatten and get off at Luchre stop close to hostel. Or walk ¾ mile to hostel.

ZOFINGEN HOSTEL

General Guisan-Strasse 10, CH-4800 Zofingen

Telephone Number: 062–752–2303

Fax Number: 062–752–2316
E-mail: zofingen@youthhostel.ch
Rates: 26 SF (about $17.30 US) per HI member; doubles 69.40 SF (about $46.25 US)
Credit cards: MC, VISA
Beds: 60
Private/family rooms: Yes
Kitchen available: Yes
Season: March 1–December 15

Office hours: 7:00 to 10:00 A.M.; 5:00 to 9:00 P.M.
Affiliation: Hostelling International
Extras: Breakfast, meals ($), meeting room

Best bet for a bite:
Supermarket close by

Insiders' tip:
Olten has a nice old town

What hostellers say:
"Not much to do but sit."

Gestalt:
Swiss mouse

Hospitality:

Cleanliness:

Party index:

A beautiful country house beneath shade trees, this hostel's best and worst feature is its quiet location—that and the groups who invade it regularly.

Dorms are four- or six-bedded, breakfast is included with the price of your bunk, and they serve meals, too. There's a conference room waiting in store for the inevitable vanload of kids, so we might head for another joint instead—maybe a bit farther west, over in French Switzerland. This area isn't that interesting, anyway.

How to get there:

By bus: Call hostel for transit route.
By car: Call hostel for directions.
By train: From Zofingen Station, walk ¼ mile to hostel.

PAUL AND MARTHA'S PICKS

THE BEST HOSTELS
IN AUSTRIA & SWITZERLAND

FOUR HARDBODY HOSTELS

EIGHT GREAT SKI HOSTELS

ELEVEN GREAT FAMILY HOSTELS

SEVEN KNOCKOUT ROMANTIC-VIEW HOSTELS

. . . TWO HARD-ROCKIN' PARTY HOSTELS

ABOUT THE AUTHORS

Martha Coombs is a translator, writer, and photographer who works in North America and abroad.

Paul Karr is an award-winning writer, writing coach, and author or coauthor of two dozen guidebooks. He contributes regularly to magazines, and writes screenplays when he's not traveling. He has twice been named a writer-in-residence by the National Parks Service. You can contact him directly at this e-mail address:

Atomev@aol.com